Political economy has been an essential realm of inquiry and has attracted myriad intellectual adherents for much of the period of modern scholarship. The discipline's formal split into the distinct studies of political science and economics in the nineteenth century, while advantageous for certain scientific developments, has biased the way economists and political scientists think about many issues, and has placed artificial constraints on the study of many important social issues.

This volume calls for a reaffirmation of the importance of the unified study of political economy and explores the frontiers of the interaction between politics and markets. Recent research in political economy has frequently failed to incorporate the full power of modern economic and political analysis, generally leading to unbalanced development. In contrast, this volume, which brings together intellectual leaders from various areas, draws on state-of-the-art theoretical and empirical analyses from each of the underlying disciplines. Each chapter, while beginning with a survey of existing work, focuses on profitable lines of inquiry for future developments. Particular attention is devoted to fields of active current development, including domestic and comparative regulation, macroeconomic and international economic policy, budgetary rules, economic transition, legal decision making, and the fundamentals of institutions.

MODERN POLITICAL ECONOMY

POLITICAL ECONOMY OF INSTITUTIONS AND DECISIONS

Editors
James E. Alt, Harvard University
Douglass C. North, Washington University in St. Louis

Other books in the series
James E. Alt and Kenneth Shepsle, eds., *Perspectives on positive political economy*
Alberto Alesina and Howard Rosenthal, *Partisan politics, divided government and the economy*
Yoram Barzel, *Economic analysis of property rights*
Robert Bates, *Beyond the miracle of the market: the political economy of agrarian development in Kenya*
Peter Cowhey and Mathew McCubbins, *Structures and policy in Japan and the United States*
Gary W. Cox, *The efficient secret: the cabinet and the development of political parties in Victorian England*
Jean Ensminger, *Marking a market: the institutional transformation of an African society*
Murray Horn, *The political economy of public administration: institutional choice in the public sector*
Jack Knight, *Institutions and social conflict*
Michael Laver and Kenneth Shepsle, *Cabinet ministers and parliamentary government*
Leif Lewin, *Ideology and strategy: a century of Swedish politics (English Edition)*
Gary Libecap, *Contracting for property rights*
Mathew D. McCubbins and Terry Sullivan, eds., *Congress: structure and policy*
Gary J. Miller, *Managerial dilemmas: the political economy of hierarchy*
Douglass C. North, *Institutions, institutional change, and economic performance*
Mark Ramseyer and Frances Rosenbluth, *The politics of oligarchy: institutional choice in Imperial Japan*
Elinor Ostrom, *Governing the commons: the evolution of institutions for collective action*
Jean-Laurent Rosenthal, *The fruits of revolution: property rights, litigation, and French agriculture*
Charles Stewart III, *Budget reform politics: the design of the appropriations process in the House of Representatives, 1865–1921*
John Waterbury, *Exposed to innumerable delusions: public enterprise and state power in Egypt, India, Mexico, and Turkey*

MODERN POLITICAL ECONOMY

Old topics, new directions

Edited by
JEFFREY S. BANKS

ERIC A. HANUSHEK
University of Rochester

CAMBRIDGE
UNIVERSITY PRESS

Published by the Press Syndicate of the University of Cambridge
The Pitt Building, Trumpington Street, Cambridge CB2 1RP
40 West 20th Street, New York, NY 10011-4211, USA
10 Stamford Road, Oakleigh, Melbourne 3166, Australia

First published 1995

Printed in the United States of America

Library of Congress Cataloging-in-Publication Data
Modern political economy: old topics, new directions / edited by
Jeffrey S. Banks, Eric A. Hanushek.
    p.   cm. — (Political economy of institutions and decisions)
Includes index.
ISBN 0-521-47233-4 – ISBN 0-521-47810-3 (pbk.)
1. Economics – 2. Political science – I. Banks, Jeffrey S.
II. Hanushek, Eric Alan, 1943– . III. Series.
HB74.P65M63   1995
330 – dc20   94–39766
                                                                        CIP

A catalog record for this book is available from the British Library.

ISBN 0–521–47233–4 Hardback
ISBN 0–521–47810–3 Paperback

Contents

Contributors

Alberto Alesina
Department of Government and
   Department of Economics
Harvard University
Cambridge, MA 02138

David P. Baron
Graduate School of Business
Stanford University
Stanford, CA 94305

Randall L. Calvert
Department of Political Science
   and W. Allen Wallis Institute of
   Political Economy
University of Rochester
Rochester, NY 14627

John Ferejohn
Department of Political Science
Stanford University
Stanford, CA 94305

Edward M. Gramlich
Institute of Public Policy Studies
University of Michigan
Ann Arbor, MI 48109

Raymond Riezman
Department of Economics
University of Iowa
Iowa City, IA 52242

William H. Riker*
Department of Political Science
   and W. Allen Wallis Institute of
   Political Economy
University of Rochester
Rochester, NY 14627

Pablo T. Spiller
Haas School of Business
University of California
Berkeley, CA 94720

David L. Weimer
Department of Political Science
   and W. Allen Wallis Institute of
   Political Economy
University of Rochester
Rochester, NY 14627

John D. Wilson
Department of Economics
Indiana University
Bloomington, IN 47405

*Deceased

Series editors' preface

The Cambridge series on the Political Economy of Institutions and Decisions is built around attempts to answer two central questions: How do institutions evolve in response to individual incentives, strategies, and choices, and how do institutions affect the performance of political and economic systems? The scope of the series is comparative and historical rather than international or specifically American, and the focus is positive rather than normative.

An earlier volume of essays on the state of the field in this series, *Perspectives on Positive Political Economy,* mainly addressed organizational development. Now, Banks and Hanushek have assembled an exciting collection of papers in which formal theories of political economy are applied to the interaction between institutions and public policy. The chapters cover regulation, privatization, and the construction of credible property rights in economic transformations, as well as the political economy of economic policy in industrial societies (trade policy, macro policy, and budget policy). All of these are significant areas where politics and markets – or political and economic forces – interact. Each of these chapters summarizes a recent research program, integrating a variety of approaches and findings while pointing out the need and direction for future research. Additionally, two chapters address theoretical developments relating to the role of equilibria in institutional choice. Both of these chapters, one on the political economy of law and the other on institutions more generally, focus on problems of cooperation and coordination, and point the way to rigorous microfoundations for institutional analysis.

Nevertheless, despite the apparent diversity of approach and content, all the chapters in this volume share the underlying purpose of integrating the concerns of economics and political science in areas where the interdependence of the two is evident.

Preface

The study of political economy typically involves individual researchers following their own instincts about productive ways to expand on the way we think about specific political and economic phenomena. At least as practiced in the United States, institutional impediments frequently stand in the way of appropriate training and research when that research is very different from traditional approaches. Such is particularly true when the new approach falls across the boundaries of existing disciplines.

This volume represents a first step in altering some of these existing institutional impediments. The essays contained here were commissioned for presentation at the Inaugural Conference of the W. Allen Wallis Institute of Political Economy at the University of Rochester. The Wallis Institute was the natural outgrowth of the efforts of the economics and political science departments at the University of Rochester to foster closer intellectual ties than usually exist across these disciplines. The research lines sketched in this book constitute a starting point for the development of new approaches to research and training. This development has been supported and encouraged by the University of Rochester, which has dedicated resources to the development of the Wallis Institute.

The Wallis Institute is named in honor of W. Allen Wallis. He is a former president of the University, but more than that, his career is a personal model of political economy in action. Trained as a statistician, he achieved wide acclaim for innovative statistical approaches − achievements recognized, for example, by his election as President of the American Statistical Association. His career, however, was not narrowly defined by statistics. He ranged from academe to government while maintaining close relations with business and industry. He helped develop the national statistical system; he advised presidents from Eisenhower through Bush; he served as undersecretary of state for economic affairs; and he served on corporate boards across the country. The fact that we are creating a new institution for the study of political economy named after him is no accident. Neither was it an accident that the inaugural conference was timed to celebrate his 80th birthday.

We hope that future volumes sponsored by the Wallis Institute will expand on this starting point.

Introduction

JEFFREY S. BANKS AND ERIC A. HANUSHEK

Political economy, to paraphrase the editors of an earlier volume in this series, is the study of rational decisions in a context of political and economic institutions.[1] Its central tenent is that a comprehensive understanding of economic phenomena requires knowledge of the political institutions, actors, and incentives present in the decision-making process. Conversely, these same political variables are best studied with the rational actor orientation of economics and with a continual eye toward the economic consequences of political choices.

While politics and economics coexisted as the single discipline of political economy for much of the period of modern scholarship, these fields were formally split in the late nineteenth century. It is now apparent that this split, while advantageous for certain scientific developments, has biased the way in which economists and political scientists think about many issues. The separate disciplines, with their own views on appropriate methods and the most productive lines of research, place artificial constraints on the study of many important social issues. The reconstitution of political economy is designed to reunite the separate perspectives in those areas where the interaction of individuals, institutions, and markets is paramount.

The division of economics and political science into separate disciplines can be traced back to a variety of factors. To take one prominent example, the development of the neoclassical model in economics emphasized behavior of individual consumers and firms in perfectly competitive markets, at the expense of any sort of political considerations. Indeed, one of the founders of the neoclassical movement, Stanley Jevons, was an early advocate of replacing "the old troublesome double-worded name for our science," namely, political economy, with the much more concise label of "economics."[2] Whatever the cause, by the late nineteenth century professional organizations devoted solely to the study of economics and to the study of political science had emerged, and along with these organizations came a development of separate academic departments at the major universities. While this path followed a different timing across schools, largely based on their own internal dynamics, the division of the disciplines was virtually complete early in the twentieth century.

The most important implication of this division was a movement toward a high degree of specialization. Economists concentrated on market activities and, for the most part, took the political and institutional structures as given. Political scientists, on the other hand, devoted their energies to how institutions interacted with individuals and were shaped by individuals in essentially nonmarket situations. Such specialization has obvious and considerable advantages; in particular, by restricting the scope of inquiry, a wide range of analyses become more tractable. Moreover, because the modes of theoretical development, the kinds of data required for empirical analysis, and the types of expertise required for understanding the separate areas differ, divisions into "politics" and "economics" promoted the rapid development of knowledge in each area. The problem comes, of course, when the divisions of inquiry mask important issues. If, for example, the market forces themselves influence the institutional structure, say, through the politics of law and regulation, then analyses that take the institutional structure as given may be quite misleading.

A rejoining of political science and economics into political economy has been in progress in areas where the disciplinary divisions are most distorting. The fruits of this research are already substantial and its promise is greater than ever. Two separate but related aspects of the movement toward a new political economy stand out. First, this movement provides a natural way to cross-fertilize the separate disciplines and, essentially, to import approaches and thinking across disciplinary lines. This aspect of political economy does not really change the underlying boundaries of inquiry. It merely provides a natural way to expand and improve existing lines of economic and political science inquiry. The political scientists' emphasis on institutions and their effects has helped economists recognize how the structure of economic institutions effects economic performance. Conversely, the economist's individual choice perspective has made political science examine more critically its theories about the formation, evolution, and maintenance of institutions. The understanding that results from such interdisciplinary exchange has without doubt improved the way we address important policy problems, ranging from the management of firms to the design of constitutions.

Second, and more exciting, is the true integration of the two lines of analysis. As noted, the clean conceptual separation of markets, politics, and institutions is inappropriate in a variety of important situations. For example, analysis of the economic effects of regulation cannot be complete without careful attention to how market and political forces determine the institutional structure itself. In simplest terms, regulatory institutions and their rules do not appear as some sort of gift from on high. Instead, they are designed, implemented, and modified by the body politic, which includes the regulated, the regulators, and the general public (i.e., consumers and voters). Analyses of firm behavior in the face of a given set of regulations may miss entirely the most important issues by failing to consider the origins and development of the institutions themselves. Moreover, what analysis is done might be seriously biased by assuming that the regulatory structure is given. As another example, economists interested in international trade and tariff formation have typically not been sensitive to the politics of campaign contributions and interest group lobbying; similarly, political scientists are naturally led to explore tariff formation as a case of distributive politics, but are usually naive about the underlying economic forces driving the distributional consequences of trade restrictions. Though specialization is often desirable for scholarly research, it can promote lopsided perspectives on problems of social interaction. The unified approach of political economy is promising for its natural relevance to the problems of government economic policy making, regulation of industry, legislative structure and performance, and the development or conversion of economic and political systems.

The initial stages of the resurgence of political economy tended quite naturally to be unbalanced. Economists, for example, tended to take well-developed maximizing models of individual economic behavior and graft on simplistic models of politics. The models of politics tended to be "black boxes" that returned a political solution without describing its genesis. To the extent that political actors were included, these actors tended not to be optimizers – in sharp contrast to the economic actors. Political scientists, on the other hand, tend to graft on distorted models of market outcomes in their development of models of political behavior. By not fully appreciating the subtleties of market interactions, they tended to neglect market adjustments to any political changes. Indeed, in the early development, when traditionally trained economists or political scientists attempted to publish in the other's journals, they were typically met with a certain disdain for their simplistic modeling approaches.

The most recent period of development has moved toward more balanced treatment of the various parts of issues of public behavior. The most innovative and potentially important areas of development in political economy concentrate precisely on the interactions of politics and economics through institutions. They include models with rational actors

3

on both sides and, in many forms, allow for considerable endogeneity of the institutional structure. The subsequent chapters in this book highlight this new phase of intellectual development.

The development of political economy has varied by specific area. The most appropriate analytical structures for dealing with financial regulation issues almost certainly differ from those for considering the spread of tariffs and quotas. One theme is present in almost all contexts, however: the importance of the extent of commitment that can be expected from the political system for understanding individual and collective behavior. Once the political system produces an institutional structure – whether related to the elements of contract law or to the determination of governmental fiscal policy – will the system stay in place? Or is it likely to change, perhaps based on the future choices of individuals operating within the existing political system? If the political system will not, or cannot, commit to the future, then the optimal choices for an individual are likely to differ dramatically from the choices under complete commitment.

This theme of commitment pervades most areas of political economy. Institutional design confronts the topic directly. For example, when approaching the problem of how a government should encourage private investment in plant and equipment, the ultimate impact of any program will depend crucially on whether investors think nationalization of industry or changes in liability laws are likely. And this simple example demonstrates the central themes of political economy: large private investment in industries makes nationalization more attractive to politicians, but the likelihood of attracting investment will depend critically on the ability of the government to credibly commit not to nationalize. The design question concerns how such commitments can be made credible in the face of the short-run incentives facing the government. Similarly, the response of individuals, say public utility investors, to various regulations on rate of return to investment will depend on their expectations about a stable set of returns in the future. Or the savings behavior of individuals in an economy will be affected by what future tax regimes the government can commit to maintaining. Or the likelihood that individual voters will respond to politicians' promises about economic policy will depend crucially on whether the voters have reason to believe that the politicians will carry through on their promises.

The actual application of this notion of political commitment also varies with the topic of study. The ways that governments can use international organizations and agreements to achieve commitments about trade policies clearly differ from the ways that the national government can develop credible commitments about fiscal policy and taxes. Nevertheless, the ideas of commitment are central to most inquiries into the boundaries between economics and politics, and so constitute a common theme among the chapters to follow.

In this volume we attempt to provide guidance about future developments in political economy. The volume is not meant to be just a review of what has been done in the past, although that is a part of the motivation and development. Rather, it is meant to describe a series of productive and useful lines of research, lines that are likely to expand our understanding of the underlying political and economic behavior. Further, the selection of topics covered in the volume is not so much comprehensive as it is illustrative. We have commissioned analyses of areas with common characteristics. They are inherently important in that they directly impinge on the welfare of a large number of individuals. They have received considerable past attention, yet important issues remain to be resolved. They are, for the most part, areas where the interplay of theory and empirical work is important. At the same time, the separate chapters diverge in their primary attention to political or to economic outcomes; in the importance of different kinds of economic agents (individuals, firms, or nations); and in the kind of political activity that is most central. Other examples and illustrations than those chosen could be included or substituted. Yet the important element of the current collection is that they illustrate the primary analytical and modeling approaches that fall within the domain of modern political economy.

In Chapter 1 David Baron surveys and synthesizes research on governmental regulation of firms and industries. One prominent line of work in this area focuses on the regulation of monopolies (e.g., public utilities) in the presence of asymmetric information, where such information is valuable in identifying a regulator's optimal decision. Earlier models in this vein posited regulators interested in economic efficiency and able to commit to long-term output and pricing arrangements. More recent studies have relaxed both of these assumptions, allowing for distributive and other considerations to enter the regulator's decision calculus, allowing for bargaining between regulators, the regulated firm, and their political overseers, and allowing for a lack of commitment on the part of any and all concerned parties. Other lines of research are considered as well; for example, the regulatory models associated with the Chicago school focus not so much on the efficiency-enhancing talents of government as on its ability to redistribute income from some groups of individuals to others. Baron brings these and other features of regulation research together into a coherent description of extant results and open questions.

Regulation is addressed in Chapter 2 as well. Here, Pablo Spiller looks at the attempts by various Latin American countries to privatize their utilities. He finds that, consistent with Baron's discussion in Chapter 1, the implementation of efficient regulatory schemes relies critically on the government's ability to commit to a "fair" rate of return. Thus, those countries that lack constitutional or other protections against governmental expropriation are typically the ones that have a relatively painful, unsatisfactory, or nonexistent privatization experience. Conversely, those countries possessing such protections have been able to privatize, thereby demonstrating in dramatic fashion the economic consequences of political institutions.

William Riker and David Weimer examine the issue of political commitment in the context of the emerging democracies of Eastern Europe in Chapter 3. Specifically, they look at how different countries' attempts at establishing a secure system of property rights has determined to a large extent each country's success in easing the transition from socialism to capitalism, and from authoritarianism to democracy. Underlying any neoclassical model of exchange and production, as well as the consequent efficiency properties of equilibrium allocations, are the assumptions of well-defined rights to the ownership and control of resources. Hence, the positive effects of the free market system predicted in the wake of the collapsed communist regimes in Eastern Europe required satisfactory answers to questions concerning "who owns what." Furthermore, raising such questions necessarily raises distributional issues as well, in that identifying ownership automatically assigns the gains from such ownership. The difficulty in Eastern Europe, then, stems from the attempt to specify a system of property rights and simultaneously to affect the short-term winners and losers under the system, and doing so in a still-developing political regime predicated on democratic ideals. As with the discussion of regulatory practices in Chapters 1 and 2, here again we see how the ability of the government to commit to a system of property rights, and to garner sufficient political support for such a system, are critical variables in the equation identifying a country's economic success.

Chapter 4, authored by Raymond Riezman and John Wilson, analyzes the ability of private firms to influence the trade policies of their host countries. Neoclassical economists from Adam Smith on down have supported the notion of free trade without tariffs, quotas, and the like among nations. Yet these impediments to trade have long been in existence. Furthermore, their existence appears to depend in a systematic fashion on the industries and the countries in question. This inconsistency of theory with data is defused when the model of the government as "benevolent planner" found in many neoclassical models is replaced with one in which political decision making is sensitive to the demands of electorally important groups of constituents. Specifically, from the perspective of a single firm or industry within a country, the benefits of protection can be quite large even if such protection inhibits efficiency, and hence firms will have an incentive to invest time, effort, and money into the political process to secure such benefits. This chapter thus focuses on the political environment within which decisions concerning trade policy are made, with competition for votes among parties and candidates being a principle determinant of the policy outcome.

The effects of political institutions on macroeconomic variables such as inflation and unemployment is addressed by Alberto Alesina in Chapter 5. As with the preceding chapter on trade theory, the central idea here is that macroeconomic policy is not determined by efficiency (or other) considerations alone, but rather is the result of a political process by which a consensus on policy is somehow achieved. Most of the political models of macroeconomics have simplified this process by positing a single representative (e.g., the president) having complete control over policy, and then studying the influence of political competition or party ideology on the policy outcome. For example, "opportunistic" models assert that the incumbent representative modifies policy while in office so as to maximize the chances of being re-elected; under such a model one should observe "political business cycles" during a representative's time in office (e.g., booms prior to an election). On the other hand, "partisan" models are built around the presumption that different parties naturally follow different policies, given their intrinsic preferences for certain types of policy outcomes; here, movement through a cycle is correlated with the party affiliation of the incumbent. Alesina reviews the theory and supporting data (or lack thereof) for both classes of models, as well as their "rational expectations" successors.

Edward Gramlich tackles the politics and economics of fiscal policy and deficit control in Chapter 6. In particular, he considers the pros and cons of a balanced budget amendment to the U.S. Constitution, in light of previous attempts to mitigate the federal government's profligate debt financing through legislation such as the Gramm–Rudman–Hollings Act of 1985. The temptation for politicians to spend for today's benefits with tomorrow's dollars is readily apparent: today's politicians need not be around when today's bill comes due. (Indeed, one relevant question is not why deficits are so large today, but rather why haven't they always been so.) Gramm–Rudman set target levels for successive budgets that in theory could not be missed under penalty of sequestor. Yet, as was seen in earlier chapters, the issue of commitment comes into play: no one Congress can tie the hands of another, so when the targets became binding the current Congress would simply alter the targets. The appeal of a balanced budget amendment, then, is that it would supposedly inhibit changes in the targets by making such changes more costly to implement. Gramlich addresses the forcefulness of this argument, in part by considering experiences at the state level, where 49 out of the 50 states require a balanced budget.

In most of the chapters, the political institutions involved in the decision making are contained within either the legislative or the executive branches of government. For example, the single representative selected by the electors in the macroeconomics models in Chapter 5 or the trade models in Chapter 4 can be thought of as the president, whereas the balanced budget discussion in Chapter 6 dealt primarily with legislative decision making. In Chapter 7, John Ferejohn argues for the extension of these and other rational choice models of politics to include the judicial branch as well. That the courts have a distinct and measurable impact on legislative and executive policy decisions and outcomes is beyond question; judicial review of legislative statutes and administrative law governing executive agencies guarantees such. The innovation of these emerging rational choice models of courts is the employment of many of the fundamental tools from the legislative and executive models (preferences, strategies, agenda control, etc.) in the analysis of the courts, thereby expanding the institutional scope of these earlier models in an analytically parsimonious manner. This innovativeness runs in the other direction as well: by considering factors such as the interpretation of laws, classical legal issues and arguments breathe life into the otherwise stale policy choice models of legislatures.

Finally, in Chapter 8 Randall Calvert takes a step back from the applications-oriented studies of the other chapters and analyzes more generally the notion of political and economic institutions as endogenously determined phenomena. The key insight here is that, at a certain level, all institutions have a potential problem of enforceability; that is, they must have some means by which the rules and processes of decision making can credibly constrain individual and collective behavior. To take an example from Chapter 6, passing a balanced budget amendment would not in and of itself generate a balanced budget, because no mechanism exists to preclude all of the relevant political actors (including those found in the judiciary) from simply ignoring the amendment. On the other hand, such a maneuver may be quite costly to the parties involved in terms of, say, how predictable future governmental decisions would be (recall the Chapter 2 discussion). Therefore it is not the amendment itself, but rather the behavior of the political actors involved, reacting to the incentives present, that generates a balanced budget. Effective institutions, then, can be seen to possess the trait of self-enforcement, in that the participants have an incentive to maintain the institution. And this criterion of self-enforcement leads inexorably to a game-theoretic modeling strategy for the understanding of the emergence and stability of institutions. Calvert models economic and political institutions as equilibrium outcomes of certain collective action or coordination games, and demonstrates how communication can foster cooperative outcomes in such games.

Each of these chapters strips away many of the structures of political and economic analysis that have comfortably survived decades of development. Each points to how traditional disciplinary specialization falls short of dealing with a number of very important issues of society. The rigid boundaries of the constituent disciplines simply constrain analysis and, too frequently, bias results in the important issues taken up here.

The essays, however, are best thought of as beginnings to new lines of research. Each describes the current state of knowledge and research in its own area, criticizing shortcomings and pointing to profitable directions for the future. But the uncertainty and rudimentary nature of much of the thinking must also be recognized.

In many ways the success of this volume will be measured by how quickly it becomes obsolete. Success in the modern development of political economy will move us beyond these introductory stages and onto paths yet to be considered. While not the normal view of authors, we hope that obsolescence comes quickly, for it will be a clear sign that political economy is successfully re-emerging and intruding on the way we think about the world around us.

NOTES

1. J. Alt and K. Shepsle, eds. *Perspectives on Positive Political Economy*, Cambridge University Press (1990), p. 2.
2. Quoted in B. Clark, *Political Economy: A Comparative Approach*, New York: Praeger (1991), p. 32.

1

The economics and politics of regulation: perspectives, agenda, and approaches

DAVID P. BARON

INTRODUCTION

This essay provides perspectives on research on regulation, identifies an agenda of research topics, and discusses approaches to some of those topics. The focus is on a set of presently identified issues on which social science research may be able to make a contribution, irrespective of how amenable the issues are to study with our present set of analytical tools. The essay thus focuses more on research opportunities and less on where progress is most likely to be made. Many of these research opportunities are suggested by regulatory practice and emerging concerns.

One approach to regulatory research focuses on the identification of market failures and on market-like mechanisms for correcting those failures. This perspective is necessarily normative and measures performance in terms of efficiency. Major advances in the theory of regulation have resulted from treating as endogenous the behavior in the regulatory relationship. This includes not only treating the behavior of the firm as endogenous, but also making the choice of a regulatory policy endogenous. The research challenge, however, is broader than that of providing advice about efficient regulatory policies and includes the prediction and explanation of actual regulatory behavior.

A second approach to regulatory research, that of political economy, adopts a positive perspective. In its simplest form, the political economy approach views regulation as demanded and supplied as a function of the interests of those who incur the distributive consequences of policy alternatives.[1] The political economy perspective thus does not require a market failure for regulation to be supplied. This perspective is not divorced

This research has been supported by NSF Grant No. SES-9109707. I would like to thank Justin Adams, Susanne Lohmann, Pablo Spiller, and Robert Wilson for their helpful comments.

from the market failure perspective, however, since the presence of a market failure and a policy to correct it generate distributive consequences. Those distributive consequences provide incentives for political action both in support of and in opposition to a policy, but if the policy is not Pareto dominant and side payments cannot be made, no simple resolution of the conflicting interests is possible. Resolution then rests with a political institution.

The political economy approach is not inconsistent with normative theory, since normative theory should incorporate the political behavior that invariably accompanies policy choice and implementation. In economics, moral hazard or adverse selection are taken into account in the design of a regulatory policy. In the political economy approach, regulatory policy should be designed in light of the present political activity and the possible opportunistic political action intended to change the policy as a result of information gained through experience with that policy. This perspective is developed more fully in the section "Political Design of Regulatory Policy."

The past twenty-five years have witnessed an explosion of research on economic, or industry, regulation. This has been driven by a number of forces. One has been regulatory performance, as concerns were raised about the effect of regulation on costs in industries such as airlines, trucking, and public utilities. This research has focused not only on whether competition would yield better performance than regulation, but also on how the regulatory process itself affects performance. Although deregulation has prevailed in a number of industries and regulation has diminished in importance for others, price regulation may be returning, propelled by political forces resulting from the distributive consequences of industry performance. Price regulation has recently been enacted for basic cable television service and could be on the horizon for prescription pharmaceuticals. The pressures resulting from rapidly increasing expenditures on health care, for example, could lead to regulation and price controls on a range of health care products and services.

The dramatic expansion of social regulation beginning in the early 1970s has not generated a body of regulatory research commensurate with its importance. The theory of safety, health, and environmental regulation has not advanced as rapidly as has that for price, entry, and conditions of service regulation. Although cost-benefit analysis has been applied to the evaluation of certain aspects of social regulation, a principal complication to this type of research is the considerable uncertainty about both the underlying phenomenon itself and the consequences of policy alternatives. This complication is often due to scientific uncertainty, but it may also be due to the contrast between the efficiency concerns of economists and the concerns of legislators and regulators, which often

11

seem to focus on rights and protecting people from their own actions and the actions of others.

Scientific advance and technological change have also brought attention to hazards that had in the past been poorly understood, giving rise to calls for expanded protection or more stringent regulation. Although these calls may not result in the creation of new regulatory agencies, they are likely to result in a continuing evolution of social regulation. If history is an indicator of the future, that regulation will evolve in the direction of greater stringency.

This essay is organized as follows. In the next section, normative theory is considered, and the political economy approach is addressed in the third section. The institutional context of the first two sections is the economic regulation of industries, whereas social regulation is considered in the fourth section. Policy analysis and evaluation are the subjects of the fifth section, and the sixth section discusses comparative research. A summary is also provided by addressing research issues in the regulation of pharmaceuticals.[2]

NORMATIVE THEORY

Information economics and regulatory mechanisms
In the past three decades, the theory of regulation has been extended by incorporating a number of features of the regulatory environment ranging from characteristics of institutions and institutional choice to informational and observational asymmetries.[3] This theory has focused on optimal second-best regulation, where "second-best" refers to institutional restrictions or restrictions arising from asymmetric information or observability, and "optimal" refers to the choice of the best policy relative to those restrictions.

A rich literature has developed around the complications that arise from incomplete information and imperfect monitoring of performance in regulatory relationships. This research program has generated theories that have deepened our understanding of the design of regulatory policies and has identified some of the limitations of regulation in addressing market failures. It has also provided guidance for the design of regulatory incentive mechanisms, although the actual designers of those systems have generally chosen to emphasize simplicity and transparency over complexity and finely tuned incentives.[4] That is, regulators have chosen systems, such as price caps, that have relatively few observables and loose monitoring, over more detailed incentive mechanisms.

The basic model of information economics as applied to regulation begins with the observation that the regulated firm has information about some aspect of performance, such as its cost of production or the demand for its output, that is superior to the information the regulator has. (This is referred to as incomplete, private, or hidden information.) In the simplest setting, a regulator must set the price for the output of a regulated monopolist that is better informed about its marginal cost than is the regulator. For example, the regulator knows the probability distribution of possible marginal costs, whereas the firm knows its marginal cost exactly. If the regulator knew the marginal cost, it would set price equal to marginal cost and provide a lump-sum transfer equal to the fixed costs of the firm. In the context of U.S. institutions, that transfer is paid by consumers through, for example, monthly charges that are independent of the quantity consumed. In other institutional contexts, the transfer could be provided by the government budget and funded through the tax system.[5] With the former approach, the regulatory objective is typically expressed as a linear combination of consumers' and producers' surpluses. With the latter, the objective is usually formulated as consumers' plus producers' surplus less the cost of the economic distortion due to the taxes levied to cover the transfer. Under both approaches, the firm is assumed to have the right to choose whether to participate, that is, to produce or withdraw.[6]

The regulator is assumed to have legal authority to regulate the price and, because of that authority, is typically assumed to move first by making a take-it-or-leave-it offer to the firm. The offer is a price at which the good will be sold and the transfer paid to the firm. If the regulator were to set the price and transfer too low, the firm would choose not to participate, in which case the good would not be supplied. To ensure that the good is supplied, the regulator can set a price equal to the highest possible marginal cost and provide a transfer equal to the fixed cost. The loss in consumer surplus could be substantial, however, because of the high price. Furthermore, the firm would earn a profit equal to the quantity demanded at that price multiplied by the difference between the highest possible marginal cost and the firm's true cost.[7] The issue then is whether the regulator can do better than this by choosing a low price when the firm has low costs and a high price when the firm has high costs.[8]

The regulator's problem then is to find the optimal trade-off between control of the rents of the firm and the surplus of consumers. Although the regulator does not know the firm's marginal cost, it does know the probability distribution of that cost and can use that information to design a price schedule or mechanism, consisting of a set of price and transfer combinations, and allow the firm to choose the combination it prefers based on its private information. The optimal price schedule includes alternatives ranging from a low price and a high transfer to a high price and a low (possibly negative) transfer. The schedule is chosen so that a firm with a low marginal cost will have an incentive to choose a low-price/high-transfer combination and a firm with a high cost will have an incentive to choose a high-price/low-transfer combination. In the optimal price schedule, the price corresponding to the lowest possible marginal cost can be set equal to that cost, but for any higher cost the price exceeds marginal cost. The difference between the price and marginal cost is the marginal information rent, which depends on the probability distribution of the possible marginal costs. The transfer is chosen to achieve two objectives. First, it is chosen so that the firm prefers to produce rather than to withdraw. Second, it is chosen to structure the incentives so that if the firm has a marginal cost of say 10 it will choose the price-transfer combination designed for a marginal cost of 10. The firm then has the incentive to select the price-transfer combination designed for its costs, and with that combination its profits are nonnegative, so it will chose to produce.

This type of theory can be extended in a number of directions. One natural extension is to incorporate actions, such as the choice of factor inputs or managerial effort, that the firm can take to affect its costs. If those actions are observable, the regulator can require, as a condition of being allowed to produce, that the firm take the most efficient actions. A more realistic assumption is that the ability of the regulator to observe the actions of the firm is limited and thus that the actions are hidden from the regulator. The regulator may, however, be able to observe, perhaps imperfectly, the actual costs of the firm *ex post* and draw inferences about those actions. The regulator thus must design the price schedule taking into account the hidden actions and its ability to observe costs *ex post*. It does so by basing the transfer on the observed cost and perhaps, depending on the model, by distorting the price schedule as well.

Although considerable progress has been made in extending the theory of regulation under incomplete information in a number of directions, there are a number of issues that warrant additional attention. This section addresses some of those issues and suggests additional research questions.

Moving first and counteroffers.   As indicated earlier, much of the theory of optimal regulation under hidden information and hidden actions has been developed using screening models in which the regulatory agency moves first in promulgating a policy to which the firm responds. This type of model seems natural because agencies have the authority to impose policies at their discretion, subject, of course, to due process requirements. Regulated firms, however, also have the opportunity to initiate regulatory actions and provide information without being commanded or induced by incentives to do so.⁹ The resulting model then is one of signaling.

The equilibria of these two classes of models can be quite different, yet intuition suggests that they should not be so different, since in the real world the sequence in which parties may move is not restricted a priori. The difference in these theories presumably centers on the ability of a player to commit to a strategy. For example, in screening models the regulator is assumed to be able to commit credibly to the menu of policies it offers to the regulated firm. Commitment means that if the firm responds with a message that is not in the specified message set or if the firm refuses to participate, the regulator can commit to having the firm not produce. That is, if the firm can earn at least its reservation value by participating, it is assumed to do so. But what if the firm chooses not to participate or if it makes a counteroffer? Will the regulator be able to keep its commitment not to make another offer to the firm? And if the firm is not absolutely certain that the regulator will never make another offer, it may refuse to participate by, for example, not investing in facilities. This might be more likely if the firm has high costs, since in a screening model a firm with high costs earns small rents relative to a firm with low costs. In a signaling model, similar concerns can arise. For example, what happens if the regulator refuses to listen to the communication of the firm?

This suggests that the ability of the regulator to commit not to revise its offer in the face of an unanticipated response by the firm and the ability not to listen to communication from the firm are the central differences between screening and signaling models. A theory that reconciles screening and signaling theories of regulation is needed. Some type of bargaining model in which commitment is not completely credible and the sequence of moves is not prespecified could produce a theory in which regulators choose policies, but firms have an opportunity to communicate before the policy is chosen by the regulator and can make counteroffers. Such a unifying theory would increase the confidence that we have been studying the design of regulatory policies with an appropriate framework.

Commitment. Regulatory policies generally remain in effect indefinitely yet are subject to revision either by the regulatory agency itself (subject to due process requirements), Congress, or the president. In many cases, the revisions are in response to industry, interest group, or public pressure. The theory of incentive regulation under incomplete information and moral hazard can be extended in a straightforward manner to a multiperiod framework under the assumption that the regulatory agency can make credible commitments to a policy for the entire horizon. This type of extension can also incorporate information that evolves over time, so optimal regulatory policies can be adaptive, flexible, and responsive to information that becomes available and to developments such as technological change.[10] The assumption of credible commitment limits the extent to which a party can engage in opportunistic behavior and hence provides a basis for reliance. Commitment can fail, however, because of a change in government, opportunistic behavior on the part of either the regulatory agency or the regulated firms, or pressure from interest groups. When commitment is not fully credible, firms have greater difficulty making long-term plans and weaker incentives to make long-term and irreversible investments.

If commitment is not credible, characterization of the optimal policy or equilibrium is extremely difficult if not impossible, as Laffont and Tirole (1988) have shown.[11] Determining an optimal policy in the absence of commitment may be infeasible, but multiperiod and dynamic policies are sufficiently important to warrant additional attention. The nature and direction of this line of research is less clear, however. One possibility is to view the regulator and the firm as negotiating an agreement that can be enforced by a third party or in which opportunistic behavior can be limited by due process or procedural requirements. Political intervention from Congress or the president, however, can never be precluded, so such measures provide only limited assurances of the continuity of policy.

One approach might be to focus on simple, but nonoptimal, policies, such as linear policies, that are transparent and not burdensome to implement or comply with. Such policies may be less likely to generate the forces that can lead to changes in policies because change is smoother and easier to explain to external parties. Such policies may provide limited commitment. Schmalensee (1989) and Gasmi, Ivaldi, and Laffont (1991) have evaluated what they refer to as "good" regulatory policies. The notion of good, but nonoptimal, policies assessed by numerical methods holds some promise for finding multiperiod policies that might be both implementable and sustainable. One objective of this type of research is to determine how close simple policies can come to an optimal policy. If they are close, then attention can focus on choosing the simple policy that increases the likelihood that it will remain in force, thereby giving firms incentives to make long-term investments.

A more direct approach is to focus on mechanisms to make commitment more secure. These could include institutional features ranging from the use of due process requirements, to greater independence from Congress and the executive branch, to legislative procedures, such as those contained in fast track procedures, which limit the alternatives available to legislators.[12] Mechanisms to make commitment more likely could also take the form of external bonding that is difficult to undo because of administrative procedures that take considerable time to complete or because penalties could be imposed by third parties such as consumers if policies are changed dramatically.[13] Similarly, through the use of particular types of incomplete contracts, the regulator may be able to restrict its ability to take advantage of information it learns over time from the firm. That is, if the regulator can limit its ability to observe regulatory performance, opportunistic behavior may be less likely. This, of course, has to be balanced with the potential gains from using information that becomes available through performance.[14]

One proposal for limiting opportunistic behavior is the fair bargain proposed by Baron and Besanko (1987) in which the regulated firm agrees to participate and satisfy demand, and the regulator assures it a fair profit that does not opportunistically take advantage of sunk investments. Such a bargain could be enforceable by the courts. Klevorick (1991) views this type of bargain as intended to respect process values of fair treatment that make policies more credible and opportunistic behavior more difficult.

The issue of commitment and opportunistic behavior is also affected by the institutional arrangement for administering the regulatory policy. Price cap systems are the current experiment, and although they have been studied extensively from a theoretical perspective, less is known about their implementation.[15] As experience is gained with these systems, evidence will become available to evaluate their design and implementation, as well as their ability to withstand opportunistic behavior.

In a variety of regulatory contexts, anecdotal evidence suggests that firms moderate their actions in an attempt to reduce the pressure for changes in regulatory policies, either opportunistic or planned, and avoid more stringent regulation. For example, British Telecom was believed to have moderated its price increases prior to the five-year review of the RPI-X price cap system, so that its rate of return would not appear to be "excessive" and hence warrant a higher estimate of the rate (X) of technological progress.[16] The issue is why such behavior, if it does occur, has any influence on the regulator. That is, if this behavior is the result of a pure strategy, the regulator should be able to invert the policy and infer the firm's underlying information. This would not be the case if the moderation were in the context of a pooling equilibrium, a randomized strategy, or coarse observation, since although the regulator would not be fooled in equilibrium, opportunism would be limited by the imperfect inferences that could be drawn. A theory of strategic moderation grounded in the strategies of firms would be instructive.

Learning from limits, limits of learning, and focal points. As indicated earlier, the mechanism design approach to the study of regulation has been successful in developing insights into optimal second-best regulatory policies when commitment can be assured, but since regulation takes place over time, it is important to take into account a series of regulatory decisions in which commitments to future policies have only limited credibility. One approach to studying regulatory relationships with limited commitment and the periodic choice of a regulatory policy is that of repeated games. The representation of the regulatory relationship by a repeated game has the advantage that no assumption is made about a long-term commitment to a policy, and a policy is chosen at each stage given the history of play up to that stage.[17] The theory of these models has (at least) two types of limitations, however. One is that they typically have an infinite number of equilibria that can differ considerably in their properties. This limits their predictive powers. Second, in models with incomplete information, the characterization of reasonable equilibria can be quite difficult because information is revealed over time and beliefs must be updated at each stage. Repeated game models, however, should be capable of yielding insights into regulatory relationships with repeated encounters, so means of drawing reasonable conclusions from these models are needed.[18]

One means of addressing the limitations of the theory of repeated games is to study the limit properties of their equilibria. Two approaches have recently been developed. For stochastic games of complete information, Rausser and Simon (1991) study the limit equilibria of finitely repeated bargaining games such as those that might be used to represent an unstructured relationship involving a regulator and a regulated firm in which the player who has a move at a given stage is determined randomly. The intuition underlying the approach is that the farther away is the (finite) horizon, the more expectations smooth out the future. The limit can be an exact equilibrium or a cycle among a set of equilibria, or it can remain unknown. Although the limiting equilibria must be determined by numerical methods, this approach provides insights into the types of equilibria that can be limits of finite equilibria. Their approach can be thought of as a search for a focal point for the limit game.

Another approach to identifying a focal point in an infinitely repeated game is to adopt the perspective that players are likely to focus on simple rather than complex equilibria (unless the simple equilibria have unreasonable properties).[19] One means of formalizing the notion of simplicity is to represent the strategies of players by finite automata and then ask which strategies can be implemented by the simplest automata. Baron and Kalai (1993) show that the simplest equilibrium in a complete information, majority-rule bargaining model of division is the stationary equilibrium characterized by Baron and Ferejohn (1989).[20] This type of bargaining model can be applied to the study of repeated regulatory

18

encounters, as considered in the section "The Stringency of Social Regulation."

Infinitely repeated games of incomplete information are more complex and allow even more equilibria than infinitely repeated models of complete information. Kalai and Lehrer (1991) show that in an infinitely repeated game of incomplete information, the players will eventually play the Nash equilibrium of the complete information, infinitely repeated game. The folk theorem, however, establishes that there are an infinite number of equilibria, so there can be an infinite number of limiting equilibria. McKelvey and Palfrey (1992a,b) study an infinitely repeated game of incomplete information and focus on belief stationary equilibria in which players play the same strategy in each subgame in which they have the same beliefs about the type of the other player. This can be thought of as a model of a regulatory relationship in which the regulator and the firm have private information. McKelvey and Palfrey show that in spite of the belief stationarity restriction, the equilibria can exhibit a chaotic pattern, although that pattern is interpretable. Although their results are somewhat discouraging, experimentation with other restrictions on beliefs or strategies may be more fruitful in yielding plausible equilibria from the focal point perspective.

Since repeated models are reasonable representations of certain regulatory relationships, understanding the properties of their equilibria is important. The search for focal points, although perhaps not compelling from a theoretical perspective, may provide reasonable insight into workable regulatory relationships in the sense of the fair bargain concept discussed earlier.

Unforeseen contingencies. One of the principal obstacles to the design and implementation of long-term regulatory policies is, as history reveals, that not all events can be foreseen. When unforeseen events occur, regulatory policies are often revised in light of those events. Revision may be appropriate, but it can lessen the credibility of any long-term policy. What is needed is a choice theory for situations in which unforeseen events may occur. Kreps (1992) presents a choice theory that incorporates unforeseen events and constitutes a first step in such a line of inquiry. The hope is that further research along this line will provide a basis for the formulation of regulatory mechanisms that fully take account of foreseen events and have procedures for addressing unforeseen contingencies.

Multidimensional information. Most models of optimal regulation represent private information by a unidimensional parameter.[21] This provides tractability and clarifies intuition, yet in any complex regulatory relationship information surely has many dimensions. For example, a

19

regulator may have incomplete information about both demand and cost (Lewis and Sappington 1989) or the firm might have multiple products with costs depending on parameters associated with each product (McAfee and McMillan 1988).

Multidimensional screening models, however, are quite difficult to analyze because of integrability requirements. Recent advances by Armstrong (1991) and Wilson (1993) provide some hope that analytical characterizations of optimal policies can be obtained and, when they cannot be characterized analytically, that numerical methods can be used to determine optimal policies.

Multiple principals. Many, if not most, firms are regulated by more than one agency. In some cases, there may be a separation between the various regulatory policies, but this is not the case for firms subject to cost-based regulation. Electric power companies are subject to environmental regulation that substantially increases the costs of electricity, and those costs thus indirectly link environmental regulation and price regulation. The cost of environmental compliance affects prices, and those prices affect the quantity produced and hence the pollution emitted. Although environmental regulation and price regulation interact, the regulatory policies are chosen by different agencies, which typically act independently of each other. The regulated firm thus has multiple, and independent, principals. Yet optimal environmental regulation and price regulation should be determined jointly.

The research questions include the following. Is there some form of transfer price among the agencies or coordination mechanism that would achieve optimal regulation? If not, what is the second-best regulatory policy? On which side, environmental or price regulation, is the inefficiency the more pronounced? Does the efficiency of the regulation depend on which agency moves first, or is performance institutionally independent?

Baron (1985a,b) has investigated regulation with multiple principals and incomplete information.[22] He studied models involving a firm subject both to environmental regulation of emissions and fair-return regulation with the control of prices as the instrument. In the model, the environmental regulator has the authority to move first in setting an emissions standard, and the economic regulator sets prices taking into account the costs of environmental compliance. A Stackelberg equilibrium between the regulators is characterized under the assumption that communication by the firm to the public utility regulator is observable to the environmental regulator. A number of important issues remain. One pertains to whether the environmental regulator is indifferent between observing the communication to the public utility regulator and having the firm communicate directly to it. Another is the relationship between the equilibrium among the regulators and the firm and its implications for the structure of the regulated firm. Related issues are considered in the section "Organizational Structure and the Scope of Control."

Hierarchies and regulation.   Regulation involves an administrative process that is both controlling and controlled. Agencies regulate aspects of the operations of firms, but those agencies are also controlled by political principals. The natural model thus is hierarchical with a firm regulated by an agency and the agency either controlled by or given objectives by a political principal such as a legislature.[23] Incentive problems can be present at both levels of the hierarchy. More importantly, a hierarchical structure can provide an opportunity for hidden gaming in which, for example, the political principal designs a structure for the regulation of the firm, but the regulatory agency can also choose an incentive mechanism through implementation rules that are not fully observable to the political principal.[24] Regulation takes place largely in the public view, so the ability of a political principal to monitor the regulator's actions limits the hidden gaming. Monitoring and communication thus should be central to the study of hierarchies and regulation. The following section discusses a related issue of regulation and organizational structure.

Organizational structure and the scope of control.   The theory of regulation has largely been developed from models that treat the firm as a unitary entity, yet the internal organization of the firm and of its production can affect performance, particularly when information is incomplete. Regulated firms also enter into a variety of relationships with suppliers and in some cases with distributors, and regulatory performance may be affected by the structure and efficiency of those relationships. When there are informational asymmetries, the organizational structure, the locus of information, and the nature of communication can affect organizational performance and hence the regulator's choice of the scope of control. For example, the performance of a regulated firm may depend on how it is organized both internally and externally, and hence regulation should take that organization into account.

Production may be organized in separate firms, consolidated in a single firm, or arranged in a hierarchy in which one firm is regulated and contracts with another firm under a delegation structure. Production in a number of regulated industries is characterized by complementarities with units producing components that are combined to form the final product or service. Gilbert and Riordan (1992) give the example of the

21

regulation of the transmission of electricity and contracting for the supply of bulk power. The supply of power and transmission are complements that can be regulated together, separately controlled, or one (e.g., transmission) controlled and the other delegated. The Public Utility Regulatory Policies Act of 1978, for example, requires utilities to purchase electricity from independent power producers. This relationship could be regulated in any of the three manners just mentioned. Another example is the regulation of natural gas transmission and the supply of gas. A third is telephone service, which requires at least five components: a local connection, switching, a trunk connection, switching at the receiving end, and a terminal local connection. These examples illustrate the potential scope (or breadth) of regulatory control and indicate that the theory of regulation of a firm should encompass its supply arrangements and its internal organization in the design of a regulatory mechanism.

In the model studied by Baron and Besanko (1992), each of two units has private information about its own costs and produces a component, and the two components are then combined to form the regulated service. The units can be organized as a consolidated unit, as separate or decentralized units, or in a hierarchy in which one unit is regulated and supervision of the other unit is delegated to the regulated unit. When the units have private information, the organizational form interacts with their information. For example, consolidation of the units implies consolidation of their information about costs. A regulator designing an optimal mechanism thus faces a different problem than if it were dealing with separate units each of which has private information unknown to the other unit.

When communication between the units is observable, Baron and Besanko show that the regulation of one unit and delegation to it of the contract with the other unit is as efficient as the direct regulation of the two units as separate entities.[25] This result obtains because the hierarchically superior unit must extract the cost information of the other unit and can do so as efficiently as can the regulator. This is true even though the hierarchically superior unit has an informed principal problem. This result implies that if communication can be observed, only limited regulation in a hierarchy is required, and regulatory authority need not be extended to the hierarchically subordinate unit. Indeed, if there are transactions costs associated with regulation or noneconomic considerations are involved in the design of regulatory arrangements – for example, minimizing the restrictions on liberty – delegation with monitoring may be preferred.

When the sum of the costs of the two units is a sufficient statistic for the decentralized organizational structure, the regulator prefers consolidation of the two units.[26] This results because consolidation reduces the information rents that the units can earn on their private information. The expected prices are the same (in general), but efficiency is improved by consolidation. This results because consumer surplus is convex in price, and when the costs are uniformly distributed, regulation establishes a lower price for low cost realizations and a higher price for high cost realizations. Although there are benefits from consolidation, the regulator may not have the authority to consolidate the units, and the units may not have an incentive to consolidate.

When communication in a hierarchy is not observable to the regulator, delegation can result in considerable inefficiency. This results because unobservable communication allows the regulated firm to engage in hidden gaming in which it can structure the incentives of the other unit to serve its own interests by undoing the incentives the regulator would like to establish for that unit. Kofman and Lawarée (1993), Laffont (1990), and Tirole (1986, 1994) study the opportunities for collusion in this setting, and Baron and Besanko (1994) consider firms that may join together and privately share their information. All find that the hidden game results in inefficiency because the set of contracts that can be implemented is restricted. The observability of communication thus is an important factor determining which organizational form a regulator prefers and the efficiency of regulation.

This line of work has only begun and many issues remain unexplored. Other organizational forms and production technologies with a degree of substitution should be studied to determine the generality of these results. More interesting questions may lie in the nature and role of communication among and within organizations. To the extent that efficiency depends on organizational structure, regulatory monitoring of supply and other arrangements may be warranted. A more general issue is whether, and under what conditions, there is a separation theorem for the internal organization of the regulated firm and optimal regulatory policy.

Neoclassical theory

The application of neoclassical methods to the study of regulation has yielded rich theories of firm behavior under regulatory constraints, second-best pricing, dynamics, the optimal control of externalities, and the provision of public goods. There remain a number of important research topics centering on dynamics, the regulation of firms that also have unregulated lines of business, the design of adaptive regulatory systems, and the implementation of market-like mechanisms for the decentralized control of externalities. These theories are well codified in the literature and will not be discussed here.[27]

A continuing issue amenable to analysis with neoclassical methods is the extent to which competition can be substituted for regulation.[28] The technology of some industries may be less of an impediment to competition than it has been in the past. In local telephone service, for example, alternative local service networks are being developed by Teleport, Metropolitan Fiber, and other companies, and the recent Federal Communication Commission (FCC) decision permitting them to connect directly to local telephone offices gives them a greater incentive to expand their networks. Cellular systems also have the potential to compete directly with local networks, and cable television in some areas may also become a viable alternative. What is needed are theories of competition among a small number of firms operating with different technologies. For example, will competition be that predicted by contestable market theory? Will implicit collusion or price leadership eventually prevail? Will predatory behavior be observed and, if so, will the ability to raise capital be impaired?

Regulation as a barrier

Much of the recent theory of regulation has focused on problems of incomplete information and moral hazard. Other approaches to regulatory issues, however, are undoubtedly warranted. One such approach is that of reflected Brownian motion, which could be used to study the dynamics of firm performance under certain regulatory systems. Price cap systems impose barriers to price increases on a market basket of services but otherwise leave the firm unconstrained in its actions. One way to model the firm's problem is to represent the prices in its market basket of services as controllable; that is, the firm chooses prices or capacity, but stochastic elements characterize demand, the mix of services purchased by consumers, and the actions of competitors. In some cases, these stochastic elements might be represented as Brownian motion controlled by the firm's choices, and the price cap can be represented as a reflecting barrier requiring a price change when it is met.[29] To complete the theory, the barrier itself can be thought of as a control set of a regulatory principal.

One possible positive contribution of this type of theory is an explanation of why firms might moderate behavior prior to a review of whether the barrier, or price cap, should be changed. Whether research of this type is likely to be successful in producing either a positive or a normative theory is unclear, but experimentation with such research paradigms could be worthwhile.

The economics and politics of regulation

THE POLITICAL ECONOMY OF REGULATION

Introduction

Positive theory is intended to predict and explain behavior, and the political economy approach to regulation combines economics and political science to generate such theories.[30] The political economy approach treats as endogenous both the behavior of the firm and the regulator and looks beyond the identification of the efficient regulatory policy to incorporate the strategies of interested parties that attempt to influence the choices of regulatory policies and their implementation. A starting point for this approach is the incentives for political action generated by the distributive consequences of regulatory policies. These political actions can be thought of, in a general sense, in terms of aggregate, competing pressures. The political economy approach is developed more completely by explicitly taking into account the costs of political action and the organization of interests to economize on those costs.[31] This supply-side approach adds completeness, but the discussion here will focus on the demand rather than the supply side, since the demand side is more directly linked to regulatory policy.

Positive theory should also incorporate institutional features, and much of positive regulatory theory is naturally derived from models based on representative government. In many other countries, the government system is parliamentary with majority parties or coalitions able to implement the policies they prefer subject only to their concerns about the future electoral consequences of those policies. A general approach to regulation should be capable of accommodating alternative institutions.

The evolution of regulation

Since regulatory polices are in effect over extended periods of time, more attention to the evolution of regulation seems warranted. Most theories of regulation are static, and those that do capture a degree of dynamics often rely on strong assumptions (such as commitment) or special structures (such as repetition of identical stage games). A dynamic theory should incorporate technological change, learning, and the evolution of information as experience is gained with a regulatory policy. For example, information that had initially been hidden because of strategic considerations may be revealed through performance, and new information may also be generated through scientific discovery and technological change, as well as through exogenous events that affect costs and benefits.

The evolution of regulatory policy is also shaped by intervention. The courts, congressional oversight committees, activist and interest groups, and political entrepreneurs may attempt to change regulatory policy. For example, both the regulated firm and those seeking more stringent or broader regulation challenge regulatory policies in the courts on substantive and procedural due process grounds. EPA administrators report that 80% of their actions are challenged in court by one side, the other, or both. From a normative perspective, this can be either good or bad, although the legal costs incurred are a burden. From a positive perspective, it would be interesting to investigate the effects of prospective legal challenges on the evolution of regulation and more importantly on policy outcomes.

Reregulation

Regulatory innovation has included deregulation in a number of industries as well as the introduction of market-like mechanisms, such as franchise bidding in cable television and cellular telephone service, to deal with certain allocation problems. A service such as cellular telephones used primarily by businesses and high-income consumers does not provide a substantial base or incentives for political action either by customers or by political entrepreneurs. In contrast, cable television has a broad customer base, including many lower- and middle-income households, which provides opportunities for political action by consumers as well as for political entrepreneurs to claim credit for representing their interests.[32] These considerations can lead to reregulation.

Research on the economic and political foundations of regulation would help explain why cable TV regulation has been imposed by a congressional majority large enough for the only override of a veto by former President Bush.[33] The motivation for the regulation is surely the capture of rents. The impact of that regulation will be determined not only by the enacting legislation, but also by the FCC's administration of it. The legislation establishes price controls for basic cable service, leaving a variety of services such as premium channels and pay-per-view services, as yet unregulated. Yet cable TV is characterized by large fixed costs, low variable costs, joint products, and all the factors that made telecommunications regulation so difficult and inefficient prior to deregulation. Furthermore, competition is present both from broadcast TV and soon from telephone companies, which have been permitted by the FCC to carry video services.[34]

Regulation also establishes rights and redistributes wealth, usually by indirect means. The Cable Television Consumer Protection and Competition Act, however, redistributes wealth directly by requiring "retransmission consent" under which cable networks must pay television stations for their programming. Also, under the "must carry" provision, small television stations were granted the right to demand that cable systems carry their programs. Cable TV firms are challenging both provisions in the courts.

Reregulation can also occur as states attempt to control the consequences of federal deregulation. For example, the Clean Air Act of 1990 established a tradeable allowances system for SO_2 (sulfur dioxide) emissions. Trades, however, affect where acid rain will fall, and hence a geographic distribution of abatement benefits has become a political issue. Environmental activists in New York have backed an attempt in the state assembly to regulate the trading of allowances by New York utilities. Whether a state can regulate interstate commerce in this manner is unclear, but the incentive for local interests to reregulate what federal law has deregulated remains.

A positive theory of the political economy of reregulation is needed to predict where reregulation might occur. That theory should focus on the distributive politics of regulation and the instruments used to redistribute rights and wealth – both directly and indirectly. Such a positive theory could be accompanied by a normative theory directed at designing a regulatory system that responds to political pressures yet promotes efficiency. This type of theory is discussed next.

Political design of regulatory policy

Political action shapes regulatory policy and influences its evolution. It is present not only when policies are formulated and laws enacted, but later once the policies are implemented. In the case of a policy implemented in the face of incomplete information, performance can reveal information relevant to the *ex post* appropriateness of the policy itself. Performance can be observed not only by the regulator, but also by the interests affected by the regulation. Pressure for change thus can come from outside the regulatory relationship as well as from within it. To the extent that the political pressure can be anticipated, it can be taken into account in the *ex ante* design of a policy, that is, the political design of regulatory policy. The design of a regulatory policy should incorporate the subsequent political action, lobbying, and pressure that interests generate as information becomes available as a result of performance and experience with the policy. That political action can be anticipated but not perfectly, so *ex ante* the policy can be designed conditionally on the information revealed by performance under the policy. The following three examples illustrate how the external pressure generated by performance under a regulatory policy can be anticipated and incorporated into the initial design.

The first example of taking political considerations into account in the design of a regulatory mechanism involves the auction for SO_2 allowances under the Clean Air Act of 1990. One possibility would be to conduct a differentiated auction in which different quantities of allowances trade at different prices or alternatively to conduct a sequence of auctions during a year. These alternatives have the potential problem of leaving the traders open to criticism that they made a bad decision by selling at a price lower than the price on some other transaction, buying at a price higher than some other transaction price, or not waiting for a better price. Legislators, other public officials, and interest groups cannot commit to pass up such an opportunity for criticism when it would serve their own interests. At a minimum, such charges could result in public distrust and, at a maximum, in a regulatory decision to disallow some portion of the transaction price. The political solution to the design of the auction then is to hold a single-price auction in which all trades take place at the same price. To reduce the likelihood that intertemporal comparisons will be made, the auction can be held once a year. This is the solution used in the Clean Air Act of 1990.

A second example is the provision in the Clean Air Act allowing utilities until 1995 to keep confidential the prices and other conditions on the trades of SO_2 allowances. This provision is intended to help reduce criticism of the type just discussed. This fear of criticism is considered in more detail in the section " 'A Fear of Criticism' Hypothesis of Regulatory Inertia."

A third example is the FCC's price cap policy governing charges for access to local telephone networks. The FCC allows self-selection among two alternative regulatory policies, both of which provide for profit sharing between the firm and customers:

Under one schedule, the price cap includes an annual productivity factor of 4.3 percent for the four-year period, and the firms are allowed to keep their profits up to a rate of return of 13.25 percent. If their rate of return is between 13.25 percent and 17.25 percent, fifty percent of the profit [in that range] is returned to customers. Above 17.25 percent, all the additional profit is refunded.[35]

The other schedule has a lower productivity factor, but profit sharing begins at lower rates of return. The purpose of the profit sharing feature is to reduce political pressure to rescind the price cap system in the event of unexpectedly high rates of return.

Now, can these types of considerations be taken into account in a theory of political design? To do so, it is necessary to endogenize the political action that can overturn a regulatory policy. That political action is more difficult to incorporate when there is incomplete information or uncertain future events that can give rise to opportunistic behavior.

The distributive consequences of regulatory policies thus create incentives for political action, and regulators and policy makers are not well insulated from that action. In particular, if a regulatory change either results in adverse distributive consequences for some interest group or creates an opportunity to seek rents, political action can be expected. The initiative for political action may be taken by interest groups or by political entrepreneurs who seek to organize and lead as a means of representing, or catering to, organized and unorganized interests. Such political action is not always successful, in part because opposition is also created by distributive consequences, but often it forces revision in or adaptation of regulatory policies. The long-term commitments required to generate incentives for efficiency are thus not fully credible.

Generating the incentives necessary for efficient regulation thus requires credible commitments to long-term policies so that firms can be assured that the regulatory policies will not be changed opportunistically once the firm has sunk investments or revealed information about its capabilities. In particular, the opportunistic taking of rents and quasi-rents can distort incentives for efficiency and reduce aggregate welfare. The credibility of commitments to multiperiod regulatory policies thus should be a concern when, for example, political opportunism directed at eliminating rents to information cannot be precluded.[36] The degree of credibility of commitments thus should be an endogenous consequence of opportunistic political action motivated by the distributive consequences of a regulatory policy and directed toward revising or preserving that policy.

The model considered in Baron (1988) of the multiperiod regulation of a monopolist with incomplete information illustrates this. If the regulator could commit to a regulatory policy, the design problem is a straightforward extension of the single-period design. If a revision in the regulatory policy can occur because of political action, however, commitment is not feasible and hence not credible. In the model, the political action is assumed to be generated by an interest group that infers the true cost of the firm by observing the profit it earns in the first period. Given this inference, the interest group takes political action in an attempt to force down the price in the second period. The stronger the incentive of the interest group, the greater the profit and hence the lower the cost of the regulated firm. In an effort to maintain the price and hence its profits in the second period, the firm can take political action to counter the action of the interest group. The greater the incentive of the firm, the lower is its cost, since it has more to lose from the action of the interest group.

One modeling issue in this line of research centers on how to represent the outcome of the political competition. That outcome can be a function not only of the amount of political action, but also of institutional factors. The political action can, for example, be directed at the regulatory agency or the congressional oversight committee for the agency. Modeling the

29

interplay between political action and institutional decision-making processes can be complex. Ideally, it should be modeled based on first principles incorporating the incentives for political action, the cost of that action, and the institutional context that action takes place in. An alternative is to use a reduced form in which the probability of a change in the regulatory policy (e.g., a reduction in the second-period price) is a function of the political action. For example, it could be represented as proportional to the amount of political action of the interest group relative to the total political action of the interest group and the firm.

In the model presented by Baron, the regulatory horizon extends for two periods, and the regulator is assumed to be able to commit credibly to a policy for those two periods in the sense that the regulator cannot itself change the policy. The optimal regulatory policy with credible commitment is to use the same policy for each period with the price equal to reported marginal cost plus the marginal information rent required to induce the firm to report its cost truthfully. Although the regulator can credibly commit to this policy, interest groups can take political action at the end of the first period in an attempt to overturn the policy. They observe the performance of the firm in the first period and infer its actual marginal cost. Their incentive to take political action stems from the possibility of forcing the second-period price to be lowered to the level of actual marginal costs and eliminating the information rents the firm would earn in the second period if the regulatory policy were to remain in effect. If the efforts of the interest group are successful in overturning the policy, the second-period price is set equal to the inferred marginal cost, and the firm earns no rents. The firm has an incentive to oppose the interest groups' efforts by taking political action on its own to preserve the regulatory policy and hence its rents.

The regulator can affect the amount of political action that occurs at the end of the first period through the choice of a policy *ex ante*. The regulator's optimal response to the anticipated political opportunism is to choose a policy with a lower likelihood that political action will be taken to overturn that policy. It can do so by setting a lower price than that which is *ex ante* optimal with credible commitment. This is less efficient if the policy remains in effect but is an optimal response to the possibility of political action directed at overturning the regulatory policy.

Policy makers and designers of incentive mechanisms thus must understand the political reality for at least two reasons. First, a regulatory incentive mechanism may not lead to the anticipated performance if those affected by the mechanism have incentives to take political action to change the mechanism. Second, by anticipating political action and designing mechanisms that take into account that action, regulators can improve the chances that (second-best) efficiency will result.

The economics and politics of regulation

This type of research also has implications for the evaluation of regulatory performance. If opportunistic political action can be expected in response to regulatory policy making, regulatory performance should not be evaluated against an economic efficiency standard developed under the assumption of credible commitment. Indeed, the standard for evaluation should be that which anticipates that interest group action may force a change in regulatory policy. Furthermore, if political action causes commitment to fail, that should not be viewed as an exogenous event beyond the realm of regulatory influence. Indeed, the regulator should be evaluated in terms of the measures taken to reduce the likelihood that commitment will fail.

The theory sketched here is only one example of the design of regulatory incentive mechanisms in the presence of anticipated political action. In particular, it incorporates only one type of incentive problem resulting from asymmetric information about costs. Regulation, however, involves a wide variety of incentive problems, and the politics associated with those problems may differ from that described here. Furthermore, the model discussed here incorporates *ex post* political action, but political action is also present at the *ex ante* or design stage. A theory also should not abstract away from institutional characteristics and the preferences of institutional officeholders that can be important to whether political action will be successful in altering regulatory policies.

An opportunity for positive theory

As a consequence of the Single Market Act, the European Community (EC) adopted measures to open the airline market to competition among EC airlines. In response to political pressure from the French and others, the removal of internal barriers to competition was phased in beginning January 1, 1993, but the barriers will not be eliminated until April 1997. The principal barriers are those that prevent a carrier from picking up passengers in a foreign country and carrying them to a destination not in the carrier's home country. For example, a carrier such as Alitalia will be able to pick up passengers in Paris and carry them to Toulouse and then to Rome.

The opportunity for positive political economy is to predict the evolving structure and performance of the airlines industry as the barriers are phased out. This could focus on price and efficiency, industry structure (consolidations and bankruptcies), and national market shares. The predictions should be guided both by the theory of competition and pricing in networks and by empirical evidence on the cost structure of networks, as investigated, for example, by Brueckner, Dyer, and Spiller (1992). The focus also should be on (1) the extent to which non-EC carriers are

31

accorded the same privileges as EC carriers, (2) how countries such as the United States can use reciprocity agreements to gain access to national markets, (3) how the more competitive EC industry attempts to erect barriers to outside competition, and (4) which of those barriers become trade issues (e.g., in the context of GATT).

Another research opportunity in the EC pertains to telecommunications services, which in most European countries are provided by state-owned monopolies. In October 1992, the European Commission issued a white paper advocating competition in voice communication similar to that in the United States. The privatization movement, the Single Market Act, and the demands of business for efficient and modern services create incentives for greater competition through a restructuring of the European industry. A variety of industry structures can be imagined, and a number of transition plans are possible. These could take the form of U.S.-style ownership and regulation, the British system used for the privatization and regulation of British Telecom, or hybrids such as that which may emerge from the partial privatization of Germany's Deutsche Bundespost Telekom. A research challenge for positive political economy is to predict the evolution of the EC telecommunications industry and the form that public control will take. Such a study also provides an opportunity for a comparative study of institutions and interests.

Another opportunity for regulatory research in the EC is the decontrol of the national electric markets, which are also largely controlled by state-owned monopolies. It seems inevitable that the control of the national markets by state-owned firms will give way to at least some degree of competition. A challenge for normative theory is to design a politically feasible system for decontrol. The EC must not only determine the extent to which one firm can supply customers in another country, but also the charges that can be assessed for transmission. The European Commission has recently ruled that a private French hydroelectric power producer is to be paid the price an Italian customer is willing to pay rather than the price Electricité de France pays for power. In addition to change stimulated by decisions such as this, the antitrust authority as administered by Directorate General IV can be used to change the structure of the EC electric power industry.

SOCIAL REGULATION

The subject
Social regulation – the regulation of health, safety, the environment, the employment relationship, and so on – can be supplied in response to market failures resulting from externalities and incomplete information.

It can also be supplied in response to political pressure for redistribution and protection from hazards.

The theory required to explain social regulation is a combination of the theories of market failures, interest group politics, and institutional behavior. For example, in the regulation of the hazards of fires caused by disposable butane lighters, the interest groups included safety advocates, the producers of lighters, and the trial lawyers who represent the injured. The principal market failure was said to be an asymmetry of information about proper use, which was a particular problem with respect to children five years old and younger.[37] As another example, the section of the Clean Air Act of 1990 establishing a tradable allowances system for SO_2 emissions may have resulted from efficiency considerations, but the provision that allocates special allowances to those power plants that add a scrubber resulted from interest group politics led by Eastern coal interests.

One aspect of the study of social regulation involves comparative institutions. Both the institution of products liability and the institution of regulation can address the disposable lighter safety issue, and the characteristics of these institutions can affect the responses. Product safety regulation depends on the mandate of the Consumer Product Safety Commission (CPSC), the procedural requirements it must satisfy, the likelihood of court review of its actions, and alternatives to regulation such as voluntary standards. Furthermore, a number of the social regulation statutes enacted in the 1970s allow private parties to set the agenda of regulatory agencies. For example, individuals and interest groups can petition the CPSC and Occupational Safety and Health Administration (OSHA) requesting that a standard be set, and the statutes require the agencies to act within a specific time.[38] This has forced proceedings on issues ranging from the safety of chain saws and disposable butane lighters to cadmium exposure in the workplace.

Similarly, environmental protection statutes give individuals and others the right to file suit in federal court to force compliance with regulations or simply to impose fines on polluters. For example, the law requires firms to report spills and other inadvertent discharges to the EPA, and the Natural Resources Defense Council (NRDC) has followed a strategy of monitoring those reports and suing the reporting firms for illegal discharge under the Clean Water Act. The NRDC then negotiates an out-of-court settlement with the firms under which they make voluntary contributions to a designated environmental project. The impact of such provisions is unclear at best, and research could clarify whether they are merely a feature with little impact on efficiency or have significant efficiency effects.

David P. Baron

Market-like approaches

Social regulation is often criticized because it is an imperfect response to a set of complex problems and because the cost of compliance is often high. From an efficiency perspective, these characteristics may be a silver lining. The difficulty in applying existing regulatory approaches such as standard setting to certain externalities, such as acid rain, global warming, and ozone depletion, and the impact of high compliance costs on international competitiveness have produced two types of reactions. First, some social regulation activists, such as the Environmental Defense Fund, have searched for workable regulatory approaches to achieve their objectives, and if those approaches are efficiency enhancing, so much the better. Second, the pressures from international competition have brought greater attention to the costs of regulatory compliance. These forces have resulted in the increased use of market-like, decentralized regulatory approaches including tradeable allowances and externality taxes. The use of these approaches could well grow in the future, particularly because taxes produce revenue that can be used for other government purposes.[39]

It is difficult to identify which issues will gain saliency in the future, but some such as the international control of externalities will surely receive more attention. The Montreal Protocol on the reduction of chlorofluorocarbon (CFC) production and use, and the accords arrived at the Rio summit are examples that provide a context for both theoretical and empirical studies.

Small business and exceptions

Regulatory performance standards, compliance requirements, and reporting requirements can be chosen on a continuum ranging from uniform policies applicable to all firms to a case by case approach under which a policy is set individually for each firm. Case by case decisions are generally infeasible for issues such as worker safety and health regulation, environmental protection, pension requirements, and housing regulations because administrative costs would be prohibitive. Uniform rules have the advantage of simplicity in addition to lower administrative costs compared to case by case decisions. Uniform rules also have appeal to the extent that the benefits of regulation are similar for all firms, as might be the case in worker safety and health regulation. Uniform rules have the disadvantage, however, that compliance costs can vary dramatically among firms. Efficient regulation thus calls for different standards as a function of the costs of compliance. This is the obvious motivation for tradeable allowance and pollution fee approaches to environmental regulation. These approaches, however, may be difficult to administer for worker exposure to hazards, Employee Retirement Income Security Act requirements, equal employment opportunity requirements, and reporting requirements. Because of these complications, exceptions to general rules are often allowed. This is particularly the case for small business.

Many regulations provide small businesses with exemptions, streamlined reporting procedures, reduced compliance burdens, smaller penalties, or less stringent standards. Brock and Evans (1986, Table 4.2) list 29 federal regulatory programs that provide "tiers" of regulation based on the size of firms. Many of the tiers and exemptions were written into the initial enacting legislation. For example, the Family Leave Act of 1993 exempts firms with fewer than 50 employees. Furthermore, the Regulatory Flexibility Act of 1980 encourages regulators not to unduly burden small businesses in setting requirements. Small business receives these exceptions in part because the compliance costs, and particularly their administrative components, are disproportionately burdensome for small business. Exceptions, however, can also be viewed as the result of the effective political organization of small businesses, which because of compliance costs have an incentive to take political action to reduce those costs.

The purpose here is not to address the content of exceptions and tiered regulation but instead to consider explanations for the types of exemptions observed. One approach relies on the normative theory of optimal regulation to explain regulatory tiering as a function of the costs of compliance.[40] The theory of mechanism design under incomplete information about those costs is directly applicable, and firm size can be used as the observable on which exceptions are based, with compliance costs as the unobservable variable.

The political economy approach is also driven by compliance costs that differ across firms, but its focus is not on optimal regulation but instead on the distributive consequences on businesses and the political action they take to obtain exceptions and tiered regulations. A systematic reading of page B-2 of the *Wall Street Journal* indicates that small businesses are well organized for political action and that regulation is one of their principal targets. Small businesses are numerous, have complete coverage of legislative districts, and in the aggregate have substantial resources. Small businesses are also well organized for political purposes, with the National Federation of Independent Business and the National Small Business Association having considerable influence in Washington and in state capitols.

Despite the political strength of small businesses and their disproportionate compliance costs, exceptions are not always provided and some regulation is imposed. Research on exceptions and tiering is needed not only to identify a standard of efficiency, but to explain why specific programs have the exceptions and tiers they have. Such a study would also provide evidence on the comparative strengths of the normative and political economy approaches to the study of regulation.

"A fear of criticism" hypothesis of regulatory inertia. Social regulation has proved to be difficult to reform particularly from within the agencies that administer the laws. For example, for many years the FDA was unable to reform its drug approval procedures even in the face of stinging criticism. Why this regulation is so difficult to change might be explained by a number of factors.[41] One hypothesis is that change is difficult because any change is always opposed by some interest group, which can take political action directed at the agencies as well as at congressional committees and the courts.[42] Another hypothesis, however, is that regulation is hard to change because regulators fear criticism – in addition to the personal embarrassment – that might damage their own and their agency's future prospects. That fear could center on the risk that even an *ex ante* optimal decision might *ex post* have a bad outcome. Preferences thus presumably depend not only on the present, but also on reputation and future career opportunities. Moreover, criticism might well interact with the risk aversion of the regulator. To investigate this hypothesis, it is necessary to identify the preferences of regulators, the technology of criticism, and the administrative process requirements and institutional features that insulate regulators from criticism.

In addition, the regulation of health, safety, and environmental protection is often characterized by considerable scientific uncertainty about cause-effect relationships and the consequences of regulatory alternatives. Epidemiological evidence is often inconclusive, and the direction of causality is difficult to determine. One example is the CFC and ozone depletion issue. In the mid-1970s, the issue was examined based on theoretical considerations. Empirical evidence and knowledge of the cause-effect relationships were difficult to obtain, however, and little regulatory action was taken.[43] The scientific uncertainty about causation and consequences interacts with legislative and regulatory caution.

Criticism can come from a variety of directions on any number of issues. In part, it comes from interest groups that are able to interest the media in the issue. In part, it comes from activist and advocacy groups, some of which seek to prevent change, while others seek to promote change by forcing the agency to act. In part, it comes from political entrepreneurs in Congress or the administration who seek to advance their interests by attacking the regulator. An example of this is Representative John Dingell's use of congressional hearings to discipline regulators, among others.

Institutional parameters can affect the likelihood of criticism and the response to it. These parameters include the independence of the regulatory commission, the publicness of the issues in its jurisdiction, and the access that critics have to the commission. On the one hand, independent commissions may be less susceptible to criticism than single-administrator agencies because of their independent status. On the other hand, single-administrator agencies housed in the executive branch may be less susceptible to the extent that the executive can defend and protect them.

One type of research that might be conducted on these hypotheses would be to track the career paths of regulators and correlate them with the criticism to which they were subjected. (There obviously would be serious measurement and data collection problems involved in such a study.) One focus of this line of inquiry could be the criticism from the oversight committees for the regulatory agency. The instruments of criticism are not only critical comments but also threats of legislation to change the agency's mandate or to cut its budget. This suggests that there may be differences in behavior between careerists and political appointees. One difficulty in such a study is that, as Weingast and Moran (1983) point out, the absence of hearings is not necessarily an indication of the absence of criticism or of regulatory compliance, since in equilibrium the regulator may avoid those actions that would attract criticism.

The fear of criticism can directly affect the behavior of regulated firms. As an example, the effectiveness of the tradeable allowances system for SO_2 emissions may be impeded by the fear that criticism could be directed at the purchaser of allowances by local interests that want greater local abatement rather than the higher emissions that the purchased allowances would allow. Environmental interest groups in Tennessee criticized the Tennessee Valley Association when it announced that it had purchased allowances from a Wisconsin utility. The same type of criticism has recently been leveled at the Long Island Lighting Company for selling an option on a portion of its allowance. Moreover, the fear of criticism about the prices at which allowances are transacted can affect behavior. A consultant to utilities on environmental matters explained that "the message to engineers and planners who would have to arrange the trades . . . is that if you screw up you get shipped off to count transformers."[44]

Alternatives to standard setting

Safety and health regulation typically takes the form of standards that firms are required to attain. One alternative to standard setting is the provision of information about hazards and precautionary measures. Viscusi and Magat (1987), for example, have presented a detailed study of information provision as an alternative to regulation.[45]

A competing view is that the purpose of safety and health regulation is to protect individuals from themselves or their own failure to take care. This perspective is frequently advocated by activists who claim that incentives and information will not affect the behavior of consumers and workers. For example, former CPSC Commissioner R. David Pittle stated, "Safety campaigns may work to get people to perform a one-time act, like buying a smoke detector. But it is far more cost effective to change a product than to change the long-term behavior of millions of consumers."[46] This perspective could be understood in terms of efficiency or simply as reflecting the objective of reducing injuries. More research is needed on how effective information provision is in reducing injuries and health impairments and how costly it is relative to standard setting. More research is also needed on whether the advocates of more stringent social regulation are motivated by considerations such as rights rather than efficiency considerations.

Rights and regulation

A continuing tension in regulation results from competing philosophies. Most economists view regulation through the lens of economic efficiency. The efficiency perspective has been strengthened in recent years by concerns about U.S. competitiveness. Many activists, however, view regulation from a rights perspective that is largely independent of costs and benefits. The rights perspective appears primarily in two policy areas. One involves claims about economic rights to services such as telephone, banking, and insurance. The other is in the area of health and safety, where claims are made about the right to be free of the risk, for example, from carcinogens and other exogenously imposed hazards.

Public processes have not yet been able to reconcile these two perspectives. In the absence of transactions costs, the Coase theorem shows that the efficiency and rights perspectives are not incompatible, but the source of conflict between the two perspectives is apparent. In the absence of transactions costs, efficiency results with any assignment of rights, but the distribution of costs and benefits depends directly on that assignment. The Coase theorem treats the assignment of rights as exogenous, yet that assignment is endogenous. In either the presence or absence of transactions costs, the affected parties can be expected to take political action to capture a larger share of the rents, with the assignment of rights being the instrument to capture rents. This competition for rents can distort efficiency as it allocates rights.

The economics and politics of regulation

An example of the clash between rights-based regulation and cost/benefit-based regulation is the removal of asbestos insulation. Cost-benefit analysis frequently concludes that it is more harmful to remove asbestos than it is to leave it in place. Of course, the harm and the cost fall on different individuals, so the proponents of the right to be free from potential harm from asbestos have little reason not to insist that those potential victims have the right.[47] The costs are borne by the owners of the buildings and by those who remove the asbestos, although the latter are compensated to some extent through wages. In this case, those who demand rights seem largely to have prevailed against the cost-benefit advocates, apparently because the issue involves health and safety. More needs to be known about how health, safety, and environmental protection policy depend on claims about rights and on the political action of those seeking those rights.

The study of rights and regulatory policy could be guided by the study of the evolution of the institution of liability. That institution is based on a rule under which a party incurring damages is compensated based on the actual damages. The concept of liability has been broadened, its burden has been shifted, and the concept has been "deepened." The deepening involves pressures to move toward a standard of absolute liability in which an individual will be compensated for damages regardless of the care he or she took. A product then essentially has an insurance policy attached to it. This places the entire burden of injuries and preventive measures on the producer.

Coupled with the increasing willingness of juries to impose punitive damages and provide compensation for pain and suffering, these changes would bring the liability system closer to that of a rights-based system. Indeed, the pressure for a standard of absolute liability seems to be based on the notion that individuals have an entitlement to safety that is protected by a property rule enabling them to force the elimination of certain hazards by making them prohibitively costly.[48] This is analogous to individuals having a right to safety or environmental protection or to be free from exposure to health hazards. The role and impact of rights-based arguments on regulatory policy enactment and its implementation should be the subject of more research.

The stringency of social regulation

One focus of the political economy approach to regulation is the explanation of where regulation is found in the economy and what its stringency is. Considerable attention has been given to the economic regulation of industries, but less attention has been given to social regulation. The three principal issues regarding social regulation pertain to what is regulated, what the stringency of that regulation is, and how that regulation is implemented. The theory of market failure provides one explanation for what is regulated, but the Coase theorem shows that regulation may not be required if transactions costs are low. The theory of externalities predicts that the scale of regulation would be that which most efficiently corrects the market failure, and the Coase theorem indicates that a market-like mechanism can be the instrument.

In contrast, the political economy perspective explains the stringency of regulation as a function of interests and the associated political action. For example, in the Clean Air Act of 1990 environmental regulation was applied to SO_2 emissions of existing coal-fired power plants in the Midwest, South, and Mideast regions. The stringency of that regulation corresponds to the aggregate quantity of emissions allowed, and the political economy perspective explains the stringency in terms of the actions of environmentalists, firms, and their supporters. Implementation involved the design of a system of tradeable allowances with special attention given to distributive considerations. The allowances were given free to power plants, so that consumers in the areas served by the plants would not experience as large a price increase under the regulatory pricing policies used by state public utility commissions. Also, special allowances were given to plants that added a scrubber and hence were more likely to use high-sulfer eastern coal and save the jobs of eastern coal miners.

The stringency of regulation can be studied formally from the perspectives of both market failures and political economy. The market failure perspective focuses on the stringency that produces the greatest excess of social benefits over social costs. The political economy perspective incorporates those benefits and costs but considers the policy chosen in the context of a political institution such as a bureaucracy or a legislature, as influenced by political action. The model discussed here applies this perspective to the choice of a policy by a majority-rule legislature.

A political economy theory of the stringency of social regulation should have a number of properties. First, it should allow for choices of policies by legislatures and rules by regulatory agencies and commissions. Second, the theory should take into account the distributive as well as the efficiency consequences of regulatory alternatives. Third, it should incorporate some central institutional features. For example, as applied to legislatures, the theory should incorporate majority rule, agenda setting, bicameralism, and a presidential veto. As applied to regulatory commissions, it should include agenda setting, congressional oversight, rule-making procedures, substantive and procedural due process requirements, and the possibility that policies will receive scrutiny by the courts.

Two other features of regulation should be incorporated in a model. First, regulation is typically applied to ongoing economic activity, so the status quo is relevant to the legislative choice. Second, time preferences can be important in regulation. That time is a relevant consideration in regulatory policy making is indicated by the observations that the amendments to the Clean Air Act took nearly a decade to enact. Similarly, the CPSC was not reauthorized for a decade and functioned under continuing resolutions.

Unfortunately, no theory with all these features yet exists, but a possible precursor to such a theory will be sketched to illustrate some of these properties. This precursor is based on noncooperative game theory as developed in the sequential bargaining literature and not on the social choice approach to collective choice in which all alternatives are compared simultaneously. The game should incorporate institutional details, but in any model, the more institutional detail incorporated, the more difficult the model is to analyze. The model discussed here thus is sparse in institutional detail but is suggestive of the type of analysis that can be conducted.

The model is based on that in Baron (1993b, 1994) and represents a majority-rule, unicameral legislature that chooses the stringency of regulation. Regulation has the characteristics of a collective or public good, which can be thought of as a policy applicable to some characteristic of economic activity such as the quantity of pollutants allowed, the level of allowable exposure to a hazard, or the number of safety features required on a product. The policy yields costs and benefits that can vary across political jurisdictions, and those costs and benefits depend on the stringency of the regulatory policy. The legislative process is represented as a sequence of proposals and votes, ending when a regulatory policy is approved by majority vote. The stringency of regulation is denoted by z and is assumed to be one-dimensional ($z \in [0,\infty)$). The benefits to political jurisdiction i are denoted by $B_i(z)$, $i = 1, \ldots, n$, where n is the number of districts represented in the legislature, and the costs borne in district i are denoted $C_i(z)$, $i = 1, \ldots, n$. These are not costs that appear in government budgets, but instead are incurred by firms and individuals in the districts.

The model of the legislative process is simple and symmetric. In each session, a legislator or committee is selected to make a proposal, which is followed by a vote on that proposal. If the current proposal is rejected, the status quo prevails for the current session and the legislature continues on to the next session with another member selected to make a proposal. If the current proposal is approved, it takes effect in the current session and becomes the status quo for the next session. That policy can last forever, in which case the legislature acts no further, or the policy can last for some finite number of sessions followed by new proposal making.[49]

There is little in the theory of collective choice that suggests that efficient regulation will be chosen in this type of setting. Yet the intuition provided by the median voter theorem for collective goods is that the outcome should be centrally located in the space of the ideal points of legislators. The equilibrium in this model is parameterized by the impatience of legislators and the status quo. If legislators are not impatient (the discount factor is one), the equilibrium outcome is the median of the ideal points of the legislators, provided the status quo is also at that point. If the status quo differs from the median, the committee that makes a proposal can propose an equilibrium stringency closer to its ideal point. Similarly, for any given status quo, the committee can propose an equilibrium stringency closer to its ideal point the more impatient are legislators. The greater the power of the committee to make a proposal that serves its interests, the farther away is the status quo and the more impatient are legislators. When the regulatory stringency can be changed at each session, the equilibrium proposals have the property that they are contained in sets of decreasing size that converge to the ideal point of the median legislator. Whenever the median legislator can make a proposal, she proposes her ideal point, and the policy never changes thereafter. That ideal point thus is an absorbing state. Until it converges, the regulatory policy will oscillate based on whether the proposer is to the left or right of the median voter. If political parties are such that those who prefer less stringent regulation (lower z) belong to one party and those who prefer more stringent regulation (higher z) belong to the other party, a change in the majority in the legislature will be associated with a change in regulatory policy.[50]

Incorporating the electorate

The preceding analysis is based on a utilitarian calculus in which the aggregate costs and benefits in each district motivate legislative behavior. If legislators are concerned about reelection and voters cannot transfer their votes, then legislators may be concerned about the numbers of voters who will incur positive or negative net benefits as a result of a regulatory policy. The stringency of regulation then depends on intra-district consequences that fall disproportionately on certain voters. For example, much of the costs of regulation will be borne through higher prices. Rents will also be affected, since the costs of social regulation often fall on firms, their owners, and their employees. This is evidenced by the extensive lobbying by small businesses to be exempted from the requirements of social regulation. Since regulatory policy can be a source of electoral competition, these effects should be incorporated through a model that links policy to votes.

The economics and politics of regulation

POLICY ANALYSIS AND EVALUATION

Regulatory review

Recent administrations have imposed a regulatory review process on executive branch agencies. This began with the Regulatory Analysis and Review Group and evolved to include the Office of Information and Regulatory Affairs and the Competitiveness Council in the Bush administration. These groups have rejected a number of regulations and forced revisions in others. The cumulative impact of these executive branch reviews should be assessed to determine if they have been an effective screen on regulations that were likely to produce a low level of benefits relative to costs. Viscusi (1992) has provided an initial study of the effectiveness of the Office of Management and Budget review of regulation of hazards.

Empirical studies of incentive regulation

The past half dozen years have witnessed considerable experimentation with incentive regulation in telecommunications, electric power, and natural gas. In the United States, this experimentation has taken place at the federal level as well as in nearly half the states. A number of other countries have also experimented with various incentive regulation systems often in conjunction with the restructuring or privatization of state-owned firms. One of the most prominent systems is the price cap mechanism used for British Telecom.

The number of incentive regulation systems and the years of experience with them may now have generated sufficient data to evaluate their performance and relate that performance to specific incentive features. This research should seek to identify the transitory and permanent components of performance. Particularly in industries such as interstate telecommunications, incentive regulation is intended to govern the transition from a regulated monopoly to oligopolistic competition. When the price cap mechanisms now in place will be replaced by competition is unclear, but the incentive features of those mechanisms could be studied under an alternative hypothesis about their duration.[51]

The application of information economics to regulation has provided a set of predictions about optimal regulation. Testing these theories is complicated because of the importance of the distribution of private information that is not observable to the econometrician yet is central to the predictions of the theory. The test for this type of theory is to take into account the distribution of information. It is also necessary to take into account the monotonicity condition necessary to ensure separation in the self-selection. Wolak (1991) and Wolak and Feinstein (1991) have devel-

43

oped and conducted what appears to be the first test of this type of theory. More research of this type is warranted.

Drawing conclusions about the efficiency of regulation when information is incomplete, however, is complicated in the absence of systematic empirical evidence. For example, the observation of the actual price and the actual marginal cost does not yield a clear conclusion about the efficiency of regulation. Baron (1989, p. 1439) identifies one dimension of this difficulty:

Suppose that, after the fact, the econometrician had data on actual costs and the price that had been set in a period. If the price were equal to the actual marginal cost yet information had been incomplete at the time the price had been set, the conclusion that should be drawn is that regulation was inefficient, since price should have been above marginal cost (except in the case of the lowest conceivable cost). Similarly, if the price had been above actual marginal cost, the econometrician could not conclude that regulation had been inefficient. Distinguishing between these two cases may be possible using other data. For example, the econometrician could use data on the profits (rents) of the firm to judge whether regulation had been efficient. . . . Profits are useful here because, unlike prices, they do not depend directly on the information available to the regulator at the time that prices were established.

One problem in the evaluation of regulatory performance is the alternative to which a regulatory policy is compared. The benchmark discussed earlier is second-best regulation conditional on the information structure. Another benchmark is competition, but the appropriate theory of industry performance with a small number of firms and incomplete information is not always obvious. Research on appropriate benchmarks is needed as well.

As deregulation has progressed in a number of industries, firms increasingly have developed unregulated as well as regulated businesses. In some industries, these businesses are independent. In others, there are interrelationships that complicate regulation. In others, a regulated line of business may be in competition with an unregulated industry. The economics of these situations is an important subject for research, as is the empirical evaluation of their performance.[52]

Another problem in empirical studies centers on the effect of the regulatory mechanism on the characteristics of the output. In particular, to the extent that service quality is endogenous, output must be measured multidimensionally. Any empirical evaluation of incentive systems should attempt to take into account induced changes in quality.

Risk analysis, compliance costs, and indirect effects

Activists have skillfully used advocacy science to advance their claims for more stringent environmental, health, and safety regulation. ("Advocacy science" refers to the selective use of scientific evidence [often combined with alarm] to support a cause.) When analysis of these claims is undertaken, it often is based on the method of risk analysis in which risk reduction alternatives are compared against each other rather than evaluated in terms of costs and benefits. Some critics of highly stringent regulation argue that protecting a life at a very high cost reduces wealth. Since better health and safety are positively associated with higher wealth, any estimate of risk reduction for regulation should take into account the increase in risks that result because the costs of regulation make people poorer. Risk analysis thus, it is argued, should include the risk consequences of wealth effects. Not surprisingly, this is a controversial argument, because of both the asserted link between wealth and health and the less favorable risk reduction measures that would result from adoption of this perspective. That compliance costs have wealth effects cannot be denied, but the relation between decreases in wealth and the impairment of health and loss of life requires considerably more study to determine if it is significant enough to be taken into account in risk analysis.

The evaluation of tradeable allowances systems

The Clean Air Act of 1990 established the first large-scale market system for trading emissions allowances. The South Coast Air Quality Management District in California has also embraced the idea of tradeable allowances, and proposals have been made for international tradeable allowance systems to address carbon dioxide emissions. The time for tradeable allowances may have arrived, and that should be accompanied by the evaluation of the performance of these systems to guide the design of other systems and document the efficiency gains and abatement achieved.

COMPARATIVE RESEARCH

Introduction

Most studies of regulation involve institution-specific research focused on the conduct and performance within the jurisdiction of a specific agency or commission. Comparative research can also be informative. One form of this research involves comparative institutions within a country. In the field of social regulation, product safety regulation can be evaluated relative to the institution of products liability. Comparative research should also involve the study of regulation in different political jurisdictions. A comparison of telecommunications regulation across the states can be made as can an international comparison of telecommunications regulatory systems.

Comparative research should focus not only on performance but also on institutional factors that affect performance. For example, one focus could be on the implications of the due process requirements of the U.S. Constitution relative to the procedures used in other countries. The U.S. regulatory system gives interested parties the opportunity to participate in regulatory processes and also provides a basis for legal challenges. It is also a largely public process with most of it observeable to interest groups, politicians, and the media. It thus may be more susceptible to direct political forces than is the regulatory process in, for example, a number of European countries, where regulatory decisions are made within ministries or state-owned firms and beyond the view of the public and the media.

Comparative institutions and cumulative regulation

In the case of social regulation, the institution of liability serves to internalize, albeit imperfectly, the social costs of private actions. The liability system can be effective when the damage is specific and who incurs it can be identified. For example, efficient levels of product safety can in principle be induced through the liability system. Regulation is also used in the case of product safety, but the number of mandatory and voluntary safety standards promulgated by the CPSC has been small. Liability remains the principal institution.

More attention should be given to the choice among institutions, but more realistically, in much of social regulation a mixture of regulation and liability is used. Regulation is often used to impose standards with the role of liability being to compensate those who incur damages. The institutions thus can be viewed as cumulative. This may result in protection levels, and hence compliance costs, that are higher than socially efficient as producers both comply with standards and attempt to avoid liability. Research is needed on whether this cumulative regulation results in excessive care and compliance costs.

Harmonization of regulations and mutual recognition

Under the Single Market Act, the EC has worked to harmonize regulations across its member states. The lessons learned during this process can be important for future regulatory issues. For example, an issue that is likely to be of increased saliency in the future is the effect of environmental regulation on international competitiveness. This issue could well be a focus on the next GATT round, and insight into the effect on competitiveness can be obtained by studying the effects of EC efforts to harmonize environmental standards.

The economics and politics of regulation

One industry in which harmonization, mutual recognition, and reciprocity have become important is financial services. The globalization of the financial services industries has resulted in mutual recognition policies in which domestic and foreign financial services firms are accorded equal treatment within a country, although the treatment across countries differs because of the laws and practices of the host country. This means that at least for the short-term the regulatory systems and industry structures for financial services will differ among countries even though the same technology is available to all. This provides an opportunity for comparative research.

The approach of mutual recognition may find considerably more widespread use in the next decade as the globalization of business increases and trade barriers are reduced. At some point harmonization of regulations across countries will be needed. This is likely to be driven not by governments but by firms seeking economies of standardization. The Uruguay Round of GATT may provide a framework for this process, but that framework could well be only a cautious step toward mutual recognition and harmonization.

Public enterprises and public regulation

In many countries, public enterprises are the counterparts of private ownership and public regulation. Laffont and Tirole (1993) study regulation using models incorporating transfer payments, which are costly to society because of distortions resulting from the taxes used to fund the transfers. A number of models of U.S.-style regulation adopt the framework of a two-part pricing structure, with the regulatory objective modeled as a weighted-surplus measure. The qualitative results of these models are the same, which raises the issue of whether there is a fundamental difference between the performance of public enterprises, such as those found in European countries, and public regulation as found in the United States. This issue can be investigated from both economic and political perspectives.

From an economic perspective, the U.S. system of private ownership and public regulation of firms means that tax revenues are not used to subsidize firms. This affects pricing, since the firm must cover its costs from revenue provided by customers. If the firm can use a two-part tariff and the fixed charges do not affect demand, consumers can be thought of as subsidizing the firm through lump-sum payments in exchange for the lower unit price. If demand is affected by the lump-sum charge, however, or fixed charges cannot be used, pricing becomes more complicated. With public enterprises that do not have to cover all of their costs with revenues from consumers, pricing is less constrained, and hence, prices

47

may have a different structure in countries with public enterprises than in countries with regulated private firms. This issue is intertwined with the inefficiency that often accompanies public ownership, as evidenced by the privatization wave sweeping developing countries. Indeed, privatization provides both longitudinal and cross-sectional data that can be used to enrich a comparative study.

This pricing issue can also work in the other direction. That is, fair return regulation in the United State requires regulated firms to reduce their prices to yield only an allowed return. With public enterprises, prices can be set to exploit monopoly power, and the profits can be used to subsidize other government activities. For example, excess profits from public telecommunications enterprises can be used to subsidize the postal service in a country in which both services are provided by the same firm or ministry. As another example, a number of countries have opposed reductions in the "accounting charges," which substantially increase the price of international telephone calls. The opposition results because reductions would directly impact government budgets.[53] In the United States, similar effects result through regulation. Profits from one class of service (e.g., business telephone service) can be used to cross-subsidize another class of service (e.g., residential telephone service).[54]

As another example of a comparative topic, under U.S.-style regulation environmental protection costs are borne directly by firms and indirectly by consumers. Public enterprises, however, can have their environmental compliance costs subsidized. An empirical investigation of the practices across countries and the corresponding performance would be informative.

The differences between public regulation and public enterprise can have significantly different efficiency, as well as distributive, consequences. The nature of these differences and their relationship to the structure of the public enterprise (e.g., a separate entity or combined with another entity such as a postal service) should be a subject of comparative research. Such a study could also incorporate political dimensions and in particular the nature of the governmental institutions involved with these enterprises. In addition to its empirical contribution, a comparative study could also inform theoretical research, since researchers should understand how assumptions about ownership or bureaucratic status may be directing their results.

RESEARCH ISSUES IN PHARMACEUTICALS

Introduction

Regulation in pharmaceuticals is more of a potential than an actuality (other than for new drug approval by the FDA), but it has the potential to encompass both economic regulation (the control of prices) and social regulation (the availability of pharmaceuticals and the direction of research and development). The potential regulation of pharmaceuticals can be studied using normative theory (the design of a price control mechanism tied to costs and research and development expenditures), positive theory (the political action of activists to lower the price of AZT and to streamline the drug approval process), and political economy theory (the design of a price control system that mitigates the political action to lower opportunistically prices on those drugs that are successful). This research can be done in the context of the U.S. institutional system, but comparative research would also be useful in the study of alternative drug approval systems and price control systems.

Pharmaceutical price regulation

In the United States, pharmaceutical prices have come under attack on both economic and political grounds. On economic grounds, health care costs account for more than 12% of GDP, and the share continues to increase. Pharmaceuticals often have unique therapeutic properties and hence enjoy a relatively inelastic demand. Furthermore, insurance and government programs cover much of patients' costs of drugs. Not surprisingly, purchasers of health care products and services have begun to pressure pharmaceutical companies through managed care programs, competitive bidding, and demands for discounts.[55] The political pressure on pharmaceutical prices has also increased. This pressure takes a variety of forms ranging from legislative actions, to presidential orders (e.g., vaccines for children), to private political pressure such as that by AIDS activists directed at the price of AZT and other drugs.[56] President Clinton has also publicly criticized high pharmaceutical prices.

In response to pressure, a number of pharmaceutical firms have adopted "free drug" programs to provide drugs to those who cannot afford them. Under pressure from the People With AIDS Health Group and other activists, Lyphomed donated substantial quantities of pentamidine for use by patients without insurance.[57] Similarly, when its drug Diflucan was approved by the FDA, Pfizer donated 6,000 bottles of it to health care facilities that treat AIDS patients. With large numbers of people not covered by insurance, the possibilities of further pressures on pharmaceutical companies can be expected, although individuals with other diseases are generally less well organized for political purposes.

Political officeholders have also found pharmaceutical prices to be an attractive, as well as an important, issue. This interest has led to criticism by government agencies. For example, the Office of Technology Assessment (OTA) (1992) has recently criticized the Genzyme Corporation for the price of its drug Ceredase, which is used to treat Gaucher's disease. The OTA questioned whether the government should support research and development under the Orphan Drug Act when the government has no say in the pricing of the drugs developed with that support. Similarly, the General Accounting Office (1992) issued a report concluding that prescription drug prices are higher in the United States than in Canada. These examples suggest that in addition to formal regulation, there is a developing system of informal regulation with pressure and threats as the instruments. A systematic study of regulation by pressure would be of considerable interest.

In addition to informal regulation, a number of bills have been introduced and promoted in Congress to control pharmaceutical prices. For example, revisions in the Orphan Drug Act were sought to shorten the seven-year exclusive marketing provision and otherwise introduce more competition for orphan drugs. Another bill to impose the Canadian pharmaceutical price consultation system received congressional attention.

The pharmaceutical industry has responded by attempting to reduce the pressure. In 1990 in the midst of congressional consideration of legislation to reduce government expenditures on drugs, "Merck announced a goal of keeping future price increases within the rate of inflation in the United States and of generally limiting price actions to one per year, given stable market conditions and government policies that are supportive of innovation."[58] This is equivalent to a voluntary price cap system. A number of other pharmaceutical companies made similar pledges, and for 1993 Pfizer pledged that its price increases would be limited to 3 percent.[59]

Under its Equal Access to Medicines Program, Merck also offered to give state Medicaid programs the same discounts it gives to the Veterans Administration.[60] In exchange, Merck sought broadened eligibility (Medicaid formulary approval) of its drugs for use in those programs.[61] The Merck offer was in part a response to the pressures on pharmaceutical companies and in part an effort to forestall pending legislation. In light of Merck's action and the imminent congressional consideration of legislation, however, the Pharmaceutical Manufacturers Association (PMA) adopted a policy opposing "proposals to tie the availability of prescription drugs to the willingness or ability of companies to grant discounts or rebates."[62] Merck's offer was also criticized by some industry members because Merck had not previously offered discounts. Merck, however, stepped up the pressure on other firms. Merck chairman Dr. P. Roy Vagelos urged the industry to recognize the pressure for price controls, and stated, "I detest [federal] regulation but it may be brought on by my colleagues [other firms]."[63] The pressure for price controls is likely to mount if the pressure for national health insurance increases.

The economics and politics of regulation

As part of a budget deficit reduction effort, the Omnibus Budget Reconciliation Act of 1990 contained Medicaid Prudent Pharmaceutical Purchasing provisions, which took effect on January 1, 1991. The provisions require pharmaceutical firms to give state Medicaid programs the lowest price offered elsewhere.[64] The Congressional Budget Office estimated that the extension of discounts to Medicaid programs would reduce expenditures by $3.3 billion over five years. The legislation also orders state Medicaid programs to make drugs available under their programs, which is basically the "equal access" policy advocated by Merck.

The possibility of price controls on drugs provides an opportunity for the application of the mechanism design approach to regulatory policy formulation. Any price control system must recognize that there is incomplete information about the cost not only of producing drugs but of developing new drugs. In addition, the therapeutic benefits from a research and development program are quite uncertain. The regulatory design problem thus is to construct incentives to encourage research and development yet limit the prices of existing drugs. Any price control mechanism will distort the incentives for research and development, and the ability to monitor the research and development process — its cost, and its results — is highly limited. The mechanism design problem thus involves both hidden information and hidden actions.

One important aspect of pharmaceutical price regulation would be the difficulty of the government in committing to a regulatory scheme. The possibility of political opportunism cannot be precluded, as the experiences with AZT and other AIDS drugs have shown. The design of incentives in the face of limited commitment is a central characteristic of the political design of regulatory mechanisms, as considered in the preceding section "The Political Economy of Regulation." The price control issue offers an opportunity to contribute to both the theory and the application of mechanism design and public policy.

From a positive perspective, an important research topic is the political economy of the movement toward price and expenditure controls. Interest group activity is broad and intense, involving doctors and other health care providers, insurance companies, medical equipment manufacturers, patient advocate groups, health care purchasers such as employers, and pharmaceutical firms. A complex set of institutions is likely to be involved as will state legislatures, Congress, executive branch agencies, and procurement agencies.

End runs

Regulation takes place through a set of established public processes, but in some cases there are ways to avoid those processes. For example, pharmaceutical firms have the opportunity to turn to Congress when frustrated by the FDA's regulatory processes. The PMA has supported regulatory provisions to obtain extensions of patent lives and to restrict the ability of generic drug companies to compete.[65]

An example of an end run is the successful effort of MicroGeneSys, Inc. to advance the approval process for its AIDS vaccine GP-160. Frustrated with the speed at which its vaccine was being reviewed by the FDA, the company undertook a political strategy directed at advancing trials on the vaccine. The company hired former Senate Finance Committee Chairman Russell B. Long to lobby in Congress and was successful in including in a Department of Defense appropriation bill an appropriation of $20 million for human trials of the drug. This type of end run has the potential to affect the nature of the regulatory process. A study of regulatory end runs could be helpful in understanding regulation in its broader context.

Regulatory process innovation and evolution

Regulatory change takes place as a result of a variety of factors including scientific advancement and technological change. The biotechnology revolution has provided a number of challenges to the FDA's regulatory processes by bringing new issues, technologies, and products in both drug and food areas.[66] The pioneering firms have precipitated regulatory innovation and evolution, and their initiatives affect the regulatory process for the firms that follow them. A study of those pioneering experiences could provide considerable insight into regulatory processes and the strategies of those trying to influence them. With respect to the regulatory process, the questions that might be asked include whether the regulatory process becomes more streamlined or more complicated over time as the agency gains experience with the products. A second question is whether the burden, in terms of out-of-pocket costs and length of proceedings, decreases or increases over time.

One way to study these changes is through case studies of the events associated with innovation. For example, in 1994 the FDA finally approved for commercial sale the first genetically engineered food, a tomato developed by Calgene, Inc. A case study that focuses both on the FDA's development of an approval process for genetically engineered foods and Calgene's efforts to speed that development would be illuminating. The regulatory process and regulatory burden associated with this process can also be studied to determine the importance of the FDA's previous experience with biotechnology drugs on the process for reviewing and approv-

ing foods. This could be extended to other agencies to develop comparative data. Calgene, for example, has also developed the first genetically
engineered plant, a herbicide-resistant cotton, to receive approval from
the USDA for field testing.

An alternative approach also holds promise. That approach focuses on
the impact of changes in regulatory policies on the activities of firms by
considering firms in different stages of their development and hence in
their experiences with the FDA. This approach could focus on a cross-
section of firms in the biopharmaceutical industry. Genentech was the
first firm to carry a biotechnology drug through the FDA's regulatory
process. Firms such as Amgen and Biogen received final FDA approval for
their first drugs some years later, and they presumably faced lower regulatory compliance costs than did Genentech for its first drug. A study of the
experiences with the approval process by firms approaching it at different
points in time could provide insight into the evolution of the regulatory
burden on firms and the effects of the development and refinement of the
approval process on their research and development activities.

Comparative regulatory systems

Pharmaceutical prices are regulated in most countries, and the regulatory
systems differ considerably. Many of these systems are integrated with a
national health insurance program in which the government has roles
both as a purchaser and a regulator. Both politics and economics thus are
involved in the control of pharmaceutical prices.[67]

Pharmaceutical sales in Japan are made directly by physicians and, not
surprisingly, Japanese per capita consumption of pharmaceuticals is the
highest in the world. The sale of pharmaceuticals is said to represent
approximately 50 percent of doctors' incomes. Pharmaceutical prices are
set by the Ministry of Health and Welfare (MHW), and prices in the
distribution channel are set as discounts from the MHW price. Price
setting is done under guidelines established by the Central Social Insurance Medical Council. Budget pressures on the MHW have caused it to
lower the prices of many drugs, which has squeezed doctors' incomes.
Since the margins on new drugs generally are higher than the margins on
older drugs, Japanese doctors often switch quickly to prescribing a new
drug.

Australia has a constitution that many believe does not grant the federal government the authority to regulate prices.[68] Through its national
health insurance program, the government uses its ability to offer "subsidies" to reduce the price of eligible pharmaceuticals to retirees and the

poor. This system is independent of the drug approval process, and firms are permitted to sell drugs on the market at unregulated prices.[69]

The Australian approach is basically to negotiate with the producer a per-dose subsidy so that the effective price of a drug is reduced substantially below the price the producer charges on the open market. This approach is said to explain in part why pharmaceutical prices, including the subsidy, are substantially lower in Australia than they are in the United States and many other countries. From the perspective of economic theory, the subsidy is intended to lower the price toward the level of marginal cost, thus increasing demand and reducing the deadweight loss that would otherwise result from pricing above marginal cost. The subsidy, in principle, would leave the firm with profits that are at least as large as the profits it would earn at the unsubsidized price. The Australian government, however, has incentives to reduce the amount of the subsidy payment received by the firm and can do so through bargaining with the firm for a lump-sum reduction in the subsidy. The bargaining power of the government results from its ability to choose which drugs to subsidize.

If there is more than one drug for a particular therapeutic application, the government can play one producer off against another by offering to include in the subsidy program the drug for which the total subsidy cost is the lowest. Since the market demand for the competing drugs is interdependent, subsidization of the price of one drug can reduce the sales of the other drug. This interdependency of demand yields a prisoner's dilemma structure giving the government substantial bargaining power that can be used to reduce the budgetary cost of the subsidization program. The government's bargaining power is strengthened by bargaining in secret, so firms have an incentive to agree to the government's terms.

The British system of pharmaceutical regulation involves an implicit contract between pharmaceutical firms and the government. This is formalized in the Voluntary Price Regulation Scheme agreed to by the Department of Health and Social Security and the Association of the British Pharmaceutical Industry. This system results in drug prices set annually for each firm to provide the firm with an appropriate return, as determined by factors including research and development expenditures, exports, and value added.

An important element of a comparative study of the pharmaceutical industry is to relate the nature and stringency of regulation to industry characteristics such as whether the country has pharmaceutical firms that conduct research and development on new drugs. Another dimension is to relate the form of regulation to the nature of the health insurance system, the compensation system for doctors, and the organization of the medical care delivery system.

NOTES

1. See Stigler (1971), Posner (1971), and Peltzman (1976) for early examples of this approach.
2. The subject of regulation is too broad to be covered in its entirety here. This essay thus is selective. It does not address the regulation of financial services, health care provision, and government procurement. It also does not address the legal dimensions of regulation or the related field of antitrust.
3. See Baron (1989) for a survey and Laffont and Tirole (1993) and Spulber (1989) for extended treatments of these considerations.
4. In perhaps the first use of self-selection in industry regulation, the Federal Communications Commission has allowed the seven regional Bell operating companies and GTE to choose between two incentive mechanisms that offer different combinations of price caps and profit sharing. See Baron (1993a, pp. 270–1).
5. Laffont and Tirole (1986) take this perspective, whereas Baron and Myerson (1982) take the perspective that consumers provide the transfer. In their simplest forms, these two assumptions yield essentially equivalent theories.
6. Sappington (1983) considers the case in which the firm can choose not to produce if *ex post* it will not earn a profit.
7. Since in this theory the profit is derived solely from the private information of the firm, it is typically referred to as an information rent.
8. This is desirable because consumers' plus producers' surplus is a strictly convex function of price, so low prices contribute more than is lost through correspondingly high prices.
9. See Banks (1989) and Banks and Weingast (1992) for models of this type.
10. As discussed later, this type of extension is based on the assumption that all future events can be anticipated and assigned a probability.
11. They consider a two-period model in which neither the firm nor the regulator is able to commit in the first period to its actions in the second period. The mechanism design becomes dramatically different in this case because the incentive compatibility conditions can bind both upward and downward. They show that no mechanism can be separating on any interval with positive measure. Furthermore, the equilibrium can have an infinite number of discontinuities.
12. This line of reasoning is susceptible to the inheritability problem discussed by Riker (1980).
13. An additional complication here, of course, is that in practice changes could be made retroactively. The Supreme Court has traditionally not applied the takings clause of the Constitution to such cases, but it has recently ruled that a state may have to compensate an individual for an economic loss due to a regulatory policy.
14. An example of the political design of regulatory policies is discussed in the section "Political Design of Regulatory Policy."
15. For the theory of price cap regulation, see Einhorn (1991), Sappington and Sibley (1992), and the 1989 symposium in the *RAND Journal of Economics*.
16. The value of X was increased modestly at the review.
17. For example, Salant and Woroch (1992) consider a long-term regulatory relationship that has equilibria that perform well.
18. See Gilbert and Newberry (1993) for an application to regulation.

19. For example, even in a sequential model of the division of a pie under majority rule, an equilibrium exists in which one player receives all the pie. (See Baron and Ferejohn 1989 and Sloth 1992.) Such an equilibrium seems unreasonable.
20. See Abreu and Rubinstein (1986) and Banks and Sundaran (1990) for related approaches.
21. The work of Rochet (1984) is an exception.
22. See also Martimort (1992).
23. See Baron (1988) for a model with an incentive problem at only one level in the hierarchy.
24. See Tirole (1986) and Laffont (1990) for the seminal works on hidden gaming.
25. Laffont and Tirole (1993) have a closely related result.
26. Gilbert and Riordan (1992) obtain a similar result for a different model.
27. See Berg and Tschirant (1988), Braeutigam (1989), Gruenspecht and Lave (1989), and Spulber (1989).
28. See Joskow and Schmalansee (1983) and Gilbert (1991) for analyses of the potential for competition in electric power.
29. See Harrison (1985) for the theory of reflected Brownian motion and Dixit (1992) and Dixit and Pindyck (1994) for economic models of irreversible investment that have some of the features discussed here.
30. See Noll (1989) for a survey of the politics of regulation.
31. See Becker (1983) and Olson (1965) for expositions of these two respective perspectives.
32. Complaints about service, pricing, and concentration in the airline industry have also led to occasional calls for reregulation.
33. Regulation is provided by the Cable Television Consumer Protection and Competition Act of 1992.
34. Bell Atlantic recently announced that it would offer a video rental service through which subscribers can select movies transmitted through existing copper wire telephone connections.
35. Baron (1993a, pp. 270–1).
36. Such takings seems unlikely to be protected by the Constitution.
37. The Consumer Products Safety Commission (CPSC) estimates that 180 people a year die from fires caused by children five years old or younger and that most of the fires result from playing with disposable lighters.
38. Typically, the agency will announce an investigation and then suspend the proceedings. The cases can take several years to complete.
39. These taxes have been used in a number of instances in the United States including for chlorofluorocarbons. A Btu tax has also been proposed in the United States to address the global warming and other problems. A carbon tax has been proposed in Germany in part as a means of raising revenues for the environmental clean-up of the former East Germany.
40. Brock and Evans (1986), for example, provide a model of optimal environmental taxes when firms have differing compliance costs.
41. The model discussed in the section "Stringency of Social Regulation" suggests that the status quo is easy to change when control of the proposal-making process is passed from one party to another.
42. See Hopenhayn and Lohmann (1992) for a theory of the regulation of hazards focusing on the role of oversight committees.

43. The use of CFCs in aerosol cans was banned in the 1970s. Du Pont, the largest producer of CFCs, pledged to stop production if a link between CFCs and ozone depletion was established. When a link was eventually established, Du Pont announced a timetable for its cessation of production.
44. *The New York Times,* January 25, 1993.
45. Also, see Magat and Viscusi (1992).
46. *The New York Times,* June 18, 1983.
47. The clean-up of certain toxic waste sites under the Superfund is similar.
48. See Calabresi and Melamed (1972).
49. One feature of regulatory policy making pertains to how long a policy remains in effect. Some regulatory statutes such as the basic antitrust statutes and the Interstate Commerce Act have remained largely intact for long periods of time, whereas others, such as automobile emissions standards, are frequently changed. Consequently, two cases in which the policy remains in effect forever and in which it remains in effect for one period should be considered. The equilibria in these two cases are qualitatively similar but can differ somewhat in their equilibrium stringency.
50. This discussion explains policy in terms of party or the legislative majority but causation may run in the other direction. Those districts that prefer less regulation may give rise to a party, and those that prefer more regulation may give rise to another party. In this sense, policy causes politics, as Lowi (1964) observed.
51. In November 1992, the Court of Appeals ruled in a case brought by AT&T that the FCC could not exempt other interstate carriers from filing tariffs given that AT&T was required to file tariffs. Bell Atlantic then petitioned the FCC to require local access carriers to disclose their prices.
52. See Braeutigam (1979) for an example of the type of theory needed and Friedlander (1992) for an empirical study of rail rates for coal.
53. See Baron (1993a, pp. 275–7).
54. See Palmer (1992).
55. For example, the California Medicaid program, the Veterans Administration, and the Social Security Administration have successfully demanded and received discounts on pharmaceuticals.
56. The case of AZT brought a new dimension to interest group activity in pharmaceuticals. For perhaps the first time, a significant portion of patients treated with AZT were either members of, or represented by, a well-organized and experienced interest group. Effective political strategies by the activists and compassion for the victims resulted in intense pressure on Burroughs-Wellcome, the producer of AZT. Advocates for AIDS victims, such as Representative Henry Waxman, chairman of the House Subcommittee on Health and the Environment of the Energy and Commerce Committee, brought direct political pressure on Burroughs-Wellcome. Congress was the subject of constituent pressure, and although it could have subsidized the purchase of AZT, budget and precedential concerns made that alternative unattractive. Instead, members of the Congress applied pressure directly to Burroughs-Wellcome. Interest group and political pressure forced Burroughs-Wellcome to reduce the price for AZT by 20 percent in 1987 and another 20 percent in 1989. Pressure for further price reductions decreased when, in 1990, the FDA allowed a reduced dosage for AZT.
57. Pentamidine is an orphan drug to which Lyphomed retains exclusive rights

for seven years. The interest group had pressured Lyphomed by purchasing the drug in the United Kingdom and bringing it into the United States illegally.
58. Vagelos (1991, p. 1083). This policy drew praise from the Senate Special Committee on Aging (1991, p. 15).
59. Senators David Pryor of Arkansas and William Cohen of Maine accused seven drug companies of breaking these promises. They used the unweighted average price increase, whereas the companies used weighted averages.
60. Bristol-Myers Squibb and Burroughs-Wellcome also indicated interest in extending discounts to Medicaid.
61. A number of states have restrictions on eligibility of drugs for reimbursement under their Medicaid programs.
62. *The New York Times,* May 22, 1990.
63. Dr. Vagelos also stated opposition to President Clinton's "play or pay" campaign proposal under which businesses that do not provide health insurance to their employees would be taxed to finance insurance for those who are not covered by their employer. He argued that the system if implemented would quickly slide into a "centralized system" that would discourage research and development.
64. An exception is that the discounts given to military depots do not have to be matched.
65. See Baron (1993, pp. 197–8) for a discussion.
66. It has also brought new issues before the U.S. Department of Agriculture (USDA) as a result of the design of new varieties and strains of plants and animals. Pharmaceuticals developed through biotechnology have also been the subject of considerable criticism by political activists, who have pressured both Congress and the FDA.
67. See Hancher (1990).
68. See Johnston and Zeckhauser (1990).
69. In a number of other countries, prices of pharmaceuticals are regulated, and agreement on the price is required before a drug is approved for sale in the country.

REFERENCES

Abreu, Dilip, and Ariel Rubinstein. 1986. "The Structure of Nash Equilibrium in Repeated Games with Finite Automata," *Econometrica,* 56: 1259–81.
Armstrong, Mark. 1992. "Optimal Nonlinear Pricing by a Multiproduct Monopolist," Chapter 3 of D.Phil. Thesis, University of Oxford, Oxford.
Banks, Jeffrey S. 1989. "Agency Budgets, Cost Information, and Auditing," *American Journal of Political Science,* 33: 670–99.
Banks, Jeffrey S., and R. K. Sundaran. 1990. "Repeated Game, Finite Automata, and Complexity," *Games and Economic Behavior,* 2: 97–117.
✔ Banks, Jeffrey S., and Barry R. Weingast. 1992. "The Political Control of Bureaucracies under Asymmetric Information," *American Journal of Political Science,* 36: 509–24.
Baron, David P. 1985a. "Noncooperative Regulation of a Nonlocalized Externality," *Rand Journal of Economics,* 16: 553–68.
✦ Baron, David P. 1985b. "Regulation of Prices and Pollution under Incomplete Information," *Journal of Public Economics,* 28: 211–31.

The economics and politics of regulation

Baron, David P. 1988a. "Regulation and Legislative Choice," *Rand Journal of Economics*, 19 (Autumn): 467–77.

Baron, David P. 1988b. "Regulatory Incentive Mechanisms, Commitment, and Political Action," Working paper no. 1028, Graduate School of Business, Stanford University.

Baron, David P. 1989. "Design of Regulatory Mechanisms and Institutions," in *Handbook of Industrial Organization*, Richard Schmalensee and Robert Willig, eds., North-Holland, Amsterdam: 1347–1447.

Baron, David P. 1993a. *Business and Its Environment*, Prentice-Hall, Englewood Cliffs, NJ.

Baron, David P. 1993b. "A Theory of Collective Choice for Government Programs," Working paper, Stanford University.

Baron, David P. 1994. "A Sequential Choice Theory Perspective on Legislative Organization," *Legislative Studies Quarterly*, (May): 267–96.

Baron, David P., and David Besanko. 1987. "Commitment and Fairness in a Dynamic Regulatory Relationship," *Review of Economic Studies*, 54: 413–36.

Baron, David P., and David Besanko. 1992. "Regulation, Information, and Organizational Structure," *Journal of Economics and Management Strategy*, 1: 237–75.

Baron, David P., and David Besanko. 1994. "Informational Alliances," Working paper, Stanford University.

Baron, David P., and John A. Ferejohn. 1989a. "Bargaining in Legislatures," *American Political Science Review*, 83: 1181–1206.

Baron, David P., and Ehud Kalai. 1993. "The Simplest Equilibrium of a Majority Rule Division Game," *Journal of Economic Theory*, 61: 290–301.

Baron, David P., and Roger B. Myerson. 1982. "Regulating a Monopolist with Unknown Costs," *Econometrica*, 50: 911–30.

Becker, Gary S. 1983. "Public Policies, Public Pressures, and Dead Weight Losses," *Quarterly Journal of Economics*, 98: 371–400.

Berg, Sanford V., and John Tschirart. 1988. *Natural Monopoly Regulation: Principles and Practice*, Cambridge University Press.

Braeutigam, Ronald R. 1979. "Optimal Pricing with Intermodal Competition," *American Economic Review*, 69: 38–49.

Braeutigam, Ronald R. 1989. "Optimal Policies for Natural Monopolies," in *Handbook of Industrial Organization*, Richard Schmalensee and Robert Willig, eds., North-Holland, Amsterdam: 1289–1346.

Brueckner, Jan K., Nichola J. Dyer, and Pablo T. Spiller. 1992. "Fare Determination in Airline Hub-and-Spoke Networks," *RAND Journal of Economics*, 23 (Autumn): 309–33.

Brock, William A., and David S. Evans. 1986. *The Economics of Small Business*, Holmes & Meier, New York.

Calabresi, Guido, and Douglas A. Melamed. 1972. "Property Rules, Liability Rules and Inalienability: One View of the Cathederal," *Harvard Law Review*, 85: 1089–1128.

Comanor, William S. 1986. "The Political Economy of the Pharmaceutical Industry," *Journal of Economic Literature*, 24 (September): 1178–1217.

Dixit, Avinash. 1992. "Irreversible Investment with Uncertainty and Scale Economies," Working paper, Princeton University.

Dixit, Avinash K., and Robert S. Pindyck. 1994. *Investment under Uncertainty*, Princeton University Press, Princeton, NJ.

Einhorn, Michael A., ed. 1991. *Price Caps and Incentive Regulation in Telecommunications,* Kluwer Academic Press, Boston, MA.

Friedlander, Ann F. 1992. "Coal Rates and Revenue Adequacy in a Quasi-Regulated Rail Industry," *RAND Journal of Economics,* 23 (Autumn): 376–94.

Gasmi, F., M. Invaldi, and J-J. Laffont. 1991. "Rent Extraction and Incentives for Efficiency in Recent Regulatory Proposals," Working paper, IDEI, Université des Sciences Sociales, Toulouse, France.

General Accounting Office. 1992. "Prescription Drugs: Companies Typically Charge More in the United States Than in Canada," Washington, DC, September.

Gilbert, Richard J., ed. 1991. *Regulatory Choices: A Perspective on Developments in Energy Policy,* University of California Press, Berkeley.

Gilbert, Richard J., and David Newberry, 1993. "The Dynamic Efficiency of Regulatory Constitutions," Working paper, University of California, Berkeley.

Gilbert, Richard J., and Michael Riordan. 1992. "Industry Organization and Regulatory Performance," Working paper, University of California, Berkeley.

Gruenspecht, Howard K., and Lester B. Lave. 1989. "The Economics of Health, Safety, and Environmental Regulation," in *Handbook of Industrial Organization,* Richard Schmalensee and Robert Willig, eds., North-Holland, Amsterdam: 1507–50.

Hancher, Leigh. 1990. *Regulating for Competition: Government, Law, and the Pharmaceutical Industry in the United Kingdom and France,* Clarendon Press, Oxford.

Harrison, J. Michael. 1985. *Brownian Motion and Stochastic Flow Systems,* Wiley, New York.

Hopenhayn, Hugo, and Susanne Lohmann. 1992. "Delegation and Regulation of Risk," Working paper, Stanford University, August.

Johnston, Mark, and Richard Zeckhauser. 1990. "The Australian Pharmaceutical Subsidy Gambit: Translating Deadweight Loss and Oligopoly Rents to Consumer Surplus," Working paper, Harvard University, Cambridge, MA.

Joskow, Paul L. 1988. "Price Adjustment in Long-Term Contracts," *Journal of Law and Economics,* 31: 47–83.

Joskow, Paul L. 1990. "The Performance of Long-Term Contracts: Further Evidence from Coal Markets," *RAND Journal of Economics,* 21: 251–74.

Joskow, Paul L., and Nancy L. Rose. 1989. "The Effects of Economic Regulation," in *Handbook of Industrial Organization,* Richard Schmalensee and Robert Willig, eds., North-Holland, Amsterdam: 1449–1506.

Joskow, Paul, and Richard Schmalensee. 1983. *Markets for Power,* MIT Press, Cambridge, MA.

Joskow, Paul, and Richard Schmalensee. 1986. "Incentive Regulation for Electric Utilities," *Yale Journal of Regulation,* 4: 1–49.

Kalai, Ehud, and E. Lehrer. 1991. "Bayesian Learning Leads to Nash Equilibrium," Working paper no. 895, Northwestern University, Evanston, IL.

Klevorick, Alvin K. 1990. "Directions and Trends in Industrial Organization: A Review Essay of *The Handbook of Industrial Organization,*" Working paper, Yale University, December.

Kofman, Fred, and Jacques Lawarée. 1993. "Collusion in Hierarchical Agency," *Econometrica,* 61 (May): 629–56.

Kreps, David M. 1992. "Static Choice in the Presence of Unforeseen Contingencies," in *Economic Analysis of Markets and Games,* P. Dasgupta, D. Gale, O. Hart, and E. Maskin, eds., MIT Press, Cambridge, MA: 258–81.

Laffont, Jean-Jacques. 1990. "Analysis of Hidden Gaming in a Three Level Hierarchy," *Journal of Law, Economics, and Organization,* 6 (Fall): 301–24.

Laffont, Jean-Jacques. 1992. "The New Economics of Regulation Ten Years After," Working paper, Université de Toulouse, Toulouse, France.

Laffont, Jean-Jacques, and Jean Tirole. 1986. "Using Cost Observation to Regulate Firms," *Journal of Political Economy,* 94: 614–41.

Laffont, Jean-Jacques, and Jean Tirole. 1988. "The Dynamics of Incentive Contracts," *Econometrica,* 56, 1153–75.

Laffont, Jean-Jacques, and Jean Tirole. 1990. "The Politics of Government Decision Making: Regulatory Institutions," *Journal of Law, Economics, and Organization,* 6 (Spring): 1–31.

Laffont, Jean-Jacques, and Jean Tirole. 1990. "The Politics of Government Decision Making: A Theory of Regulatory Capture," *Quarterly Journal of Economics,* 1089–1127.

Laffont, Jean-Jacques, and Jean Tirole. 1993. *A Theory of Incentives in Regulation and Procurement.* MIT Press, Cambridge, MA.

Lewis, Tracy, and David E. M. Sappington. 1989. "Countervailing Incentives in Agency Problems," *Journal of Economic Theory,* 20: 405–16.

Lowi, Theodore J. 1964. "American Business, Public Policy, Case-Studies, and Political Theory," *World Politics,* 16 (July): 677–93.

Magat, Wesley A., and W. Kip Viscusi. 1992. *Informational Approaches to Regulation,* MIT Press, Cambridge, MA.

Martimort, David. 1992. "Multi-Principaux avec Anti-Selection," Document de Travail 14, Institut D'Economie Industrielle, Université de Toulouse, Toulouse, France.

McAfee, R. Preston, and John McMillan. 1988. "Multidimensional Incentive Compatibility and Mechanism Design," *Journal of Economic Theory,* 46: 335–54.

McKelvey, Richard D., and Thomas R. Palfrey. 1992a. "Stationarity and Chaos in Infinitely Repeated Games of Incomplete Information," Working paper, California Institute of Technology, Pasadena.

McKelvey, Richard D., and Thomas R. Palfrey. 1992b. "The Holdout Game: An Experimental Study of an Infinitely Repeated Game with Two-Sided Incomplete Information." Working paper, California Institute of Technology, Pasadena.

Noll, Roger G. 1989. "Economic Perspectives on the Politics of Regulation," in *Handbook of Industrial Organization,* Richard Schmalensee and Robert Willig, eds., North-Holland, Amsterdam: 1253–87.

Office of Technology Assessment. 1992. "Federal and Private Roles in the Development of Alglucerase Therapy for Gaucher Disease," Background paper, Washington, D.C.

Olson, Mancer. 1965. *The Logic of Collective Action,* Harvard University Press, Cambridge, MA.

Palmer, Karen. 1992. "A Test for Cross Subsidies in Local Telephone Rates: Do Business Customers Subsidize Residential Customers?" *RAND Journal of Economics,* 23 (Autumn): 415–31.

Peltzman, Sam. 1976. "Toward a More General Theory of Regulation," *Journal of Law and Economics,* 19: 211–40.

Posner, Richard. 1971. "Taxation by Regulation," *Bell Journal of Economics,* 2: 22–50.

RAND Journal of Economics. 1989. "Symposium on Price Cap Regulation," 20 (Autumn).

Rausser, Gordon C., and Leo K. Simon. 1991. "A Noncooperative Model of Collective Decision Making: A Multilateral Bargaining Approach," Working paper, University of California, Berkeley.

Riker, William H. 1980. "Implications from the Disequilibrium of Majority Rule for the Study of Institutions," *American Political Science Review,* 74: 432–46.

Riordan, Michael H., and David E. M. Sappington. 1987. "Information, Incentives, and Organizational Mode," *Quarterly Journal of Economics* (May): 243–63.

Rochet, J-C. 1984. "Monopoly Regulation with Two-Dimensional Uncertainty," Working paper, Laboratoire d'Economie Politique de l'Ecole Normal Superieure, Paris.

Salant, David J., and Glenn A. Woroch. 1992. "Trigger Price Regulation," *RAND Journal of Economics,* 23 (Spring): 29–51.

Sappington, David E. M. 1983. "Limited Liability Contracts Between Principal and Agent," *Journal of Economic Thought,* 29: 1–29.

Sappington, David E. M. and David S. Sibley. 1992. "Strategic Nonlinear Pricing Under Price-Cap Regulation," *RAND Journal of Economics,* 23 (Spring): 1–19.

Schmalensee, Richard. 1989. "Good Regulatory Regimes," *Rand Journal of Economics,* 20: 417–36.

Sloth, Rirgette. 1992. "Voting over the Partition of a Pie," Working paper, University of Copenhagen, Copenhagen.

Spulber, Daniel F. 1989. *Regulation and Markets,* MIT Press, Cambridge, MA.

Stigler, George J. 1971. "The Theory of Economic Regulation," *Bell Journal of Economics and Management Science,* 2: 3–21.

Tirole, Jean. 1986. "Hierarchies and Bureaucracies: On the Role of Collusion in Organizations," *Journal of Law, Economics and Organization,* 2: 181–214.

Tirole, Jean. 1994. "Collusion and the Theory of Organizations," in *Advances in Economic Theory, Sixth World Congress,* J. J. Laffont, ed., Vol. 2, Cambridge University Press: 151–206.

Vagelos, P. Roy. 1991. "Are Prescription Drug Prices High?" *Science,* 252 (24 May): 1080–4.

Viscusi, W. Kip. 1992. *Fatal Tradeoffs: Public and Private Responsibilities for Risk,* Oxford University Press, Oxford.

Viscusi, W. Kip., and Wesley A. Magat. 1987. *Learning About Risk: Consumer and Worker Responses to Hazard Information,* Harvard University Press, Cambridge, MA.

Weingast, Barry R., and Mark J. Moran. 1983. "Bureaucratic Discretion or Congressional Control: Regulatory Policymaking by the Federal Trade Commission," *Journal of Political Economy,* 91: 765–800.

Williamson, Oliver E. 1975. *Markets and Hierarchies: Analysis and Antitrust Implications,* Free Press, New York.

Wilson, Robert. 1993. *Nonlinear Pricing,* Oxford University Press, Oxford.

Wolak, Frank A. 1991. "Estimating Regulated Firm Production Functions with Private Information: An Application to the California Water Industry," Working paper, Stanford University, September.

Wolak, Frank A., and Jonathon S. Feinstein. 1991. "An Econometric Analysis of the Asymmetric Information Regulator–Utility Interaction," in *Advances in Econometrics,* George F. Rhodes, ed. 9: 159–204.

2

Regulatory commitment and utilities' privatization: implications for future comparative research

PABLO T. SPILLER

INTRODUCTION

Utilities' privatization has become a booming industry. From Latin America, to Europe, to Asia and now to Africa, utilities' privatization has become a key element of reform-minded governments. Global ideological changes, fiscal concerns, and the recognition that there may not be any visible advantage for government ownership are behind this global reconsideration of the ownership role in the provision of utility services. But with privatization comes the recognition, often belatedly, that utilities are not like any other sector of the economy, where an appropriate tax treatment and a stable economic environment is enough to develop private investment in utilities. In case after case, it is being recognized that the private sector has to be "encouraged" to undertake all the investments that the public and the government expected from the utility. The need for this encouragement, however, is often seen by many governments and the public in general as a further example of the private monopolies ripping off customers, of collusion between the private companies and the governments, of the need to renationalize, and so on.

The purpose of this essay is to discuss what seems to be the crux of success for privatized utilities and what research is needed to further our understanding of the ability to succeed in regulating newly privatized utilities. In this essay I discuss the experience of some countries that have undertaken, or attempted to undertake, utility privatizations. I do not claim, however, that the discussion here is exhaustive, as I focus on a few selected countries on which I have undertaken primary research. In particular, I will say very little about the nature of privatizations in Eastern Europe, Africa, and the Far East. I believe, however, that the general conclusions developed in this essay should be applicable to those countries, once their institutional peculiarities are taken into account.

Pablo T. Spiller

THE PROBLEM IN THE PRIVATIZATION OF UTILITIES

Utilities are fragile industries. A large proportion of their assets are sunk; their technology exhibits, in general, important economies of scale; and their customers comprise the voting population of the city or state. Their pricing will always attract the local politicians' interests.[1] Such political sensitiveness to their prices implies that regulatory discretion increases the risk of administrative expropriation, as the regulators could, following public pressure, undertake various administrative actions so as to set prices below long-run average costs, *de facto* expropriating the companies' sunk costs. Indeed, history is full of examples of regulatory attempts to extract those quasi-rents, as well as of attempts by industries to fend off such actions.

For example, the current development of cellular telephony in the former socialist economies not only reflects the need to develop new telecommunications systems rapidly, but also that investors do not want to invest in assets or technologies that are extremely specific, like copper or fiber optic cables. Instead, by users undertaking a large part of the specific investments (the headsets) and companies providing the software, computer equipment, and transmission facilities (assets that are relatively fungible), companies diminish their risk of administrative expropriation. Similarly, the initial creation of state regulatory commissions in the United States seems to have been related to the inability of municipalities to commit to stable regulatory regimes.[2]

Proper management of the risk of *ex post* administrative expropriation seems to be the key for a successful privatization, for fiscal, efficiency, and political reasons. Consider fiscal reasons first. If the privatization is undertaken without strong commitment to relatively "fair" regulation, private investors will expect very low profits from the undertaking, and as a consequence, they will bid less than if the risk of administrative expropriation was limited, reducing the governments gains from the privatization. Second, lack of regulatory commitment will also have implications for investment and, hence, for pricing. As the example of cellular telephony suggests, lack of regulatory commitment implies that the private sector will limit its exposure by not investing too much out of their own resources and by investing in less specific assets, even if they are relatively inefficient.[3] Thus, congestion will not be reduced and prices may remain high. Finally, a poorly designed regulatory system lacking regulatory commitment may also represent a self-fulfilling prophecy in the sense that low and inefficient investments and high prices will build pressure to reverse the privatization.

On the other hand, economists have paid very little attention to these issues, and instead most of the modern (or information) theory of regulation has been developed around the assumption of a relatively benign government and a strategically motivated firm.[4] Indeed, only recently the problem of a strategic government has been introduced into the theoretical analysis, although in an extremely simplified way.[5] Regulatory scholarship, then, has emphasized the development of optimal regulatory schemes. The implementation of these schemes, however, requires so much regulatory discretion that, if granted, it will be impossible to deter the regulator from behaving opportunistically, and hence destroying the same incentive scheme that it was supposed to uphold.

The evidence across privatizations, however, suggests that not all countries have been able to design regulatory institutions so as to provide reasonable commitments to a "fair" regulatory process. There are two basic sources for such difficulties: first, most countries do not have constitutional protection against administrative expropriation. Second, most countries do not have a well-developed conflict resolution method. Thus, in designing regulatory institutions a trade-off has to be made between sophisticated theoretical regulatory frameworks and those that would be appropriate given the nature of the country in question.

Constitutional protection and investment

An extreme example of the lack of constitutional protection against administrative expropriation is the United Kingdom. The U.K. Parliament is sovereign, and as a consequence, courts have seldom challenged regulatory decisions by agencies. The traditional rules of voting, prevalent in the United Kingdom since the electoral reforms of the Victorian period, tend to create a two-party system. As a consequence, the party in government controls the legislature. But such control is valuable insofar as the party also controls its members, since lack of party discipline could imply the fall of the government. Thus, U.K. political parties have tended to control their members by rewarding cooperative members with their allocation of funds, patronage, and cabinet appointments.[6] Party control over the legislature and the executive implies legislative flexibility. Legislation can be amended to accommodate new technologies, new political winds, or new judicial decisions. The lack of constitutional protection, then, makes utilities particularly at risk in U.K.-like systems. Indeed, the differences in the evolution of U.K. and U.S. regulation of electricity at the turn of the century can be traced back to the development in the United States of a constitutional doctrine defense of "fair" rates of return by the U.S. judiciary,[7] coupled with the strong tradition of judicial oversight of regulatory agencies. This has reduced, to a large extent, the state regulators' discretion, providing the necessary commitment power to the U.S. regulatory system, and thus enabling utilities to expand and provide service in a relatively assured, although not necessarily efficient, environment.[8]

In the United Kingdom, on the other hand, the lack of constitutional protection meant that each utility was at risk and had to protect its investments. This protection took the place of obtaining special operating rights from parliament. But since these special operating rights were given for a limited period of time, the power sector in the United Kingdom lagged in its development well behind the United States and Europe.[9]

The fact that the U.S. judiciary developed a constitutional doctrine of protection against "arbitrary" administrative decisions is not a random event. The inherent divisions of powers in the United States, together with electoral laws limiting the dependence of legislators on the executive, is a recipe for a very strong and independent judiciary.[10] While such doctrine could have developed in other countries with relatively weak executives and constitutional division of powers, it has not, except in very special circumstances. Thus, the privatization of utilities in most countries will have to be done in the absence of a tradition of constitutional defense against opportunistic regulatory behavior.

Privatization and conflict resolution systems

Judicial review of administrative decisions, which is taken for granted in the United States, is seldom undertaken, or even understood, in most other countries. Even countries with well-developed administrative courts (e.g., France) seldom use those courts to limit the discretion of regulatory agencies. Administrative courts usually deal with procurement and government malfeasance. While the jurisdiction of these courts could be extended to regulatory decisions, courts in most countries have not developed a tradition of challenging administrative decisions on those grounds. As a consequence, using U.S.-style procedural requirements and judicial supervision to achieve regulatory stability may not succeed.

Consider, for example, parliamentary systems. Both the United Kingdom and the Caribbean countries have minimal judicial review of administrative decisions. Indeed, in the United Kingdom the grounds for judicial review of an administrative decision are its "reasonableness." U.K. regulators have, as a consequence, tended to limit the descriptions of the reasons for their decisions so as not to expose themselves to potential litigation.[11] Similarly, in the British Caribbean countries, courts do not have a tradition of challenging administrative decisions. This does not mean, however, that the Caribbean courts have not provided a check to governments. They have done so, but have resorted to constitutional grounds. That was, for example, the approach taken by the Jamaican Supreme Court when it deemed as unconstitutional Prime Minister

Manley's attempts to expropriate land without proper compensation.[12] Such constitutional challenges, however, cannot be used extensively for blatantly nonconstitutional issues without triggering a constitutional crisis.[13]

The lack of judicial oversight of regulatory agencies in U.K.-style parliaments is not surprising. U.K.-style parliaments tend to be dominated by a single party, implicitly granting the executive strong legislative powers. Other parliamentary systems, based, for example, on proportional representation, will tend to form governments based on multiparty coalitions, and thus will tend to have weaker executives and more independent-minded courts.[14]

On the other hand, presidential systems à la Latin America provide substantial discretion to the executive. The basic reason for this delegation is that their constitutions provide for presidential "regulation" of laws. That is, for a law to be implemented it needs a presidential decree that regulates the law. Unless the regulation of the law is blatantly against the language of the statute,[15] the regulation of the law is not subject to judicial review. Facing potential distortion by the executive, legislators face a trade-off among writing very specific laws that will bind future governments, writing vague laws that grant future governments substantial discretion in the area, or not writing any law at all, so as to withdraw from future governments any legislative powers on that topic. Since writing very specific laws is difficult and time consuming, policy areas will be divided into two groups, those where the government has a relatively free hand, and those where the government is prohibited from taking initiatives.[16] Because utilities are key and complex social services, Latin American legislatures have tended to defer to their executives the right to choose the regulatory framework rather than taking away their legislative powers.[17] Thus, vagueness has been the rule in Latin America's utility regulation legislation.[18]

Since the regulation of laws is undertaken by a presidential decree and not by a regulatory agency, limitation on the process by which the president regulates the law would be counter to the constitutional provision for the division of powers. Thus, challenges to a presidential decree can only be based on its constitutionality. Thus, courts in Latin America have tended to specialize in upholding contracts rather than in supervising the executive implementation of laws. In the United States, on the other hand, there is no such regulation of laws. The laws are implemented by agencies of the government and not by a presidential decree. Congress, furthermore, regulates how agencies make decisions. This regulation of the agency decision-making process, however, was not seen by the courts as a challenge to the constitutional division of powers.[19] Thus, unless legislatures start writing very specific regulatory laws (as in Chile), future governments will have substantial discretion on regulatory issues, raising questions about the ability to commit to a particular regulatory framework.

Thus, the problem of utilities' privatization is not so much how to organize the bidding process, but rather how to accommodate the privatization to the current institutional framework of the country in question.

SOME EVIDENCE FROM RECENT PRIVATIZATIONS

The recent utility privatization attempts can be divided into three groups: those that have performed well, those that have performed poorly, and those that have failed to be done. An analysis of the latter set is important because it will highlight the institutional constraints for change in the countries in question.

The good guys

There is no monopoly for successful privatizations. We find successful utility privatizations in developed and developing countries, in parliamentary and presidential systems, and in countries with strong and weak executives. I will focus here on five experiences: Chile's privatization of electricity and telecommunications, Jamaica's privatization of telecommunications, the U.K. privatization of most of its utility sector, Argentina's privatization of electricity distribution in the city of Buenos Aires, and Mexico's privatization of telecommunications.

I consider these to be successful privatizations because in each of these cases investment and service quality have increased, and prices have not increased too much.[20] As a consequence, the regulatory and ownership system is seen as politically sustainable. This, unfortunately, cannot be said from all other utilities' privatizations.

As I will discuss later, the main feature of this group of privatizations is that the nature of their regulatory systems fits reasonably well the political institutions and the administrative capabilities of the countries. As will become clear, however, there is no determinism in this analysis, as Argentina's successful privatization of electricity distribution in Buenos Aires is matched by its unsuccessful privatization of telecommunications. Indeed, successful privatizations require careful institutional design.

The bad guys

The set of relatively unsuccessful privatizations is not that large. Indeed, I know of only one privatization of utilities that has been carried through and that I would be willing to classify as a failure, using the criteria defined earlier. This is the case of Argentina's telecommunications privatization. I consider it a failure, because to privatize it, prices had to be increased in real terms by a substantial amount, investment levels were no different from prior levels, and although the privatization occurred in 1991, quality has not improved so far. Furthermore, there is substantial popular discontent with the privatization, suggesting that further regulatory and ownership changes should be expected in the near future.[21]

That the privatization would be a failure, however, could have been predicted quite well from the privatization process itself. First, there was no regulatory institution designed prior to the transfer of ownership. Bids were entered without knowing what the price-setting mechanism was going to be. Once the winners of the two licenses were assigned, the two consortia bargained with the government on setting the initial prices and negotiated a particular indexation mechanism. Interestingly, once this price was set, the revenue from the privatization of the two companies was approximately the combined cash flow for two years. Since the government sold 60% of the shares of the two companies, the private consortia were assured a three-year payout period, since in that period their shares of the companies' cash flow would be equivalent to their initial payments. Three years, however, is an unusually short payout period, reflecting the high risks involved in the transaction. While some commentators attach such a high risk to the nature of Argentina's highly inflationary economy and history of military coups, I submit that much of that high risk was the result of the prior inexistence of a credible regulatory framework.[22]

The missing guys

Privatization attempts have been blocked in several countries. Among those, Brazil, Bolivia, and Uruguay are interesting examples, since, while the governments have been determined to carry out the privatization of most of their utilities, none has been able to do so. There is, however, a common thread to the three cases. The three are presidential systems with electoral laws that promote divided governments. The large number of parties represented in the legislatures, as well as the possibility that a president is elected with only a plurality of the popular vote,[23] implies that the party in the executive will not have a strong command over the legislature, and thus, attempts to change the status quo may find strong resistance in Congress.

The case of Uruguay is most telling, for, while the legislature passed a law granting the executive the power to privatize the government telecommunications company, the losing parties in the legislature successfully implemented a popular plebiscite that overturned that legislation. Thus, as was the case in the United States, divided governments, weak and/or multiple parties, and weak executives are good recipes for the tyranny of the status quo.

These countries inability to change the current ownership structure, however, may be temporary. If an election grants a single party a majority (or a very large plurality) in the legislature, reforms could be feasible. Indeed, the current president-elect of Bolivia, who was elected without the intervention of the legislature, has already declared his support for a rapid privatization of several utilities. Similarly, President Menem's reform program was supported by the Argentinean Congress, while that of President Alfonsin's was not, simply because the former president's electoral victory was accompanied by a Peronist working majority in both houses of Congress.

PRIVATIZATION AND THE REGULATORY PROCESS

The variety of regulatory processes used in conjunction with the different privatization attempts mentioned earlier encompass three basic approaches: first, a U.S.-style public utility commission; second, extremely detailed legislation; and finally, contract law. So far none of the successful privatizations have introduced U.S.-style public utility commission (PUC) systems. To a large extent, that seems reasonable given the lack of a tradition of judicial review of administrative decisions. On the other hand, current proposals for telecommunications regulation in Argentina and Bolivia envision the creation of all-powerful regulatory commissions subject to judicial review.

As discussed earlier, extremely detailed legislation is quite difficult to write, and only Chile has used this approach since 1980 to specify the regulatory process in both electricity and telecommunications. Since then, Argentina's privatization of electricity has been based on the Chilean model, and the recent electricity law has embodied the Chilean approach. Observe, though, that telecommunications regulation in Argentina is taking a very different tack, with the law being vague and leaving its implementation to the regulatory agency.

Finally, contract law as the base for the regulatory process has been used in several privatizations, including those in the United Kingdom, the Caribbean, and Mexico. Furthermore, the regulation of the private electricity company of the city of La Paz (COBEE) in Bolivia has been based on contract law since 1912.

The way regulation can be based on contract rather than administrative law is by the firm and the government signing an agreement specifying the way by which the company's prices are to be set. If the government deviates from such a process, the company can challenge the government in the courts. In this case, the courts would be adjudicating on a contract provision rather than on their interpretation of the legislation.

Regulatory commitment and U.S.-style PUCs

In countries where judicial restraint of administrative decisions is not common, U.S.-style regulation may turn out to provide unusual discretionary powers. Consider, for example, the case of Jamaica's Public Utility Commission (JPUC) created in 1967 to regulate the electricity and telephone companies.[24] The JPUC was an independent agency, with its independence guaranteed by the appointment process. Upon creation, and in particular during the early 1970s, the JPUC introduced an investment/price increase policy whereby price increases would be allowed if the companies' investment programs achieve some unspecified levels. Since there was an inflationary environment at that time, the negotiations about whether the actual investment levels were appropriate or not implied that both companies' real rates fell drastically, bringing their profitability close to bankruptcy levels.[25] On the other hand, prior to the creation of the JPUC both companies were regulated based on contract law (see later), effectively restraining opportunistic administrative behavior.

Regulatory commitment and specific legislation

Chile's reform of electricity regulation in 1980 introduced for the first time a regulatory system in which the price-setting mechanism, including the price formulas to be used, were specified in great detail in the enabling law. The law is so specific that in specifying the way to compute the cost of capital of an efficient firm, the regulator ought to use the capital asset pricing model. The law, furthermore, specifies the exact regression to be estimated for that purpose. Since then, Chile has introduced similarly detailed legislation for its regulation of telecommunications, and Argentina has introduced it for its regulation of electricity.[26]

Since such detailed legislation is quite difficult to undertake, its advantages and disadvantages have to be considered. Its main advantage resides in the fact that the regulator is left with very little discretion. Indeed, Chile's price regulatory offices in both electricity and telecommunications employ only three full-time employees (approximately the same that the Office of Telecommunications Regulation has in the United Kingdom. The rest of the employees of the regulatory agencies deal with quality, supervisory, and planning issues. The regulator, then, has very little discretion on setting prices. Furthermore, as long as new legislation is difficult to introduce, future governments will not be able to amend the price-setting rules to the company's detriment. The rigidity of this system, however, is also its main disadvantage. As new technologies may appear, the optimal regulatory policy may change. But, if it is difficult to amend the legislation, some future socially welfare-improving regulatory changes will not be introduced.

Thus, its main advantage (commitment) and disadvantage (lack of flexibility) are present if legislation is difficult to change. This would be the case in presidential systems with fragmented legislatures. In such case, unless the party in government is able to build a strong governing coalition, drastic changes in regulatory laws will be difficult to obtain. Both Chile and Argentina, as well as Bolivia, Brazil and Uruguay, could fit that description.[27] Chile's presidents have seldom had a majority in the legislature, nor had most (democratic) governments in Argentina, Brazil, Bolivia, and Uruguay. Such a situation will persist as long as electoral rules promote small-party representation in the legislature. Thus, the current regulatory system in Chile for electricity, water, and telecommunications, as well as the electricity regulatory system for Argentina, should provide substantial commitment to private investors. It is not so surprising, then, the substantial level of private investments in Buenos Aires' electricity distribution, and in Chile's private electricity and telecommunications companies, while the telephone companies in Argentina have not invested at levels over and beyond the preprivatization levels.

Specific legislation, however, may not provide any commitment in other circumstances. Consider, for example, a two-party parliamentary system, like in Jamaica or the United Kingdom. Since the party in government can always change prior laws, regulatory laws by themselves will not provide strong commitment. On the other hand, parliamentary systems with a large number of parties (e.g., Israel or Italy) and relatively weak coalitions could base their regulatory systems on very specific and detailed legislation.

While very detailed regulatory legislation provides substantial commitment to private investors, the conditions for that to be the case (legislative fragmentation, weak executive) are the same that would make it difficult for such legislation to be introduced in the first place. Thus, regulatory systems based on very detailed legislation require historical accidents to be undertaken; namely, they require the presence of a unified government. That was the case in Chile and is true for the current Menem administration. In Chile, the regulatory reforms were introduced during the regime of President Pinochet, who controlled the legislative process. The interesting feature of Chile's regulatory regime is that it was not passed by a presidential decree that can be overruled by another presidential decree, but rather was passed as a law. Thus, if a democratic government wants to change Chile's regulatory regime it will have to get sufficient support in the legislature.

In the case of Argentina, the privatization process was initiated during the regime of President Alfonsin. Since he did not have a majority in both houses of the legislature, its privatization process was blocked. President Menem's administration, however, happened to have control over both houses of the legislature, facilitating the implementation of its privatization initiatives. In the case of telecommunications, the Menem administration's design of regulatory regime was introduced in the form of a presidential decree; it was altered several times through further decrees, and was eventually unilaterally abrogated by the introduction of a freeze on telecommunications prices. On the other hand, the regulation of electricity is not done through presidential decrees, but rather through legislation, providing substantially more regulatory commitment.

Thus, as discussed earlier, the same electoral victories that may facilitate the structural reform of utilities in countries with fragmented legislatures are the conditions needed for introducing commitment through specific legislation.

Regulatory commitment and the use of contract law

Contract law and regulation have a long tradition. Indeed, the first regulation of utilities in the United Kingdom dates back to the year 1500.[28] Since then, and until their eventual nationalization in the post-war period, U.K. utilities were regulated based on contract law. Utilities have traditionally been granted a license that stipulated the price-setting process.[29] The advantage of a license-based regulatory system rather than one based on legislation is that courts, used to adjudicating contract disputes, can also be used to solve conflicts between the government and the regulated companies. As long as the contract or license is sufficiently specific and clear, so that it can be enforced by the courts,[30] contract-based regulation may provide regulatory commitment.

Indeed, this has been the way the Bolivian Power Company (COBEE) has been regulated since 1912. Its license, that has to be renewed every 40 years, has always specified the way its prices are to be set. Since 1962 its license stipulates that its prices are to be set based on a 1962 presidential decree that created the Electricity Code.[31] Changes in the Electricity Code, however, would not affect COBEE since its license incorporates the original decree. It is then, not surprising, that the 1962 Electricity Code has not been changed yet.

Prior to the creation of the JPUC in 1967, the regulation of Jamaica's electricity and telephone companies was also based on licenses that stipulated the way their prices were to be set. Conflicts between the companies and the government were settled in court.[32] Since the privatization of the telecommunications companies in 1987, the regulatory system was again introduced in the license.[33] Since then there have been no court challenges, though.

In the United Kingdom, all utilities require a license. The licenses specify the price-setting process, in particular, they specify the nature of the price cap system (i.e., the x factor),[34] the basket of services, and so forth. While the regulator is in charge of enforcing the license, he or she cannot unilaterally change the x factor or any other term of the license.

The advantage of a regulatory system based on a license, then, is that as long as the license specifies in great detail how prices are to be set, future governments cannot easily change unilaterally the regulatory framework, providing, then, for regulatory commitment. In particular, regulatory changes that will not make the company worse off could be introduced since the firm will agree to (or even lobby for)[35] changes in the license. Changing the license against the company's will, however, may not be feasible. In Jamaica and other Caribbean countries, the license modifications require the agreement of the respective company. In the United Kingdom, however, a license modification against the will of the company may be undertaken by the regulator as long as a very specific process is followed; this involves an agreement of the Monopolies and Mergers Commission and of the Secretary of State.[36]

The use of contract law, then, provides commitment at the cost of some flexibility. In the Jamaican case, for example, the initial license granted a 25-year monopoly over domestic and international telecommunications services to Telecommunications of Jamaica (TOJ), assuring a rate of return on equity of 17.5–20%. Attempts to introduce more flexible pricing schemes will have to get the consent of TOJ, which will not be forthcoming if they will impact on its expected profitability. In the U.K. case, however, flexibility was achieved through the introduction of a license amendment process that makes use of preexisting institutions, like the Monopolies and Mergers Commission, to whom veto power is given.

KEY ISSUES FOR FURTHER RESEARCH

The discussion in the preceding sections has highlighted the importance of the nature of political institutions for the design of regulatory frameworks that will provide commitment to "fair" treatment of private utilities. In particular,it has shown that comparative studies provide fertile grounds to explore the role of commitment capabilities. Several issues have remained unexplored. A key issue is the role of federalist versus centralized governmental structures. For example, Weingast (1993) claims that a basic need for promoting private-sector development is the rise of a federalistic structure, whether formally (as in the United States during the nineteenth century) or informally (as in the United Kingdom). Not all federal structures are conducive to sustained private development, as the examples of India and Argentina show. On the other hand, Germany's power sector has had since its origins a strong private-sector component. To what extent the strong role played by the regions in the design of regulatory policy was influential in stopping regulatory opportunism remains a fascinating issue to analyze. Similarly, the extent of investment in China's power sector without the existence of Western style contract law may, again, suggest the importance of federalism as a source of commitment.

An important second issue to analyze is the role of party control in providing commitment. The experiences of two countries are particularly important here: that of Mexico and Japan. Both countries, although Japan may in the future have to be taken off the list, have political structures that traditionally support the dominance of a single party. Commitment, however, requires particular party structures that limit the potential for opportunism. The close association between party, legislative, and interest group organizations in Japan suggests such a design. A similar analysis of Mexico's party/interest group interaction could prove extremely useful to understanding its successful telecommunications privatization process.

While I have emphasized throughout this essay the role of institutions in providing commitment, economic growth may also serve as an implicit safeguarding institution. The more investment is expected in the future, the less the incentive to behave opportunistically in the present. To what extent Argentina's success in its electricity privatization is the result of a change in expectations about growth, rather than the proper matching of regulatory design to institutional features, remains to be fully explored.

Finally, in this essay I have emphasized the potential for opportunistic behavior by governments. Regulated firms, however, are neither saints nor naïve. Regulated companies have the ability to design their operations in ways that may, to some extent, counterbalance the power of the governments. For example, companies may use only expatriates as senior management and in key operational positions (i.e., only expatriates could have access to key software). In that case, the threat of withdrawing the managers may limit the governments' opportunistic incentives. Similarly, in the presence of regulatory misbehavior, a telecommunications operator could erase its proprietary software, or an electricity company could turn off power as a retaliatory measure. While I believe that the retaliatory power of private companies exists, it is also the case that if a government would make those actions legal, it would open itself to extortion, as it will be literally impossible to legislate that such actions are only legal in the face of "opportunistic behavior by the regulator."

These are all issues that regulation scholars interested in the role of transaction costs, information, and institutions can, and should, address in the near future. They present not only interesting theoretical questions, but ones with direct policy implications as well.

NOTES

1. See Goldberg (1976) and Williamson (1976).
2. See Troesken (1992) for a discussion applied to the gas sector in Chicago.
3. See Williamson (1988).
4. The *locus classicus* of the new theory of regulation is Baron and Myerson (1982).
5. For the most advanced treatment of opportunistic governmental behavior, see Laffont and Tirole (1993).
6. That U.K. legislators spend much less time on constituency work than their U.S. counterparts is then not that surprising. See Cox (1987) and Cain, Ferejohn, and Fiorina (1987) for discussions of the U.K. parliamentary system and its differences with the U.S. government.
7. *FPC v. Hope Natural Gas Co.*, Supreme Court of the United States, 1944, 320 U.S. 592, 64 S.Ct. 281, 88 L.Ed. 333.
8. This does not mean, though, that U.S. utilities, in particular electricity companies, haven't had their share of regulatory difficulties. The inflationary process, the increase in the real price of oil, and the environmental concerns that started in the 1970s required substantial changes in the regulatory process (Joskow 1974). For example, during that period electric utilities were traded at 70% of their book value (Joskow and McAvoy 1975). To some extent, though, one of the lasting effects of this period is the increase in the perceived change in the regulatory risk as capacity additions (mostly nuclear) undertaken during the oil shock period were challenged in courts by environmental groups and eventually were required to be withdrawn from the rate base. See, however, Gilbert and Newbery (1990) and Lyon (1991) for models that provide efficiency rationales for regulatory investment reviews performed with "regulatory hindsight."
9. Germany's decentralized governmental system provided utilities with substantial leverage vis-à-vis the central government, limiting in that respect the extent of central intervention in their affairs. See Müller (1993). See also Spiller and Vogelsang (forthcoming c) for a discussion of the evolution of U.K. regulation of electricity at the turn of the century.
10. Gely and Spiller (1990) discuss how the discretion of courts is limited by the homogeneity of preferences among member of the legislature and the executive.
11. See Veljanovski (1992).
12. See Spiller and Sampson (forthcoming) for a discussion of the role of courts in Jamaica.
13. For a rational choice analysis of the choice of judicial doctrine, see Spiller and Spitzer (1992).

14. For example, in the past few years, Israeli environmental groups have successfully used the courts to challenge government environmental decisions.
15. As would be the case if the regulation changes the income tax brackets from those specified by the legislature.
16. See Spiller (1993a) for a model of the choice of legislative form.
17. See, however, the discussion later on the Uruguayan plebiscite withdrawing from the government the right to privatize the telecommunications company.
18. This, however, is not the case in Chile since 1980 and recently in Argentina. See the upcoming discussion.
19. What the courts saw at a point in time as challenging the division of powers was the congressional delegation of legislative powers to the agencies themselves. This is the source of the "delegation" doctrine, which was used by the Supreme Court in reversing two major pieces of New Deal legislation. See Gely and Spiller (1992) for a rational choice approach to the conflict between the U.S. Supreme Court and Congress and the president during the New Deal.
20. See Spiller and Sampson (forthcoming) for a discussion of Jamaica's privatization of telecommunications, Spiller and Vogelsang (1993a) for a discussion of the U.K. experience in telecommunications, Abdala and Tandon (1992) for the Mexican case, and Spiller and Viana (1992) and Galal (forthcoming) for discussions of the privatization of Chile's electricity and telecommunications, respectively.
21. See Spiller (1993b) and Hill and Abdala (forthcoming) for discussions of the privatization of Argentina's telecommunication companies.
22. See Spiller (1993b) for an in-depth discussion of this issue.
23. In the case of Bolivia, if the presidential election does not provide a majority winner, then the legislature is to elect the president without respect to who obtained the largest number of votes. Coalitions then have to be formed to elect the president. While in Chile the legislature also elects the president if no candidate obtained a majority of the popular vote, so far all presidents elected by the legislature were the plurality winners. In the case of President Allende, though, his election was subject to particular prior legislation that restricted his executive powers. For a discussion of this type of presidential systems, see Shugart and Carey (1992).
24. Prior to the creation of the JPUC, there was a regulatory system based on a license that clearly stipulated the regulatory process. See Spiller and Sampson (forthcoming).
25. The government disagreed with the JPUC's demands but was unable to steer the commission toward a more cooperative mode. Eventually Prime Minister Manley's government introduced a tax on telephone calls, which was rebated to the company as a direct government subsidy. The government, in turn, received 10% of the outstanding shares of the company. See Spiller and Sampson (forthcoming).
26. For a discussion of electricity regulation in Chile, see Spiller and Viana (1992), and for a discussion of telecommunications regulation, see Galal (forthcoming).
27. See Shugart and Carey (1992) for a discussion of the nature of these presidential systems.
28. See Spiller and Vogelsang (1993) for a discussion of the evolution of the regulation of utilities in the United Kingdom.
29. It is interesting to note that the first incentive schemes I am aware of were

introduced in 1800 in the United Kingdom through what was called a price–dividend scheme, whereby firms were allowed to distribute larger dividends if they set lower prices.

30. For example, the price-setting process has to be transparent. If there is too much discretion left to the regulator in the license, then court challenges may not be successful since the courts may not be able to discern strategic from nonstrategic moves by the government.

31. See Spiller (1993b) for a discussion of this case.

32. An interesting case was one where the government did not allow a price increase to the telephone company. The telephone company sued and the court granted the price increase. See Spiller and Sampson (forthcoming).

33. The form of the privatization was by the creation of a joint venture between the government and Cable & Wireless (C&W). The initial shareholders' agreement stipulated the way the company was to be regulated. The government subsequently sold most of its shares to C&W and to the public. Prior to the sale, though, licenses were granted to the company that incorporated all the regulatory issues agreed upon in the shareholders' agreement. See Spiller and Sampson (forthcoming).

34. A simple price cap would allow average price increases for a basket of goods as long as it is less than CPI $-$ x, where CPI stands for the increase in the consumer price index, and x is a predetermined percentage. The current U.K. telecommunications price cap sets an x of 7.5%.

35. This is the current case in Jamaica, where the company wants to make the license more specific about cellular telephony.

36. See Spiller and Vogelsang (1993b) for a model of regulatory decision making in the United Kingdom.

REFERENCES

Abdala, M., and P. Tandon (1992), "The Divestiture of Telmex," Washington, DC: World Bank.

Baron, D., and R. Myerson (1982), "Regulating a Monopolist under Unknown Costs," *Econometrica*, 50: 911–30.

Cain, B., J. Ferejohn, and M. Fiorina (1987), *The Personal Vote*, Cambridge, MA: Harvard University Press.

Cox, G. *The Efficient Secret* (1987), Cambridge University Press.

Galal, A. (forthcoming), "Regulation, Commitment and Development of Telecommunications in Chile," in Levy, B., and P. T. Spiller, eds., *Regulation, Institutions and Commitment in Telecommunications: A Comparative Analysis of Five Country Studies*, Washington, DC: World Bank.

Gely, R., and P. T. Spiller (1990), "A Rational Choice Theory of Supreme Court Statutory Decisions, with Applications to the *State Farm* and *Grove City* Cases," *Journal of Law, Economics and Organization*, 6: 263–301.

Gely, R., and P. T. Spiller (1992), "The Political Economy of Supreme Court Constitutional Decisions: The Case of Roosevelt's Court-Packing Plan," *International Review of Law and Economics*, 12: 45–67.

Gilbert, R., and Newbery (1990), "Regulatory Constitutions," Berkeley: University of California Press.

Goldberg, V. (1976), "Regulation and Administered Contracts," *Bell Journal of Economics*, 426–52.

Hill, A., and M. Abdala (forthcoming), "Regulation, Institutions and Commitment: Privatization and Regulation in the Argentine Telecommunications Sector," in Levy, B., and P. T. Spiller, eds., *Regulation, Institutions and Commitment in Telecommunications: A Comparative Analysis of Five Country Studies,* Washington, DC: World Bank.

Joskow, P. L. (1974), "Inflation and Environmental Concern: Structural Change in the Process of Public Utility Price Regulation," *Journal of Law and Economics,* 291–328.

Joskow, P. L., and McAvoy (1975), "Regulation and Franchise Conditions of the Electric Power Companies in the 1970s, *American Economic Review,* 65: 295–311.

Laffont, J. J., and J. Tirole (1993), *A Theory of Incentives in Procurement and Regulation,* Cambridge, MA: MIT Press.

Lyon, T. P. (1991), "Regulation with 20–20 Hindsight: 'Heads I Win, Tails Your Lose'?" *Rand Journal of Economics,* 22: 581–95.

Müller, J. (1993), "The Evolution of the German Power Sector," The POWER Conference on International Electricity Regulations, Toulouse, France, May, 1993. mimeo.

Shugart, M. S. and J. M. Carey (1992), *Presidents and Assemblies,* Cambridge University Press.

Spiller, P. T. (1993a), "Legislative Choice in Presidential Systems with Regulation of Laws," mimeo, University of Illinois.

Spiller, P. T. (1993b), "Institutions and Regulatory Commitment in Utilities' Privatization," in *Industrial and Corporate Change,* V2, 1993, pp. 387–450.

Spiller, P. T., and C. Sampson, "Institutions and Regulatory Commitment: The Case of Jamaica Telecommunication" (forthcoming in B. Levy and P. T. Spiller, eds.) *The Institutional Foundations of Regulatory Commitment: A Comparative Analysis of Telecommunication Regulations,* Cambridge, MA: Cambridge University Press.

Spiller, P. T., and M. Spitzer (1992), "Judicial Choice of Legal Doctrines," *Journal of Law, Economics and Organization,* 8(1): 8–46.

Spiller, P. T., and L. Viana (1992), "How Not to Do It: Electricity Regulation in Argentina, Brazil, Chile and Uruguay," University of California, Berkeley, mimeo.

Spiller, P. T., and I. Vogelsang (1993a), "Regulation, Institutions and Commitment: The British Telecommunications Case," forthcoming in Levy, B. and P. T. Spiller, eds., *Regulation, Institutions and Commitment in Telecommunications: A Comparative Analysis of Five Country Studies,* Washington, DC: World Bank.

Spiller, P. T., and I. Vogelsang (1993b), "Regulation Without Commitment: Price Regulation of UK Utilities (with Special Emphasis on Telecommunications)," University of Illinois, mimeo.

Spiller, P. T., and I. Vogelsang (1993c), "Notes on Public Utility regulation in the UK: 1850–1950," University of Illinois, mimeo.

Troesken, W. (1992), "The Chicago Gas Company," University of Pittsburgh, mimeo.

Veljanovski, C. (1992), "The Future of Industry Regulation in the UK: A Report of an Independent Inquiry," London: Lexecon.

Williamson, O. E. (1976), "Franchise Bidding for Natural Monopolies: In General and With Respect to CATV," *Bell Journal of Economics,* 7: 73–104.

Williamson, O. E. (1988), "The Logic of Economic Organization," *Journal of Law, Economics and Organization,* 4: 65–93.

3

The political economy of transformation: liberalization and property rights

WILLIAM H. RIKER AND DAVID L. WEIMER

INTRODUCTION

The dramatic political and economic changes underway in Eastern Europe and the former Soviet Union present social scientists with a sobering reality and an unprecedented opportunity. The reality is that our disciplines offer very little theory of relevance to predicting the onset, course, or pace of the changes. The opportunity is a "natural experiment" that permits social scientists to study comparatively an important type of institutional transformation: in an amazingly short period of time the communist parties in a number of countries with different institutional and cultural circumstances peacefully relinquished their dominant political positions to allow democratization and the attempt to create liberal political and economic institutions. While many social scientists have been quick to offer advice about how the transformations should proceed, our purpose here is to consider how social scientists can best learn from this natural experiment.

We make two intertwined arguments about studying the postcommunist institutional transformations, specifically, and major changes in economic institutions more generally. One argument concerns what we believe to be an appropriate substantive focus for study: the evolution of property rights and their credibility. The other argument concerns the weaknesses of the disciplines as they relate to the conduct of that study and the desirability of a political economy approach for overcoming them.

An important empirical regularity motivates our focus on property

The ideas developed in this essay benefited greatly from the Seminar on Property Rights held at the University of Rochester during the 1992–93 academic year. We benefited from the assistance of Fiona McGillivary-Smith and Svetlana Basovsky. We thank Jeffrey Banks, Stanley Engerman, Tamas Fellegi, Eric Hanushek, William Hogan, and Minxin Pei for helpful comments and advice.

rights: all our previous political experience suggests that democracy is incompatible with the centralized allocation of economic resources (Lindblom, 1977, chap. 12). A market economy with substantial private property appears to be a necessary, although not sufficient, condition for the persistence of a democratic political system. Of course, the post-communist transformations, with democratization proceeding more quickly than economic liberalization, could yet refute this inductive generalization if stable democracies with socialist economies eventually emerge. In any event, economic theory points to the importance of property rights at least to economic performance.

We wish to emphasize that property systems are complex social institutions. They specify relations among those exercising various rights and those who have duties to honor the rights, as well as the mechanisms that are available for inducing the compliance of duty bearers. At a very general level, a property rights system can be described in terms of its mix of private, common, state, and open access property (Bromley, 1991). But even within a particular category, such as private property, there can be great variation in terms of clarity of allocation, alienability, security from trespass, and credibility of persistence, all characteristics of potential economic and political relevance. As is the case with most institutions, even describing the system of property rights in a meaningful way is not an easy task. Even a narrower focus on property rights than the one we propose would provide us with a rich object of study.

With respect to the adequacy of the social science disciplines for understanding such large-scale institutional transformations, we make several points. First, the social sciences have been concerned much more with transactions than with the institutions that govern the transactions. Second, as illustrated by the advice offered to the post-communist countries concerning economic liberalization, disciplinary approaches to institutional design seem far from adequate. Third, though neoinstitutional economics and social choice theory offer some insight into the efficiency and stability of alternative institutions, they are largely silent about how institutions evolve, or can be induced to evolve, from one equilibrium to another. Fourth, though political scientists have been directly concerned about democratization in South America, southern Europe, and other regions, their empirical work seems not to have led to many useful generalizations. Fifth, the new emphasis on institutions in several areas of the social sciences offers promise, as yet largely unrealized, for better understanding the post-communist transformations. Sixth, because social scientists typically work as individual scholars, and because the cross-national study of institutions is both labor intensive and demands specialization, too little truly comparative work gets done. Finally, we suggest how at least some of these current limitations in the social sciences can be over-

81

come specifically to take advantage of the natural experiment in post-communist transformation and more generally to study better institutions comparatively.

TRANSACTIONS, INSTITUTIONS, AND ECONOMIC CONSTITUTIONS

Social science consists of generalizations about two kinds of objects: transactions and institutions. By transactions we mean such things as exchanges of goods in a market, decisions on expenditures in a legislature, parental divisions of child care tasks, or, in short, all kinds of choices made jointly by two or more people. By institutions, on the other hand, we mean more or less agreed upon and relatively stable rules that guide people in carrying out their transactions. They can be thought of as sets of widely shared expectations about how people will behave in particular social, economic, or political circumstances.

In generalizing about transactions, we take some particular governing institution, or set of related institutions, as given and then describe the outcomes that result from the governed transactions. For a particular kind of transaction under a particular institution, we can describe some specific equilibrium outcome or outcomes, such as the equilibrium price for a certain good in an auction market, or the equilibrium sum of public expenditures under majority rule, or the equilibrium division of parental tasks in a particular culture.

In generalizing about institutions, on the other hand, we seek to explain theoretically why it is that some form of institution leads to a characteristic type of outcome and why it appears in some societies and not others. For auction markets we seek to explain why equilibrium price is at the point that demand exhausts supply and why some goods are traded in markets and others are not; for legislatures we seek to explain why and when choices end up close to the preference of the median voter and why legislatures take different forms in different countries; and for parents we seek to explain how lineage affects the roles of fathers and uncles and mothers and aunts and how the norms governing these roles evolved.

Unfortunately, the study of transactions and the study of institutions do not mesh together perfectly. For the sake of accuracy and efficiency in the description of transactions, our academic tradition has divided the social sciences up into specialities about particular kinds of transactions. It has assigned to economics the subject of exchanges of goods and services, to political science the subject of choices about law and leadership and government, and to sociology and anthropology the subjects of family and other small-group interactions.

Institutions, however, are not so neatly divided up in this way. The institutions that guide economic transactions not only originate endogenously in the economy; they also result from actions in the political world. Thus, for example, monopoly pricing often originates in statutes, and it is often unclear whether the motivation for these statutes arises from economic or political considerations.

Indeed, those institutions that guide transactions in the *agora,* the *acropolis,* and the *oikos* can originate in every possible combination of those places. Thus, apparently purely economic regulations like tariffs actually originate in the *agora* and *acropolis,* the apparently political norms of ideology and justice actually originate in both the *acropolis* and the *oikos,* the apparently private familial rules about the division of income in the family surely root in institutions elaborated in both the *oikos* and the *agora,* and the institutions of marriage are governed by decisions made in all three venues.

Consequently, the traditional social scientific division of labor, which works so well to study transactions, does not work so well to study institutions. For this reason we need to have programs of study that fit the actual sources of institutions. It is all a matter of appropriately combining the rubrics of transactions the better to study the rationale and reasons for institutions.

To offer a concrete example that relates to the subject of this essay, consider the matter of equilibrium prices in a market. As Harold Demsetz (1982, pp. 6–9) has so neatly pointed out:

The neo-classical inquiry into decentralization retained the price system for study, setting aside considerations of underlying systems of law. . . . The legal system and the government were relegated to the distant background by . . . [assuming] that resources were "privately owned." . . . [Thus] the model adds much to our understanding of coordination through price, but nothing to our understanding of coordination through authority.

Nevertheless, the equilibrium outcome of transactions in a market is necessarily directed by both the institutions of trade and the institutions of ownership. Whether ownership is by the state or by some group that holds in common, or by private actors like firms and individuals, surely makes a difference in the level and stability of prices. So in order to understand the institutions that guide transactions, it is necessary to study their origins in the several realms.

We call the description (and prescription) of the set of institutions that guide some particular kind of transactions the "constitution" for the activity. A constitution is in fact a kind of second-order institution, one that brings together the several institutions that govern a particular kind of transaction. Thus, the Constitution of the United States assembles a number of institutions to guide the most general kind of political decisions including, of course, essentially economic institutions like rules for the management and issuance of the public debt. For the subject of this essay, there is a constitution of the economy, which contains economic institutions for the operation of the market and political institutions for determining the ownership of goods.

Possibly the most difficult feature of social science is the study of constitutions. The explanation of how a constitution works depends especially heavily on counterfactual sentences, because the configurations of institutions of which they consist vary in many dimensions so that it is hard to associate different outcomes with specific differences in institutional components. How, for example, would a constitution work if, in its mix of institutions, it contained, in place of one institution actually present, an alternative institution? Answers to difficult questions of this sort would permit us to interpret the efficiency and stability of constitutions, which should be one of the main subjects of political economy.

INADEQUACY OF A NARROWLY DISCIPLINARY APPROACH TO POST-COMMUNIST TRANSFORMATION

The post-communist countries face the task of simultaneously creating institutions to support both democracy and market economies. The privatization of industry and trade has emerged as an especially difficult and complicated task. Most of these countries have rejected Leninist authoritarianism in political life, but they have only begun to nibble at the system of large monopolist firms, wherein, for considerable part, the old communist *nomenklatura* continues to hold office and income and indeed to substitute market monopoly for central planning. So we see the odd result that politically the revolution is perhaps over (barring fresh victories in a communist thermidor), while economically it has barely begun. That is, the central direction has been destroyed, but institutions to support an effective market economy have not yet been put in place. In some countries this odd fact allows the *nomenklatura* to regroup, which is why political resurgence by former communists is entirely possible and may very well attenuate the economic revolution. One very important question, therefore, is: "Why has the economic revolution been so slow and hesitant and up to now has involved only small proportions of the economies undergoing transformation?"

We think that one important reason is that the viewpoint of political economy has been ignored in both Eastern Europe and the West. In many of the Eastern European countries the first steps toward economic reform have been suggested, indeed supervised, by Western advisors, drawn especially from the International Monetary Fund and the academic world. Unfortunately, they have not been as alert to the political side of political economy as to the economic side. (See Boycko, Shleifer, and Vishney, 1993, on this point.) Consequently, both the advisors and the government initially proposed reforms for a well-operating market for free trade. But when these reforms were undertaken, without solicitation of popular political support for the new economic system, the voters often became hostile to the reforms, which seemed to offer immediate suffering for only the prospect of future benefits.

Only in the Czech Republic (with few advisors from market economies) did the government undertake economic reform balanced with a search for political support. In that country, the government immediately announced a privatization plan designed to give citizens a sense of participation in the reforms at the same time it began the conventional market reforms. So the "political" and "economic" proceeded hand in hand. Elsewhere, with economic advice, the initial steps were almost entirely economic – speedy privatization with widespread popular participation simply was not emphasized.[1] Only much later did Poland and Russia follow the Czech Republic in attempting to create a broad political constituency through forms of "mass privatization."

This neglect is odd considering that privatization in the United Kingdom, the most successful recent privatization in the West, was carried out in a highly political way, so much so that some observers have thought that its main purpose was political, not economic, reform (Dobek, 1993). Whatever Prime Minister Margaret Thatcher's motives, observe that her privatization began with council houses. Many people, probably previously Labour voters, acquired government assets at a cut-rate price, and many of them became Conservative voters (Dunleavy and Husbands, 1985). Most of the other privatizations in her first term were small industrial enterprises for which the main beneficiary was probably her own government, which was relieved of the cost of subsidizing them. Only in her second term did she begin large privatizations where the obvious beneficiaries were people who acquired shares at a relatively low price and became thereby supporters of the Conservative economic policy. While these actions were usually justified in economic terms, it is hard to ignore the political motivation once it is pointed out. Prime Minister Thatcher successfully carried out a new and controversial "economic" policy because she selected the steps in such a way that each one added significant new political supporters.

Most advisors from market economies and Eastern European officials seemed not to appreciate the political function of privatization at the time they launched economic reforms, though many now appear to realize its importance. We think that their initial efforts would have been more effective if they had been aware of the desirability of political balance in economic reform before they began. Of course, Eastern European governments were under a severe time constraint. The destruction of the old political system required an immediate destruction also of the political elements (central planning) of the old economic system. Just as Czech leaders recognized the political imperatives of privatization, so should the leaders, and their economic advisors, in other countries. We think the latter increased the difficulty of the task they face by following a purely economic paradigm rather than a paradigm from political economy.

INSIGHTS FROM NEOCLASSICAL ECONOMICS

Neoclassical economics offers a powerful approach for predicting the nature of transactions within markets. Models begin with the basic axiom that individuals are rational in the sense that they seek to maximize achievement of goals. Other axioms specify the circumstances of choice. Hypotheses about behavior are then deduced from these axioms. The hypotheses, which usually pertain to markets for single goods and are thus thought of as partial equilibria, provide the basis for much of positive economics.

For purposes of discussion, we distinguish neoclassical economics from neoinstitutional economics in terms of transaction costs. Neoclassical economics generally assumes that transactions can be made costlessly in markets. In contrast, neoinstitutional economics allows for the possibility that transactions may involve costs in terms of monitoring, bargaining, and enforcement. Thus, whereas the focus of neoclassical economics is usually on transactions in the idealized market, the focus of neoinstitutional economics is typically on more complicated transactions like contracts.

Extension of the neoclassical approach to model stylized economies provides a basis for normative economics. Under certain assumptions about consumer preferences, production technology, goods, factors of production, information, and the existence of competitive markets, it can be shown that a general equilibrium in prices and quantities exists and that it is Pareto efficient. This result, known as the first fundamental welfare theorem, formalizes the notion of the "invisible hand."

An important assumption of the general equilibrium model is private property: individuals have ownership of all goods, factors, and firms. Ownership is clearly specified and includes rights of use, freedom from trespass, and alienation. Perfect private property and a complete set of perfectly competitive markets are the only institutions of the general equilibrium model. As neither courts nor the coercive powers of government appear explicitly in the model to support the institution of private property, we can only assume that all individuals somehow share a norm of compliance.

Two of the traditional market failures, open access resources and externalities, illustrate the consequences of imperfectly private property in the context of partial equilibrium analyses. In the case of open access resources, the absence of exclusive ownership results in trespass that leads to overconsumption and underinvestment in terms of Pareto efficiency. In the case of externalities, Pareto inefficiency results when economic actors are involuntary parties to transactions that affect their consumption or production through other than market prices. The neoclassical framework suggests one obvious approach for correcting these market failures: the establishment of private ownership. In either case, the private property solution requires that some way be found to allocate ownership to individuals and guarantee that the rights of ownership are respected by other potential users. With the exception of Coase's theorem, which applies only to situations involving neither transaction costs nor wealth effects, neoclassical economics does not address the design or operation of alternative forms of the institution of private property.

The limitations of the neoclassical framework for understanding change become apparent even when considering the response of existing institutions to exogenous shocks. Comparative statics analysis assumes that an economy can move costlessly from one equilibrium to another. But if some prices are not free to move, such as nominal wages under long-term contracts, the relative prices needed to support the new equilibrium cannot be instantaneously reached (Ball, 1987). The result can be substantial transitional costs, such as involuntary unemployment, that are not accounted for in the comparative statics.

The assessment of welfare changes in an economy moving from central planning to market allocation raises a number of conceptual and practical problems that deserve greater attention from political economists (Berg, 1993). Consider the difficulty of establishing a pretransition benchmark. How should one take account of the queuing and rent-dissipating activity induced by administered prices? Obviously, even if the quantities of goods were to remain exactly the same after marketization, one would certainly attribute a benefit to reductions in queuing. Similar considerations arise with respect to changes in income risk, product quality and selection, environmental amenity, asset values, and economic opportunity, all of which can be significant along the path of transition. In a structurally stable economy, changes in some aggregate measure of economic performance, such as gross domestic product, provide a reasonable indication of changes in welfare only because these factors tend to remain fairly stable in the short run. Changes in the same measure are likely to be much less satisfactory for indicating changes in welfare in an economy in transition.

These conceptual problems are likely to be complicated by the practical problems of establishing effective national income accounts during transitions. Consider, for example, the gross national product per household head in China, a country undergoing a relatively slow transition to a market economy. The official estimate is about $380 per head in 1992, yet valuing physical output at world prices or comparing selected output levels per head with other countries suggests a substantially higher figure (*Economist,* 1992).

Macroeconomic and growth theories, though not entirely within the neoclassical framework, are fundamentally dynamic. But they typically have only vaguely specified institutions that are represented as fiscal, monetary, or investment rules. The empirical work in macroeconomics tends to be somewhat richer institutionally, but still offers little insight about the consequences of alternative political and economic institutions, aside from the importance of credibility in monetary and fiscal policy. Economic historians pay great attention to the role of institutions in economic growth, but growth theorists tend not to consider institutions at all.

These limitations have not stopped economists from proposing sequences for the reform of socialist institutions (see, e.g., Fischer and Gelb, 1991). Even putting aside that such proposals are largely apolitical, we can also question whether they are firmly based in economic theory. (The theory of the second best warns us not to be too optimistic about any single reform – of course, total and immediate reform is simply impossible in a real economy.) In any event, without a more sophisticated appreciation for the role of institutions, such advice is likely to be overly simplistic.

INSIGHTS FROM NEOINSTITUTIONAL ECONOMICS

By explicitly taking account of the structure of property rights and transaction costs, the emerging framework of neoinstitutional economics is beginning to provide a more sophisticated view of institutions. We follow Thrainn Eggertsson (1990) in viewing neoinstitutional economics as an extension of neoclassical economics to more explicit modeling of constraints on transactions, limitations in information that open the possibility of costly transactions, and quality dimensions of goods, while preserving the concepts of rational action, fixed preferences, and equilibria. One consequence of neoinstitutional economics has been to raise questions about welfare economics. Several authors have noted that explicit comparison of institutions, which may have substantial wealth effects, brings into question the standard normative construct of separating distributional concerns from those about efficient organization (Bromley, 1990; Murrell, 1991). Nevertheless, neoinstitutional economics has at least drawn attention to theoretical issues of potential relevance to understanding institutional transformation.

Consider, for example, the question of the origin of property rights. Harold Demsetz (1967) proposed that property rights emerged to internalize externalities that became significant because of changes in relative prices or technologies. The work that followed Demsetz has gradually become more neoinstitutional by explicitly considering the costs of specifying, monitoring, and enforcing property rights (Furubotn and Pejovich, 1972; Umbeck, 1981; Wiggins and Libecap, 1985; Libecap, 1989).

Economists, and philosophers like Locke, generally see private property rights as originating from the rights claimants themselves. Political scientists and legal scholars more often see private property rights as originating from political authorities (Riker and Sened, 1991). We think that rights claimants can often create a weak form of private property. But, because the essence of property rights is the relationship between right holder and duty bearer, these rights are only as effective as the mechanisms – fear of retaliation or hope for reciprocity – that motivate duty bearers. Trade practices enforced by the hope of reciprocity probably do encourage something like property rights within small groups. But in larger groups, in general, we expect that the capacity and willingness of the state to enforce rights and duties is needed to make private property rights secure and therefore supportive of efficient use. Consider, for example, Hernado de Soto's (1989) account of the creation of informal housing in Peru. Groups organize to "invade" and maintain settlements on state-owned or even private land. Members of the group are often able to gain an "expective" right to the land. But they usually must expend considerable resources protecting their expective right. Uncertainty about whether the expective right will become a legal right limits the investments people are willing to make in buildings. It is only after the government recognizes the right, that investment and sales bring the land to its most highly valued use. A similar process operated in the latter half of the nineteenth-century United States with respect to public prairie lands that were transferred to settlers noncompetitively through the various preemption acts (Gates, 1973).

One can draw obvious parallels between these "invasions" and the spontaneous privatization of assets by the *nomenklatura* in the post-

89

communist countries. More generally, we are likely to see claimants establish expective property rights in many spheres. (For instance, on the emergence of commodity exchanges in Russia see Frye, 1995.) Observing the course of these expective rights allows us to test the validity of the hypotheses that expective rights generally evolve into actual rights and that this evolution has important consequences for the efficient use of resources.

In general, we expect that fully effective property rights require effective political institutions to prevent trespass and provide credibility of persistence, taking us beyond neoinstitutional economics to the study of constitutions.

INSIGHTS FROM SOCIAL CHOICE THEORY

Social choice theory is concerned with mechanisms of collective choice. Like neoclassical economics, it assumes rational actors and fixed preferences. Its focus is on the characteristics of social orderings. Kenneth Arrow's (1963) possibility theorem tells us that, with three or more alternatives and two or more individuals, no social choice rule satisfying some minimal conditions of fairness can guarantee a transitive social ordering of the alternatives. Of course, the social intransitivity opens the possibility of disequilibrium. Indeed, with two- or higher-dimensional space and majority rule voting, in all but a trivial case there exists no alternative that cannot be defeated by some other alternative (Plott, 1967; McKelvey, 1976). Thus, unless some institutional structure forces separate choices along individual policy dimensions or otherwise restricts the agenda, no equilibrium will exist (Shepsle, 1979).

Peter Ordeshook (1992) applies these social choice concepts to the design of constitutions. While he offers a large number of rules to constitutional engineers in Eastern Europe and the republics of the former Soviet Union (Ordeshook, 1993), we mention just two here. The first is motivated by Russell Hardin's (1982) suggestion that institutions be thought of as coordinating devices that are self-enforcing: constitutions should be simple and concise to serve as effective coordinating mechanisms. Second, more relevant to our concerns with property rights, "Constitutional specifications of rights should be viewed as an attempt to remove issues from the domain of politics so as to reduce the opportunities to create unstable social outcomes" (Ordeshook, 1993; p. 216). Thus, we would expect there to be greater political stability when property rights are settled constitutionally. Removing the rights from the political domain also would make them more stable and therefore more effective (Comisso, 1991; Riker and Weimer, 1993).

We embrace these and most of Ordeshook's other rules as desirable characteristics of constitutions. But we believe that Ordeshook does not sufficiently appreciate that constitution writing is a political process, and we hypothesize that the political process that produces the constitution influences whether or not it will provide an effective framework for governing economic and political transactions. Property rights have important distributional consequences that cannot be reasonably separated from politics. Thus, Ordeshook's rules sketch a desirable equilibrium, but like neoclassical economics, they do not tell us how to reach it.

WEAKNESS OF THE POLITICAL SCIENCE LITERATURE ON TRANSITIONS

Finding neoclassical economics, neoinstitutional economics, and social choice theory insufficient for understanding post-communist transformations, we might naturally turn to disciplinary political science with its traditional concern for describing and understanding processes of collective choice. Indeed, an extensive literature specifically dealing with transitions between authoritarianism and democracy can be found in the field of comparative politics. It offers some insight into the immediate transitions from rule by communists parties. Unfortunately, limitations of scope, methodology, and theory render it almost useless for understanding post-communist transformations.

The literature has been largely concerned about political transformations in Latin America and southern Europe. Early work, motivated by democratization in many South American countries and Italy after World War Two, searched for structural conditions for democratization. In particular, economic development was seen as a prerequisite for democracy (Lipset, 1959). Presumably, as economies developed, democratization and stable democracy was likely to follow. Yet through the next two decades, despite economic development, Latin America actually saw transformations largely from the new democracies to authoritarian regimes. The structuralists then searched for explanations for the emergence and persistence of authoritarianism related to socioeconomic and international conditions (O'Donnell, 1973), finding substantially more explanations than cases (for a review, see Remmer, 1991). Despite, or perhaps because of, this over-determination, the structuralists failed to predict the widespread democratization that took place in the 1980s. Nevertheless, structuralist generalizations continue to be offered – the income threshold for stable democratic rule in Latin America is $250 per capita in 1957 dollars, and the socioeconomic threshold is reduction of illiteracy to below fifty percent (Seligson, 1988) – and questionable empirical approaches (often based on data only from countries that have undergone transitions) continue to be pursued (Diamond, Linz, and Lipset, 1989).

91

William H. Riker and David L. Weimer

The predictive failure of structuralism shifted the attention of many researchers to the process of regime transition (Dahl, 1971; Karl, 1990; Huntington, 1992). Though some of the process-oriented work considers the "consolidation" of new regimes (Baloyra, 1987), much of it has a narrow focus on the transitions themselves. Daniel Levine (1988) suggests that many of those who have studied transitions do so from the perspective of dependency theory, which holds a certain disdain for the usual outcomes of liberal democracy, and therefore they have chosen not to consider the link between the processes of transition and the democratic systems that result. In any event, the narrow scope of much of this work reduces the usefulness of its generalizations for understanding the transformations that will follow the accomplished transitions from communism.

But this work offers very little in the way of generalizations because it has been largely atheoretical. Consider, for example, the project led by Guillermo O'Donnell, Philippe C. Schmitter, and Laurence Whitehead to study transitions from authoritarian rule. It produced four volumes over seven years with contributions from over twenty authors. In the final volume, O'Donnell and Schmitter (1986; p. 3) report: "We did not have at the beginning, nor do we have at the end of this lengthy collective endeavor, a 'theory' to test or to apply to the case studies and thematic essays in these volumes." Aside from a somewhat reluctant normative statement that democracy per se constitutes a desirable goal, they emphasize as themes the "extraordinary uncertainty of the transition" and the inappropriateness of the "normal science methodology" for studying transformations. Aside from some characterizations of the stages of transitions such as the negotiation of pacts to set rules and guarantees for elites, they offer few generalizations of any sort.

Their disregard for "normal science methodology" includes a downplaying of the roles of popular groups and institutions in favor of a particularistic focus on elite actors. Subsequent work on transitional processes has moved to overcome some of these self-imposed limitations. For example, there are a number of studies that provide detailed consideration of aspects of popular participation in the southern European transitions (Bermeo, 1986; Foweraker, 1989). Josep Colomer (1991) formally models the strategic choices of group elites in the Spanish transition to go beyond particularistic accounts of what happened. Giuseppe Di Palma (1990) less formally considers strategies, but incorporates the notion of elites accomplishing the transition through the crafting of democratic rules, that is, through the conscious choice of political institutions.

Adam Przeworski (1991) provides the most useful extension of the transitional process approach. In addition to being specific about elite strategies, he also extends his analysis to consider the interaction between political and economic reforms, looking specifically at Eastern Europe as well as Latin America. His concern, therefore, is as much with consolidation as with transition. He considers the role of institutions, especially their distributional implications, and he links the behavior of elites to popular interests including the distribution of short- and long-term costs of economic reform. Przeworski, contrary to many observers, predicts that political developments in Eastern Europe will be similar to those in Latin America (1991, p. 190). He sees economic liberalization proceeding but falling far short of ambitious plans formulated by the new post-communist governments. Unfortunately, his conclusions follow importantly from arbitrary assumptions about the relative costs over time of the status quo, moderate economic reform, and radical economic reform.

Przeworski's rescue of the transitional process approach takes it beyond a particularistic elite focus to consider strategic actors linked to popular interests implicitly through institutions. It is an explicit emphasis on institutions, which draws on the work of political scientists and economists, that we think offers the best prospect for generalizing about post-communist transformations.

INSTITUTIONAL APPROACHES

As we previously noted, neoinstitutional economics and social choice theory are developing insights into the consequences of alternative institutional structures. Other economists, relaxing somewhat the core assumptions of neoclassical economics, consider institutions as governance structures for transactions (Williamson, 1985). The demands for explicit specification of the information and choices available to actors in the application of extensive-form noncooperative game theory, which is increasingly important in both economics and political science, naturally lead to consideration of institutional issues. Indeed, some scholars interpret institutions as equilibria in repeated games (Hardin, 1982; Axelrod, 1984; Taylor, 1987; Milgrom, North, and Weingast, 1990, and Calvert, this volume). A number of fundamental institutional concepts, such as the significance of credibility, the distinction between coordination and cooperation, and the importance of expectations about out-of-equilibrium behaviors are emerging from these approaches.

We think that consideration of the credibility of property rights illustrates the potential usefulness of the institutional approach (Riker and Weimer, 1993). The efficient use of economic resources requires not only that rights to property be currently effective (clearly allocated to individuals, alienable at low cost, and secure from trespass), but that those now exercising the rights believe that they will continue to enjoy their effectiveness in the future. In other words, they must believe that they have a credible commitment from government to preserve the rights. The less credible the commitment, the less willing will be individuals to forgo current consumption to accumulate capital and preserve the economic value of natural resources, activities that contribute to future private and social wealth. A fear that one will not be able to enjoy the potential future gains from risky efforts to invent, adapt, and adopt new technologies, both in production and organization, slows the innovation that drives long-term economic growth.

We thus hypothesize that the greater the credibility of a right to property, the greater will be the investment in improving the economic productivity of the property. Though one could imagine trying to measure credibility through surveys to see if they correlate with investment patterns, our strong prior belief in this hypothesis suggests that we might instead look at investment patterns as a proxy measure for credibility, not just of the property right but of the political institutions that support it.

The post-communist countries face severe problems in establishing the credibility of their systems of property rights for several reasons. First, their governments have yet to achieve levels of stability that make policy at least somewhat predictable. Because institutions for the new political systems are just being created, almost all issues are subjects of debate and bargaining. The central role of the state under socialism as owner, employer, and focus for opposition seems to provide a weak base for the emergence of political organizations that might play a stabilizing role by articulating interests and facilitating explicit and politically supported compromises over policy. Until constitutions take hold to give structure to political processes, policy is likely to be unstable and therefore not credible.

Second, although there seems to be a general belief among the populations and elites of these countries that market economies offer the prospect for a better life, there does not seem to be a broad and deep understanding of the role of private property in market economies. Based on a survey of attitudes in eleven countries (Russia, Poland, Slovenia, Bulgaria, Hungary, the Czech Republic, (East and West) Germany, Holland, Japan, the United Kingdom, and the United States), David Mason (1992) found that majorities of residents of the post-communist countries supported values and policies associated with the socialist system, even though large majorities also expressed disfavor toward socialism. A recent national survey conducted in the former Soviet Union illustrates the persistence of socialist values: only seven percent of respondents favored the abolition of existing restrictions on entrepreneurship and almost fifty percent held beliefs that the state should not permit the existence of millionaires (Bialer, 1990, p. 25). (A study by Schiller, Boycko, and Korobov, 1991,

however, found very similar attitudes toward the fairness of price allocation and income inequalities among New Yorkers and Muscovites!)
There may thus be significant disagreements about the social desirability
of any particular system of property rights, giving maneuvering room to
those who wish to preserve the use rights that they now enjoy. Consequently, even were there well-developed political institutions, we might
expect considerable uncertainty about the stability of the policies they
produce.

Third, both the historical and current experience of these countries
undermines credibility. Each country has some citizens who actually witnessed the expropriation of private property at the onset of socialism. In
view of the great difficulty of the task these countries face in establishing
effective property rights, it will not be surprising if any number of false
starts occur. Correcting these false starts risks undermining the credibility
of whatever system of property rights is created. Underdeveloped bodies
of tort and contract law, and the absence of a well-established judiciary to
enforce them, raise uncertainty about the security of property and encourage private means of protection that may slow the development of the
rule of law. Many observers have pointed with alarm to the growth in
Russia of "mafia" that engage in activities ranging from the provision of
security services to extortion.

While unstable political institutions pose difficulties for the establishment of effective and credible property rights, such rights, if once established, would enhance political stability in several ways.

First, by facilitating economic growth and the creation of wealth, effective and credible property rights facilitate political compromise. It becomes at least possible for the political system to adopt policies that
improve the positions of all groups in society, thus facilitating compromise within democratic institutions. Further, Aaron Wildavsky (1988)
argues that greater wealth makes societies more resilient to all sorts of
shocks that might otherwise strain political institutions. Of course, these
plausible assertions are really hypotheses that might be tested in cross-
national comparisons.

Second, as we have already noted in our discussion of social choice
theory, credible property rights contribute to stability by reducing the
number of dimensions of policy over which political systems must rou-
tinely make choices. If a right to property gains constitutional status, or
at least enjoys immunity against simple majorities, it is less likely to be
the subject of policy debate. In terms of spatial voting theory, we can
think of credible property rights as fixing policy choices at specific points
along certain dimensions, thus reducing the range over which cyclical
majorities are likely to occur.

Third, the wealth creation facilitated by effective property rights provides a resource for political participation that can help prevent the concentration of political power in the state. Wealth gives individuals voice. It also makes it easier for organizations to operate without direct support from the state so that these organizations are less susceptible to state control. While such independence might make it harder for the government to implement policies, it also makes it easier to resist the efforts of any one party to use government to eliminate competition from other parties.

Thus, effective and credible property rights facilitate the creation of wealth; stable political institutions facilitate the establishment of effective and credible property rights, which, in turn, help give stability to political institutions. The profound problem facing the post-communist countries is that they currently have neither stable political institutions nor effective and fully credible property rights.

In terms of the game-theoretic notion of institutions, the fundamental question is how can the strategic interaction of economic and political actors lead to an equilibrium involving beliefs by economic actors that they have credible property rights? We think that the answer may lie in features of the political system, such as the representation and mediation of competing interests, that make it costly for political actors to renege on commitments.

But if the institutional approach is going to help us understand the course of post-communist institutional transformations, it must do more than elucidate the threats to liberalization. A theory of institutional change is needed.

Douglass North (1990) offers the concept of path dependence to explain why different institutions with varying degrees of performance and distributional consequences can be found in different societies. He summarizes in broad terms:

Long-run economic change is the cumulative consequence of innumerable short-run decisions by political and economic entrepreneurs that both directly and indirectly (via external effects) shape performance. The choices made reflect the entrepreneurs' subjective modeling of the environment. Therefore, the degree to which outcomes are consistent with intentions will reflect the degree to which the entrepreneur's models are true models. . . . Even the most casual inspection of political and economic choices, both throughout history and today, makes clear the wide gap between intentions and outcomes. However, the increasing returns characteristic of the institutional matrix and the complementary subjective models of the players suggest that although the specific short-run paths are unforeseeable, the overall direction in the long run is both more predictable and more difficult to reverse. (p. 104)

The path dependency perspective helps explain how political actors may agree to constitutions that later come to disadvantage them. It also offers two insights of potential relevance to post-communist transformations. First, the simultaneous change in political and economic institutions suggests that politicians' subjective models may be quite poor – especially as most have neither electoral experience nor first-hand familiarity with the variety of institutions that undergird market economies. Ex post outcomes are therefore quite likely to deviate from ex ante expectations so that there may be regret about initial institutional choices.

Second, the initial choices constrain future action to some extent. For example, election rules agreed to in advance by interested parties behind the "veil of ignorance" may have some legitimacy even if they produce an unexpected electoral result. Those who prosper under the electoral rules gain an interest in keeping them in place or using their position to further tilt them to their advantage. Therefore, to have any hope of predicting the course of transformations, we must have knowledge of the existing institutional structures so that we can take account of the constraints that they impose. In the case of the post-communist transformations, we face the difficulty of assessing the relative influence of a mix of new and old institutions imposing rules and creating incentives that may be inconsistent.

What theoretical perspectives might help us further narrow the range of possible paths? Several possibilities are worth considering: interest group development, Heresthetics, public choice, and asymmetric bargaining.

Mancur Olson (1982) argues that problems of collective action make it difficult to organize interests for political activity. Yet once groups with similar interests discover mechanisms to overcome the collective action problem, they tend to persist. If these organizations have "encompassing interests," that is, if their gains are positively related to gains in aggregate social output, then economic growth is facilitated. If they have special interests that are negatively related to aggregate social output, then they may form distributional coalitions that slow economic growth. Arguing that the breakdown of socialist institutions at least temporarily weakens encompassing interests relative to special interests, he predicts a decline in economic growth in the post-communist countries before the reestablishment of individual rights sets the stage for a reemergence of encompassing interests and a resumption of economic growth (Olson, 1992). Olson's perspective suggests that close observation of interest group formation is necessary to predict the path of the post-communist transformation.

The Heresthetical perspective views politics as a continual struggle by those out of office to introduce a new political dimension that upsets the equilibrium enjoyed by those in office (Riker, 1982, 1986). From this perspective, regime transitions simply represent introductions of new dimensions that precipitate changes in political institutions rather than just changes in officeholders. It suggests that one way to predict the course of change in political institutions is to consider the size, interests, and resources available to groups that are out of office. Situations in which a large number of people or well-organized groups see themselves as net losers are fertile for the discovery of equilibrium-breaking dimensions. Obviously, the performance of economic institutions affects the distribution of interests and resources, and thus the stability of political institutions.

The public choice perspective emphasizes that political institutions consist of rational individuals. Officeholders, public employees, and clients (suppliers and benefit recipients) may behave in ways that lead to predictable institutional actions, such as legislative efforts to protect incumbency and bureaucratic efforts to expand budgets. Understanding the interests of individuals within political institutions may thus help us predict how those institutions will evolve. For example, consider Fred McChesney's (1990) analysis of the history of privatization of land on American Indian reservations. From 1887 to 1934, individual American Indians were able to claim an imperfect (restrictions on alienation and encumberment, unclear rights of inheritance) private ownership, and tribes were able to sell unallocated reservation land to nontribal members. McChesney shows that each major policy change during this period contributed to a larger budget for the Bureau of Indian Affairs: the initial policy required preparations of parcels for private ownership; the replacement of a fixed trustee period with competency testing for full ownership further expanded the bureau's workload; finally, the end of privatization, as allotments and expirations of trusteeships began to shrink reservations, ensured the bureau's control over substantial numbers of American Indians in the long term. We should not be surprised if the agencies created in the post-communist countries to oversee privatization follow a path similar to that of the Bureau of Indian Affairs. More generally, McChesney's analysis suggests that consideration of institutional interests provides some purchase for understanding institutional transformation.

Jack Knight (1992) generalizes the interest group and public choice theories by arguing that institutional change should be viewed as a process driven by resource asymmetries and the desire for distributional gains. Those with resource advantages, such as Olson's special interests or McChesney's institutional actors, have a stronger position in bargaining over changes in formal rules than those with fewer resources. Whereas North sees inefficiency as the result of high transaction costs blocking moves to Pareto efficient institutions, Knight sees inefficiency as a possible result of bargaining among parties with asymmetric resources. By considering the origins and distributional consequences of inefficient institutional changes, one might be able to distinguish between their explanations. Only if the change could be attributed to miscalculation would it be consistent with North's theory; if its distributional consequences were consistent with the resource advantages of the decision makers, then it would support Knight's theory. If it came about through the introduction of a new policy dimension and resulted in gains by those who were resource disadvantaged, then it would be more consistent with Riker's Heresthetics than Knight's theory.

If we are to determine the usefulness of these perspectives on institutional transformation, or perhaps discover even more useful ones, we must be able to make comparisons across institutions so that we can begin to distinguish between that which is systematic and that which is idiosyncratic.

THE COMPARATIVE STUDY OF POLITICAL ECONOMY

The comparative study of institutions poses a number of challenges. Because institutions are complex bundles of formal and informal rules, it is very difficult to describe them meaningfully in terms of quantitative, or even qualitative, dimensions. Even identifying what features are salient requires not only a theoretical perspective but also a detailed knowledge of how the institutions function. Researchers can rarely rely on information collected for other purposes, so the effort is usually very labor intensive. Especially with respect to the study of constitutional issues, meaningful characterization of institutions often requires very specialized knowledge such as familiarity with local languages, cultures, and histories. The demands of intensity and specialization make it difficult for individual scholars to study institutions comparatively.

While much research into institutions tends to focus on one or a small number of cases, both political scientists and economists have attempted to make some institutional comparisons across a larger number of countries. For example, G. Bingham Powell (1982) relates constitutional provisions to such political outcomes as participation, stability, and violence in 29 nations with democratic regimes for at least five years between 1958 and 1976. His more recent work considers the relationship between constitutional structure and attributes of the political system such as accountability and representation (Powell, 1989). Others address issues of political economy more directly by looking cross-nationally at industrial conflict (Robertson, 1990), political business cycles (Lewis-Beck, 1988; Alesina, Cohen, and Roubini, 1992; Remmer, 1993; see Alesina, 1988, for a review), authoritarian versus nonauthoritarian development strategies (Pourgerami, 1992), and budget deficits (Roubini and Sachs, 1989; Edin and Ohlsson, 1991). Many economists have included policy and political variables in cross-national studies of economic growth, but questions have been raised about the robustness of the findings reported in this literature – most results seem especially sensitive to changes in model specification (Levine and Renelt, 1992). Some work even has a primary focus on such institutions as central banks (Alesina, 1988; Blackburn and Christensen, 1989; Goodman, 1991) and budgetary rules (von Hagen, 1992).

The institutional variables in these cross-national studies are generally too simple to give us much confidence in assessments of relative performance. Intranational comparisons offer the possibility for greater specification of institutional characteristics. For example, Stephen Cornell and Joseph Kalt (1991) provide fairly detailed descriptions of institutional variation across American Indian tribes, and Jürgen von Hagen (1991) provides a hierarchy of budgetary constraints across U.S. states. By focusing on a very specific type of institution, it becomes feasible to rely on the accounts of other researchers so that comparisons can be made across a large number of cases. An exemplary illustration of this narrow focus approach is Elinor Ostrom's (1990) study of common property resources. Her cases are sufficiently detailed and numerous so that she can address issues of institutional change and stability, identifying design features that appear to make common property institutions long enduring. For example, she reports that initially modest but increasingly severe sanctions for violations of rules by a member of the institution appear more effective than fixed penalties, perhaps because they increase the willingness of other users to report and punish violations.

We think that the record of empirical work in comparative political economy, and our previous discussion of the political transitions literature, suggests several considerations for organizing to study postcommunist transformations.

First, the demands of specialization and intensity suggest that the project should be collaborative. Few scholars have sufficient country-specific knowledge to document institutional change in more than one or a few countries. A group of scholars is needed to provide a larger number of cases so that hypotheses can be investigated and generalizations made.

Second, even relying on each scholar for investigation of institutional transformation in only one country, the complexity of the changes underway call for a more specific common focus. We have argued throughout this essay that a focus on the evolution of property rights is substantively and theoretically appropriate.

Third, the scholars should approach their research with a common theoretical perspective of appropriate scope. The failure of the transitions research on Latin America and southern Europe to produce interesting generalizations shows the dangers of country specialists proceeding particularistically without a common theoretical perspective. Of course, in view of our limited knowledge, the theoretical perspective should not be so narrow as to rule out inductive generalizations that might help us predict constitutional transformations in other contexts.

Fourth, while political scientists with country specializations are generally best prepared to conduct detailed institutional studies, they tend not to have strong backgrounds in political economy. Consequently, recruiting an appropriate team of scholars may involve providing some training in political economy to team members.

Fifth, changes in constitutions are certainly jointly dependent with economic and political performance. Yet we must reduce the complexity of the phenomena we are studying in some way. The standard approach in the study of transactions of treating institutions as exogenous is obviously inappropriate. Instead, we propose to treat the property rights system as the major dependent variable in the first phases of study. Once somewhat stable systems emerge, then we have some hope of treating them as an independent variable to explain economic and political outcomes.

Sixth, there can be considerable variation in property rights systems even within the same country, allowing for intranational comparisons. For example, privatization in Russia appears to be greatly influenced by policies set at the levels of *oblast* (region), city, and even *raion* (city district). This variation offers the possibility of focusing on particular property forms in an approach similar to Ostrom's study of common property resources.

CONCLUSION

In this essay we have set out the case for the desirability of studying a particular subject in political economy, the evolution of property rights in post-communist countries, as well as an approach, a cooperative project involving area specialists coordinated by a common theoretical perspective, for carrying out the study. We have argued that the disciplinary perspectives of neither economics nor political science provides an adequate basis for studying changes in economic constitutions of the sort we are witnessing in the post-communist countries today. But we intend our argument to be broader, applying more generally to the study of change in important political and economic institutions. We think that the particular project we sketched could serve as the model for studying other major institutional transformations occurring simultaneously in several countries. In any event, we hope that we have conveyed the opportunities as well as the difficulties involved in the study of comparative political economy.

William H. Riker and David L. Weimer

APPENDIX:
STUDYING CONSTITUTIONAL CHANGE
AT THE WALLIS INSTITUTE

An example of the sort of research on comparative political economy that we have outlined is currently underway at the W. Allen Wallis Institute for Political Economy at the University of Rochester. With support from the Wallis Institute and a private foundation, we have recruited three post-doctoral and four pre-doctoral fellows from U.S. graduate programs in area studies, a Russian-trained lawyer, and a Rochester doctoral student in political science to participate in a comparative study of the evolution of property rights in post-communist countries and China. The fellows offer specializations in the Czech and Slovak Republics, Hungary, Poland, the former Soviet Union, the former East Germany, and China. We include East Germany as a case in which the transformation of political institutions was quickly settled; we include China as a case in which the Communist Party maintains its control of political institutions. We thus have the capacity for detailed institutional study in a number of countries.

To prepare the fellows for the project, we assembled in September 1992 for a seven-month seminar on the political economy of property rights. During the first phase of the seminar, we developed basic analytical skills (microeconomics, social choice theory, and game theory), shared historical background on the countries that are the subject of study, and began assembling information about the transformations of property rights in these countries. The second phase of the seminar involved the development of theoretical perspectives and a common research protocol. During the spring and summer of 1993, the fellows executed the research protocol in their countries of specialization. The seminar reconvened briefly at the Wallis Institute in early 1994 to begin preparing a truly comparative volume on the evolution of property rights and post-communist transformations.

The central focus for empirical research arising from the seminar concerns the question of how property rights become credible. We see the degree of credibility as resulting from strategic interaction among economic and political actors. For a right to be credible, economic actors must believe that the government will maintain and enforce it. We expect that rational economic agents will only believe the government's promises concerning a right to the extent that maintaining it is consistent with the interests of important political actors. Our specific hypotheses about credibility concern factors, such as the degree to which there is an effective "separation of powers," that make it more or less costly for political actors to take away or to fail to enforce rights.

The political economy of transformation

Aside from exploiting the post-communist natural experiment to learn about institutional transformation, we hope that the project demonstrates both the intellectual advantages of political economy for studying constitutional change and the practical advantages of fully coordinated joint research. We also hope that the Wallis Institute will provide a home for similar endeavors in the future.

NOTES

1. An interesting example can be found in two papers on Poland by Jeffrey Sachs, who is probably the most publicized of U.S. advisors in Eastern Europe: Lipton and Sachs (1990) and Sachs (1992). Sachs (1992) praised the economic liberalization that led to considerable development of small-scale private business. But his main theme was that Poland had so far failed to privatize the large industrial organizations, almost all of which continued to operate under pulling and tugging among ministries, *nomenklatura,* and workers' councils. And with this molasses-like rate of privatization, support for privatization had waned, especially when accompanied by the "continuing industrial crisis." Lipton and Sachs (1990), however, gave relatively little attention to privatization. They praised the government for stabilization and urged citizens to endure the recession because of promising long-run prospects. While the authors devoted considerable space to privatization, they contemplated that large enterprises would remain state property for some years. There was no apparent recognition that, politically, the government, if it wished to remain in office, needed to give the voters some sort of compensation for enduring recession.

REFERENCES

Alesina, Alberto. 1988. "Macroeconomics and Politics," in Stanley Fisher, ed., *NEBR Macroeconomics Annual* (Cambridge, MA: MIT Press), pp. 13–52.

Alesina, Alberto, Gerald D. Cohen, and Nouriel Roubini. 1992. "Macroeconomic Policy and Elections in OECD Democracies," *Economics and Politics,* 4 (1): 1–30.

Arrow, Kenneth. 1963. *Social Choice and Individual Values,* 2nd. ed. (New Haven, CT: Yale University Press).

Axelrod, Robert. 1984. *The Evolution of Cooperation* (New York: Basic).

Ball, Laurence. 1987. "Externalities from Contract Length," *American Economic Review,* 77 (4): 615–29.

Baloyra, Enrique A. (ed.). 1987. *Comparing New Democracies: Transition and Consolidation in Mediterranean Europe and the Southern Cone* (Boulder, CO: Westview).

Berg, Andrew. 1993. "Measurement and Mismeasurement of Economic Activity during Transition to the Market," in Mario I. Blejer, Guillermo A. Calvo, Fabrizio Coricelli, and Alan H. Gelg, eds., *Eastern Europe in Transition: From Recession to Growth?* (Washington, D.C.: World Bank), pp. 39–63.

Bermeo, Nancy G. 1986. *The Revolution within the Revolution: Workers' Control in Rural Portugal* (Princeton, NJ: Princeton University Press).

103

Bialer, Seweryn. 1990. "Is Socialism Dead?" *Bulletin, American Academy of Arts and Science,* 44 (2): 19–29.

Blackburn, Keith, and Michael Christensen. 1989. "Monetary Policy and Policy Credibility: Theories and Evidence," *Journal of Economic Literature,* 27 (1): 1–45.

Bromley, Daniel W. 1989. *Economic Interests and Institutions* (New York: Basil Blackwell).

Bromley, Daniel W. 1991. *Environment and the Economy: Property Rights and Public Policy* (Cambridge, MA: Basil Blackwell).

Boycko, Maxim, Andrei Shleifer, and Robert W. Vishney. 1993. "Voucher Privatization," Center for the Study of the Economy and the State, University of Chicago, Working Paper No. 85.

Colomer, Joseph M. 1991. "Transitions by Agreement: Modeling the Spanish Way," *American Political Science Review,* 85 (4): 1283–1302.

Comisso, Ellen. 1991. "Property Rights, Liberalism, and the Transition from 'Actually Existing' Socialism," *Eastern European Politics and Society,* 5 (1): 162–89.

Cornell, Stephen, and Joseph P. Kalt. 1991. "Where's the Glue? Institutional Bases of American Indian Economic Development," Project Report Series, Malcolm Wiener Center for Social Policy, Harvard University.

Dahl, Robert. 1971. *Polyarchy* (New Haven, CT: Yale University Press).

Demsetz, Harold. 1967. "Toward a Theory of Property Rights," *American Economic Review,* 57 (1): 347–59.

Demzetz, Harold. 1982. *Economic, Legal, and Political Dimensions of Competition* (Amsterdam: North Holland).

de Soto, Hernando. 1989. *The Other Path* (New York: Harper and Row).

Diamond, Larry, Juan L. Lintz, and Seymour Martin Lipsett, ed. 1989. *Democracy in Developing Countries, Volume 4: Latin America* (Boulder, CO: Lynne Reinner).

Di Palma, Giuseppe. 1990. *To Craft Democracies: An Essay on Democratic Transitions* (Berkeley, CA: University of California Press).

Dobek, Mariusz Mark. 1993. "Privatization as a Political Priority: The British Experience," *Political Studies,* 41 (1): 20–36.

Dunleavy, Patrick, and Christopher T. Husbands. 1985. *British Democracy at the Crossroads: Voting and Party Competition in the 1980s* (London: Allen and Unwin).

Economist, "When China Wakes," November 28, 1992, China Survey, pp. 1–18.

Edin, Per-Anders, and Henry Ohlsson. 1991. "Political Determinants of Budget Deficits: Coalition Effects versus Minority Effects," *European Economic Review,* 35 (8): 1597–1603.

Eggertsson, Thrainn. 1990. *Economic Behavior and Institutions* (Cambridge University Press).

Fischer, Stanley, and Alan Gelb. 1991. "The Process of Socialist Economic Transformation," *Economic Perspectives,* 5 (4): 91–105.

Foweraker, Joe. 1989. *Making Democracy in Spain: Grass Roots Struggle in the South* (Cambridge University Press).

Frye, Timothy. 1995. "Caveat Emptor: Institutions, Contracts, and Commodity Exchanges in Russia," in David L. Weimer, ed., *Institutional Design* (Boston, MA: Kluwer Academic), pp. 37–62.

Furubotn, Eirik, and Svetozar Pejovich. 1972. "Property Rights and Economic

Theory: A Survey of Recent Literature," *Journal of Economic Literature,* 10 (4): 1137–62.

Gates, Paul W. 1973. *Landlords and Tenants on the Prairie Frontier* (Ithaca, NY: Cornell University Press).

Goodman, John B. 1991. "The Politics of Central Bank Independence," *Comparative Politics,* 23 (3): 329–549.

Hardin, Russell. 1982. *Collective Action* (Baltimore, MD: Johns Hopkins University Press).

Huntington, Samuel P. 1992. "How Countries Democratize," *Political Science Quarterly,* 106 (4): 579–613.

Karl, Terry Lynn. 1990. "Dilemmas of Democratization in Latin America," *Comparative Politics,* 23 (1): 1–20.

Knight, Jack. 1992. *Institutions and Social Conflict* (Cambridge University Press).

Levine, Daniel H. 1988. "Paradigm Lost: Dependency to Democracy," *World Politics,* 40 (3): 377–94.

Levine, Ross, and David Renelt. 1992. "A Sensitivity Analysis of Cross-Country Growth Regressions," *American Economic Review,* 82 (4): 942–63.

Lewis-Beck, Michael S. 1988. *Economics and Elections: The Major Western Democracies* (Ann Arbor: University of Michigan Press).

Libecap, Gary D. 1989. *Contracting for Property Rights* (Cambridge University Press).

Lindblom, Charles E. 1977. *Politics and Markets* (New York: Basic).

Lipset, Seymour Martin. 1959. "Some Social Prerequisites of Democracy: Economic Development and Political Legitimacy," *American Political Science Review,* 53 (1): 69–105.

Lipton, David, and Jeffrey Sachs. 1990. "Poland's Economic Reform," *Foreign Affairs,* 69 (3): 47–66.

Mason, David S. 1992. "Attitudes Towards the Market and the State in Post-Communist Europe," paper presented at the annual meeting of the American Association for the Advancement of Slavic Studies, Phoenix, Arizona, November.

McChesney, Fred S. 1990. "Government as Definer of Property Rights: Indian Lands, Ethnic Externalities, and Bureaucratic Budgets," *Journal of Legal Studies,* 19 (2): 297–335.

McKelvey, Richard D. 1976. "Intransitivities in Multi-Dimensional Voting Models and Some Implications for Agenda Control," *Journal of Economic Theory,* 12 (3): 472–82.

Milgrom, Paul R., Douglass C. North, and Barry Weingast. 1990. "The Role of Institutions in the Revival of Trade: The Law Merchant, Private Judges, and the Champagne Fairs," *Economics and Politics,* 2 (1): 1–23.

Murrell, Peter. 1991. "Can Neoclassical Economics Underpin the Reform of Centrally Planned Economies," *Economic Perspectives,* 5 (1): 59–76.

North, Douglass C. 1990. *Institutions, Institutional Change and Economic Performance* (Cambridge University Press).

O'Donnell, Guillermo. 1973. *Modernization and Bureaucratic-Authoritarianism: Studies in South American Politics* (Berkeley: Institute for International Studies, University of California).

Olson, Mancur. 1982. *The Rise and Decline of Nations* (New Haven, CT: Yale University Press).

Olson, Mancur. 1992. "The Hidden Path to a Successful Economy," in Christopher Clague and Gordon C. Rausser, ed., *The Emergence of Market Economies in Eastern Europe* (Cambridge, MA: Basil Blackwell), pp. 55–75.

Ordeshook, Peter C. 1992. "Constitutional Stability," *Constitutional Political Economy,* 3 (2): 137–75.

Ordeshook, Peter C. 1993. "Some Rules of Constitutional Design," *Social Philosophy and Policy,* 10 (2): 198–232.

Ostrom, Elinor. 1990. *Governing the Commons: The Evolution of Institutions for Collective Action* (Cambridge University Press).

Plott, Charles. 1967. "A Notion of Equilibrium and Its Possibility under Majority Rule," *American Economic Review,* 57 (4): 787–806.

Pourgerami, Abbas. 1992. "Authoritarian versus Nonauthoritarian Approaches to Economic Development: Update and Additional Evidence," *Public Choice,* 74 (3): 365–77.

Powell, G. Bingham, Jr. 1982. *Contemporary Democracies: Participation, Stability, and Violence* (Cambridge, MA: Harvard University Press).

Powell, G. Bingham, Jr. 1989. "Constitutional Design and Citizen Electoral Control," *Journal of Theoretical Politics,* 1 (2): 107–30.

Przeworski, Adam. 1991. *Democracy and the Market* (Cambridge University Press).

Remmer, Karen L. 1991. "New Wine or Old Bottlenecks? The Study of Latin American Democracy," *Comparative Politics,* 23 (4): 479–95.

Remmer, Karen L. 1993. "The Political Economy of Elections: Latin America, 1980–1991," *American Political Science Review,* 87 (2): 393–407.

Riker, William H. 1982. *Liberalism Against Populism* (San Francisco, CA: Freeman).

Riker, William H. 1986. *The Art of Political Manipulation* (New Haven, CT: Yale University Press).

Riker, William H., and Itai Sened. 1991. "A Political Theory of the Origin of Property Rights: Airport Slots," *American Journal of Political Science,* 35(4): 951–69.

Riker, William H., and David L. Weimer. 1993. "The Economic and Political Liberalization of Socialism: The Fundamental Problem of Property Rights," *Social Philosophy and Policy,* 10 (2): 79–102.

Robertson, John D. 1990. "Transaction-Cost Economics and Cross-National Patterns of Industrial Conflict: A Comparative Institutional Analysis," *American Journal of Political Science,* 34 (1): 153–89.

Roubini, Nouriel, and Jeffrey D. Sachs. 1989. "Political and Economic Determinants of Budget Deficits in the Industrialized Democracies," *European Economic Review,* 33 (5): 903–38.

Sachs, Jeffrey. 1992. "Privatization in Russia: Some Lessons from Eastern Europe," *American Economic Review,* 82 (2): 43–8.

Seligson, Mitchell. 1988. "Democratization in Latin America: The Current Cycle," in James M. Malloy and Mitchell Seligson, eds., *Authoritarians and Democrats: Regime Transition in Latin America* (Pittsburgh, PA: University of Pittsburgh Press) pp. 3–12.

Shepsle, Kenneth A. 1979. "Institutional Arrangements and Equilibrium in Multidimensional Voting Models," *American Journal of Political Science,* 23 (1): 27–59.

Schiller, Robert J., Maxim Boycko, and Vladimir Korobov. 1991. "Popular Attitudes Toward Free Markets: The Soviet Union and the United States Compared," *American Economic Review,* 81 (3): 385–400.

Taylor, Michael. 1987. *The Possibility of Cooperation* (Cambridge University Press).

Umbeck, John R. 1981. *A Theory of Property Rights with Application to the California Gold Rush* (Ames: Iowa State University Press).

von Hagen, Jürgen. 1991. "A Note on the Empirical Effectiveness of Formal Fiscal Restraints," *Journal of Public Economics,* 44 (2): 199–210.

von Hagen, Jürgen. 1992. "Budgetary Procedures and Fiscal Performance in the European Communities," Indiana Center for Global Business, Indiana University, Discussion Paper no. 91.

Wiggins, Steven N., and Gary D. Libecap. 1985. "Oil Field Unitization: Contractual Failure in the Presence of Imperfect Information," *American Economic Review,* 75 (3): 368–85.

Wildavsky, Aaron. 1988. *Searching for Safety* (New Brunswick, NJ: Transaction Publishers).

Williamson, Oliver E. 1985. *The Economic Institutions of Capitalism* (New York: Free Press).

4

Politics and trade policy

RAYMOND RIEZMAN AND JOHN D. WILSON

The view that politics plays an important part in determining trade policy is widely accepted among international trade economists. Evidence of this can be seen in the recent surge of research activity focusing on a variety of questions concerning how the political decision-making process affects the determination of trade policy (e.g., Hillman 1989, Magee, Brock, and Young 1989, Grossman and Helpman 1992, 1994). This essay attempts to assess the problems and prospects for this literature. We begin by discussing the origins of this literature from an economist's point of view. In this discussion, we try to indicate why economists have become interested in considering the effects of politics on trade policy and what they hope to learn from this effort. We then discuss how the literature has progressed in explaining the existence of protection and what important trade policy facts need to be explained in future research. Surveys of much of this literature have been done by Nelson (1988) and Hillman (1989). Rather than provide another survey, we highlight the types of questions that have been considered and the types of models that have been used.

Unlike traditional economic theory, progress in this area will require improvements in the modeling of both economic and political activities. We discuss elements of an optimal model, describe several important trade policy issues to which such a model should be applied, and illustrate some of the key elements of the optimal model by sketching a specific illustrative model and using it to address some of the issues raised earlier.

We thank Andy Herr and conference participants for useful comments and suggestions on an earlier draft. Riezman acknowledges the financial support of the National Science Foundation under grant number SES 9023056. Wilson acknowledges the financial support of the National Science Foundation under grant number SES 9209168.

THE ORIGINS OF THE POLITICAL ECONOMY
OF TARIFFS

Since Ricardo, international trade economists have believed that free trade is desirable from a cosmopolitan perspective and, in most cases, is optimal from an individual country's point of view. Given this theoretical heritage, these economists have had some difficulty with the reality of protection. Specifically, protection has been a pervasive and persistent phenomenon. Reconciling this state of affairs with the theory of international trade, which suggests that protection should be relatively rare, has preoccupied international trade economists for some time. One response to this dilemma has been to consider that perhaps the theory is lacking and perhaps there is some theoretical justification for tariffs. A number of strains in the literature have investigated this possibility.

One such strain stresses that economies of scale might provide a justification for protection. This argument was put forward by Frank Graham in 1923. Although he was not the originator of the idea, his paper sparked a great deal of response. The basic argument concerns two similar countries and two goods, one produced under conditions of "increasing returns to scale" and the other under "constant returns to scale." Suppose that, under free trade, the "home country" specializes in and exports the constant-returns good, and the "foreign country" specializes in and exports the increasing-returns good. In this case, the home country might benefit from permanent protection on imports of the increasing-returns good since it otherwise earns no rents. Ethier (1982) carefully works out a model that demonstrates this result. He shows that the home country might be better off at autarky than free trade, so that, even with retaliation taken into account, protection might still be in the home country's interest. While this might be an explanation of some protection, it does not go very far in explaining the bulk of it.

A second strain in the literature emphasizes that large countries could benefit from protection through improvements in the terms of trade (Baldwin 1948). Johnson (1954) and Kennan and Riezman (1988) show that this terms-of-trade motivation can still exist even if there is retaliation by trading partners. This presents a second possible explanation, but it does not explain why small countries charge tariffs and does not fit well with the fact that larger countries tend to have lower tariffs.

Brander and Spencer (1985) first formulated the "profit-shifting" explanation of protection. This theory argues that countries with oligopolies can benefit from protection, because profits will be shifted to the protecting country. These extra profits can compensate for any efficiency losses incurred by the protection. Later work by Eaton and Grossman

109

(1986) and Cooper and Riezman (1989) show that retaliation makes this type of policy less likely to work. Again, while this explanation of protection could have some validity, the amount of protection it could explain is small. In general, attempts to explain protection using economic theories each have merit but, taken together, do not explain the magnitude of observed protection.

Robert Baldwin (1992), in an essay entitled "Are Economists' Traditional Trade Policy Views Still Valid?" discusses the closely related issue of whether economists still believe that free trade is best. He concludes that "the new trade theorists are very much aware of the practical limitations of their arguments, and they believe that, as a rule of thumb, free trade is the best policy for countries to follow" (p. 826). According to Baldwin, and we believe his view is widely shared, economists still believe free trade is best, from both individual and worldwide perspectives. Explanations of the widespread existence and the long persistence of protection based on purely economic considerations do not seem convincing.

The inability of trade theorists to explain protection using conventional economic theories has led economists to turn to politically based theories. The basic premise of this approach is that protection, while inefficient, exists because it is the outcome of the political process. The main goal of this literature has been to explain the existence of protection as an equilibrium outcome in a model of tariff determination, where policy decisions are made through an explicit political process.

WHY IS THERE TRADE PROTECTION?

The literature on the political economy of protection actually has its origins in Adam Smith's *Wealth of Nations*. Smith first articulated the notion that tariffs exist because of pressure politics. In his chapter on trade restraints (1981, p. 471), Smith explains:

To expect, indeed that the freedom of trade should ever be entirely restored in Great Britain, is as absurd as to expect that an Oceana or Utopia should ever be established in it. Not only the prejudices of the publick, but what is much more unconquerable, the private interests of many individuals, irresistibly oppose it. . . . This monopoly has so much increased the number of particular tribes of them, that, like an overgrown standing army, they have become formidable to the government, and upon many occasions intimidate the legislature. The member of parliament who supports every proposal for strengthening this monopoly, is sure to acquire not only the reputation of understanding trade, but great popularity and influence with an order of men whose numbers and wealth render them of great importance.

The connection between politics and protection is further elaborated by Schattschneider (1935) in his influential book, *Politics, Pressures and the Tariff*. He explains that tariffs exist because the political system is biased in favor of the concentrated interests ("pressure groups") who benefit from protection, as opposed to the disbursed, disorganized interests who lose. He writes, "Although the benefits and costs of the protective tariff, viewed in their totality, are probably very nearly equal, and theoretically the interests supporting and opposed to the legislation are, therefore, likewise approximately equal, the pressures exerted on Congress are extremely unbalanced." (p. 285).

Many of the early formal attempts to introduce political considerations into standard trade models focus on competition for the scarce rents generated from quotas and on competition to obtain the revenues generated by exogenous tariffs. Notable examples include Krueger (1974), Bhagwati and Srinivasan (1980), and Bhagwati (1982). The last study develops the general concept of "directly unproductive, profit-seeking activities," labeled "DUP," which encompass revenue-seeking, rent-seeking, and tariff-seeking activities, as well as many other similar activities. A basic goal of much of this literature is to explain how the welfare losses from trade protection are influenced by the presence of DUP activities, rather than to explain the existence of the protection itself.

The "endogenous tariff literature" assumes that trade protection takes the form of tariffs and seeks to explain why positive tariffs exist. The basic idea is that tariffs are the outcome of pressure politics in the context of rational agent models. Early examples include Brock and Magee (1978), Feenstra and Bhagwati (1982), and Findlay and Wellisz (1982). We make no pretext of offering a comprehensive view of the literature. Rather, we identify a few essays that illustrate the wide range of modeling strategies in this area, with an eye toward discussion of where the literature is headed and where it ought to go.

The Findlay–Wellisz (1982) paper offers a crude but highly influential theory of tariff formation. One group owns factors specific to an import-competing industry and therefore lobbies for a tariff. The other group owns factors specific to an industry that exports a good and therefore lobbies against the tariff. A group's lobbying effort is fully described by expenditures on the labor devoted to "political activities." The way in which these activities influence political outcomes is not modeled. Rather a "black-box," or "reduced-form," approach is followed by specifying a "tariff formation function," which relates the tariff rate to the two levels of lobbying effort. A Nash game in which lobbying efforts produce a positive tariff is described. However, the paper gives no conditions guaranteeing a positive tariff, leaving open the possibility that a negative tariff (or equivalent export subsidy) may prevail if the exported-good lobby is sufficiently strong.

A subsequent paper by Wellisz and Wilson (1986) uses a similar framework but derives conditions under which a positive tariff does exist. They posit an "unbiased" political system, in which zero lobbying by both groups implies a zero tariff. They then show that a positive tariff exists if the import-competing industry is relatively small, as measured by the share of national income possessed by its specific-factor owners. The basic idea is that a small industry is able to pass more of the deadweight losses associated with tariffs onto other members of society. This ability of the small group to "free ride" on others gives it an advantage in the lobbying game with the larger group.

In both of these papers, as well as many others, electoral politics is entirely absent (although the constraints imposed by the electorate are presumably reflected in the form of the tariff formation function). At the other extreme is Mayer's (1984) important paper on tariff formation as the outcome of majority voting. Preferences for protection depend on factor ownership. For example, voters heavily endowed with specific capital will favor protection for the industry that uses that specific factor. The result implied by the model is that tariffs will be chosen in accordance with the preferences of the median voter. This is a theory of majoritarian politics, not pressure group politics. With no uncertainty and perfect information, there is no obvious role for pressure group politics.

It is our feeling that an adequate theory of trade protection will require a model that successfully marries electoral politics with pressure group politics. There do exist attempts to do just that, but each suffers from an unsatisfactorily large amount of "black-boxism." The recent attempt by Grossman and Helpman (1994) offers an intriguing contrast to the tariff-formation-function approach. They develop a model in which the lobby problem is viewed as a common agency problem. There are many principals ("lobby groups") trying to get the agent (the government) to take actions (set tariffs) in their interest. It is the lobby groups that confront politicians with a function relating contributions to tariffs or trade subsidies, not the other way around. This function may be viewed as an inverse tariff formation function, or "contribution function," in the sense that it gives the level of contributions provided as a function of the promised tariff or subsidy. Moreover, the form of the function is not exogenously specified. Rather, all lobby groups play a Nash game in contribution functions. This game explains not only the existence of protection, but also its pattern across different groups of industries. Unfortunately, the "black box" of tariff formation functions is stripped away at a cost of removing any explicit competition between the politicians themselves. The government is treated as a single agent, with well-defined preferences over contributions and the (utilitarian) social welfare of the country as a whole. Behind this specification is the idea that contributions increase the probability of reelection, whereas the trade distortions supplied in return reduce this probability by lowering the well-being of the populace. But how exactly this happens remains a "black box."

Another attempt at combining pressure group politics with electoral politics is pursued by Magee, Brock, and Young (1989, hereafter MBY), which brings together more than a decade's worth of their own work on tariff protection. A critical essay by Austen-Smith (1991) provides an excellent critique of this work, and we recommend it to any serious student of the political economy of trade policy. The basic model has two parties, which raise campaign funds by offering trade-distorting policies to two lobby groups, each representing the interests of one of the economy's two factors, labor and capital. (The economic model uses the two-factor, two-good, Heckseher–Ohlin setup.) Here the timing of the Grossman–Helpman model is reversed by supposing that the groups respond as "Stackelberg followers" to the tariff rate announced by the protectionist politician and the export subsidy rate announced by the proexport politician, rather than the politicians responding to contribution functions. Austen-Smith (1991) views this feature as a virtue of the model, explaining that "it is illegal for interest groups explicitly to buy specific policies, so they promote politicians whose positions they support or seek to influence political decisions through nonpecuniary action" (p. 76). The two parties play a Nash game in their trade-distorting instruments, where each attempts to maximize the probability of election, specified as a function of both contribution levels and trade instrument levels. As in Grossman–Helpman, the idea here is that politicians trade off the benefits of contributions against the costs of trade distortions in an attempt to win elections. But the probability-of-election functions should be viewed as a "black box" element of the model, since they are not based on the maximizing behavior of agents in a world with a well-specified information structure.

For us, one of the most significant limitations of the model is that the assumption of two lobbies, each representing one of the two factors in the model (labor and capital), renders the model useless as a vehicle for considering competition among the many diverse groups that represent special interests in modern economies. This limitation is revealed by asking what happens as more factors are added to the model, retaining the Stackelberg structure. The answer must be that the contributions for each lobby group representing a factor must fall to zero. The reason is that a group's only goal in making a contribution in this model is to raise the probability that its candidate wins office, thereby increasing the probability of obtaining that candidate's announced trade policy. When groups become small, their influence over election outcomes becomes negligible.

A virtue of the Grossman–Helpman model as a representation of special-interest politics is that the groups are assumed to treat election probabilities as fixed.

In our own recent research (Riezman and Wilson, 1993), we have attempted to combine pressure group politics with electoral politics in a way that is consistent with the view of pressure groups as representative of special interests. We investigate whether political reforms will result in more or less protection. The surprising answer is that political reform may lead to more, not less, protection. We discuss our model more completely in the section "Optimal Model."

EXPLAINING TRADE POLICY FACTS

As was discussed earlier, the political economy literature grew out of a desire to understand the existence of protection. Having helped explain why protection exists, politically based theories should also be able to help explain the history and patterns of protection. There are many well-known stylized facts concerning protection patterns. To get a feel for where researchers must start in developing a political economy approach to explaining protection, we discuss a few of the more prominent facts.

One stylized fact is that protection declines with income growth. As countries develop, they tend to lower barriers to trade. This means that when one looks across countries, the developing countries have more protection than the industrialized countries. Conybeare (1983) argues that infant industry arguments and government revenue arguments can be used to explain why protection declines with economic development. Using tariff data from 1971 for 35 countries, he estimates the average tariff level for manufactures in 1971 (TAR) using gross domestic product per capita (GDP/P) to represent the level of economic development as one of the independent variables. The following equation is obtained:

$$TAR = 52.915 + 1.078 \text{ MF/GDP} - .018 \text{ GDP/P} + .931 \text{ XINST}$$
$$(2.177) \quad (1.429) \qquad\qquad (-3.805) \qquad\qquad (1.065)$$

$$- 4.671 \text{ RGGDP}$$
$$(-2.009)$$

$$R^2 = .396 \quad F = 4.91[1]$$

The coefficient of GDP/P is significant and has the expected sign, indicating that tariff protection declines as a country develops. In the same paper, Conybeare calculates the average tariff levels for developing countries and developed countries in the sample (p. 461). He finds an average tariff level of 50.33 percent for the developing countries and an average of 11.02 percent for the developed countries.

Presumably, one reason for this relation is that the administrative and collections costs associated with less distortionary revenue sources decline as countries develop (see Riezman and Slemrod 1984, Aizenman 1987 and Gardner and Kimbrough 1992). As a result, greater development leads countries to rely less on tariffs, more on indirect taxes such as sales taxes, and finally more on the taxation of personal incomes. However, political factors come into play in the process of moving away from tariffs as a primary revenue-raising device. These tariffs create special interests. Groups who have come to rely on protection will presumably fight the removal of these tariffs. Hence, the political decision-making process will affect how these interests are played out and, therefore, the speed with which the reliance on tariffs is reduced. It is quite possible that tariffs are history dependent in this sense. In other words, the current tariff structure may be explained, in part, by previous tariff policies. Similarly, if tariffs originally existed to protect "infant industries," similar political effects might occur as this rationale disappeared.

There is a widespread belief that as tariff rates have come down due to the successful negotiation of GATT treaties, the use of nontariff barriers (NTBs), such as quotas and voluntary export restraints, has dramatically increased. As described in Table 4.1, Laird and Yeats show that this is indeed the case. The numbers in the first column for each category of commodities represent the frequency with which NTBs were applied in 1966. The numbers in the second column for each category of commodities represent the change in this frequency from 1966 to 1986. For example, according to the first column under the category of "All Foods," 56 percent of the imports of the countries in the sample were affected by NTBs in 1966. According to the second column under the same category, this percentage increased by 36 points over 20 years, leaving 92 percent of all foods imported subject to NTBs by the year 1986. As an indication of the dramatic growth in the use of NTBs, observe that 25 percent of all commodities of the developed countries were affected by NTBs in 1966, but by 1986 the proportion of imports subject to NTBs had grown to 48 percent. Thus, the share of developed countries' imports affected by NTBs almost doubled over the 20-year period.

It could be that the nontariff barriers are used to replace tariffs that are no longer available, perhaps due to their prohibition in international trade agreements. Alternatively, the nontariff protection policies may offer political advantages over tariffs. The "transparency argument" suggests that there are political advantages to using less-observable trade barriers. NTBs may fall into this category, if voters who are hurt by protection are less able to associate their losses with protection when it takes the form of

Table 4.1. *Changes in developed countries' NTB "affected" trade indices for major product groups*
(1966 index in percent, 1966–86 change in percentage points)

Country	All foods[a]		Agr. raw materials[b]		Fuels[c]		Ores & metals[d]		Manufactures[e]		All commodities[f]	
	1966 index	1966–86 change	1966 index	1966–86 change	1966 index	1966–86 change	1966 index	1966–86 change	1966 index	1966–86 change	1966 index	1966–86 change
All countries	56[g]	36	4	37	27	0	1	28	19	39	25	23
EC	61[h]	39	4	24	11	26	0	40	10	46	21	33
Belgium[i]	68	31	1	20	96	−6	0	28	21	48	31	43
Denmark	35	65	2	5	9	0	0	37	1	45	5	32
France	56	43	4	33	22	78	0	58	6	55	16	66
Germany, FR	71	28	9	11	7	−7	0	47	12	47	24	17
Greece[j]	na	(82)	na	(10)	na	(0)	na	(24)	na	(47)	na	(26)
Ireland	na	(98)[j]	0	6	0	0	0	15	2	39	2[k]	37
Italy	72	27	0	53	0	0	1	35	9	57	27	3
Netherlands	55	43	0	21	0	93	0	71	8	50	31	48
United Kingdom	42	54	0	0	0	0	0	16	9	35	16	22

Finland	na	(70)[j]	0	55	67	28	4	−1	8	20	15[k]	36
Japan	73	26	0	59	33	−5	2	29	48	2	31	12
Norway	43	52	3	13	0	0	0	15	38	−16	31	−8
Switzerland	53	37	4	51	0	99	0	9	15	34	19	31
United States	32	42	14	31	92	−92	0	16	39	32	36	9

[a] SITCO + 1 + 22 + 4.
[b] SITC 2 less 22, 27, 28.
[c] SITC 3.
[d] SITC 27 + 28 + 68.
[e] SITC 5 to 8 less 68.
[f] SITCO to 8.
[g] Finland, Greece and Ireland are excluded from the totals since complete information on their agricultural trade barriers is not available for 1966.
[h] Ireland and Greece are excluded for the reason given in the preceding footnote.
[i] Luxembourg included.
[j] Since the 1966 data are not available, the figures in parentheses show the actual share of trade affected by nontariff measures in 1986.
[k] Barriers on food imports excluded.
Source: Laird and Teats (1990), cited in Conybeare (1983, p. 450).

nontariff barriers. In this case, the politicians responsible for providing the protection are not held responsible for the losses generated by the protection. However, they are able to enjoy the political benefits that the protection brings, such as campaign contributions. Further development of these ideas should prove helpful in understanding why different instruments are used to protect trade. This research should focus on trying to model the "transparency argument" as a problem of incomplete information.

Looking at the structure of tariffs across commodities, Deardorff and Stern (1983) find that this structure differs somewhat across countries. However, there seem to be some similarities. In most countries, wearing apparel, footwear, textiles, glass products, and chemicals have much higher protection rates than do leather products, nonferrous metals, or the printing and publishing industry. There has been extensive research trying to explain these facts by looking at the relevant economic variables (Ray 1974, 1981). However, little effort has been devoted to looking at political variables that might show that these cross-commodity differences could be the result of political forces. Is there something about these industries that makes it easier for industry groups to organize to seek protection? Is there less resistance among voters for providing protection to these industries? Explaining the differences in protection levels across commodity groups is an important goal for the political economy of protection.

Another empirical regularity of interest is that tariffs rise as the stage of production becomes more advanced. Consequently, raw materials have relatively low tariffs, while finished goods produced from those materials have relatively high tariffs. This can be seen in Tables 4.2 and 4.3. Table 4.2 shows that, in the United States, EC, Japan, and Canada, average tariff rates are quite low in raw materials industries, are higher in semi-manufactures, and highest in finished manufactures. Ray (1974) presents similar evidence for developing countries. Table 4.3 shows his comparison of tariffs on primary products with tariffs on manufactures in six different countries using both nominal and effective tariff rates. In all but one case, Malaya, he finds that tariffs are higher for manufacturing than for primary products. It remains to explain why producers of final goods are more successful in obtaining protection than more upstream producers.

Finally, we consider how protection varies over the business cycle. The commonly held view, supported by Takacs (1981), that pressure for protection grows during economic downturns and eases when economies boom. She argues that it is harder for the economy to absorb the increased imports in times of economic stress than in times of high domestic demand and economic growth. Therefore, pressures for protectionist

118

Table 4.2. *Tariffs by stages of processing.*

Industry/Country	United States	EC	Japan	Canada
All industrial products	4.4	4.7	2.8	7.9
Raw materials	0.2	0.2	0.5	0.5
Semi-manufactures	3.0	4.2	4.6	8.3
Finished manufactures	5.7	6.9	6.0	8.3

Source: Husted and Melvin (1993, p. 172).

trade policies will vary with the cyclical changes in the domestic economy. Using the number of escape clause petitions received in a given year
to measure the pressure for protectionism, Takacs runs several regressions
for the period 1949–79 with this measure as the dependent variable (see
Table 4.4). Each one of these regressions uses real GNP to represent the
level of economic activity and either the unemployment rate or the rate of
capacity utilization to capture cyclical forces. The coefficients of these
variables are significant and they have the expected signs. So, more escape
clause petitions are filed the lower the level of real GNP, the lower the rate
of capacity utilization, and the higher the rate of unemployment. Explaining why political pressures have this cyclical nature is a challenge for
future work.

THE OPTIMAL MODEL

To this point, we have seen that the political economy approach to explaining trade policy grew out of an inability of the omniscient planner
approach to explain the facts of protection adequately. An optimal political economy model would not only be able to explain these facts, but
would also be consistent with rational behavior of all agents in the economy. Given the political structure, this means that voters, interest groups,
and legislators are all behaving in a way that maximizes their respective
objective functions. This section discusses some of the essential components of such a model.

The economics of the optimal model are straightforward. Protection
affects both domestic and international conditions. Internationally, protection can have terms-of-trade effects, if countries are large enough in the
markets in which they trade. The presence of imperfect competition and
economies of scale increases the likelihood that this will be the case.
Trade policies also may be constrained by trade agreements such as
GATT, negotiated tariff reductions, or free-trade agreements such as

Table 4.3. *Tariffs on primary products and manufactures*

Country	Simple correlation between nominal and effective rates	Rank correlation between nominal and effective rates	Tariff average		Tariff standard deviation		Tariff coefficient of variation	
			Nominal	Effective	Nominal	Effective	Nominal	Effective
Brazil								
All commodities	0.88648	0.94125	60.81	110.25	55.97	137.03	0.92	1.24
Primary products	0.91179	0.91568	45.95	101.95	58.92	184.12	1.28	1.81
Manufactures	0.93246	0.92187	69.36	115.03	53.23	103.90	0.77	0.90
Chile								
All commodities	0.73928	0.90559	20.98	69.75	46.04	134.66	2.19	1.93
Primary products	0.89699	0.91356	6.16	33.00	33.12	86.39	5.38	2.62
Manufactures	0.69144	0.87704	29.52	90.91	50.56	153.09	1.71	1.68
Mexico								
All commodities	0.92190	0.89897	12.12	23.04	18.34	37.76	1.51	1.64
Primary products	0.95505	0.84084	5.32	10.79	23.36	44.20	4.39	4.10
Manufactures	0.87844	0.85571	16.03	30.09	13.62	32.14	0.85	1.07

Malaya

All commodities	0.63480	0.86879	7.08	10.36	17.79	32.46	2.31	3.07
Primary products	0.58748[a]	0.78111	9.89	8.95	27.33	48.34	2.76	5.40
Manufactures	0.91016	0.93658	5.45	11.48	8.77	19.05	1.61	1.66

Phillippines

All commodities	0.86061	0.88620	11.81	28.42	20.87	45.03	1.77	1.58
Primary products	0.81214	0.88928	5.68	20.32	17.85	49.17	3.14	2.42
Manufactures	0.90301	0.83633	15.33	33.09	21.90	42.55	1.43	1.29

Norway

All commodities	0.79193	0.82358	6.08	10.21	11.61	21.40	1.91	2.12
Primary products	0.73705	0.52323[b]	5.84	5.31	16.52	28.27	2.83	5.32
Manufactures	0.94422	0.95137	6.21	12.88	7.83	16.10	1.26	1.25

Note: All of the simple and rank correlation coefficients are significant at the 1% level of significance except for the two with superscripts [a] and [b], which are significant at the 2% and 5% level, respectively. The sample sizes are 52, 19, and 33, respectively.

Source: Ray (1974, p. 372).

Table 4.4. *Protection and the business cycle*

Constant	GNP	Unemployment rate	Capacity utilization	Trade balance	Import penetration	Lagged success rate	1962 act dummy	1974 act dummy	R^2
10.49 (3.21)**	−0.01 (−4.24)**	1.42 (2.88)**		−0.17 (−2.28)*					0.441
43.85 (4.27)**	−0.02 (−4.21)**		−0.37 (−2.95)**		190.9 (3.28)**				0.556
6.37 (2.32)*	−0.009 (−3.73)**	1.32 (2.65)*				9.39 (2.20)*			0.434
29.72 (3.23)**	−0.002 (−1.03)		−0.24 (−2.17)*				−5.67 (−5.27)**		0.694
38.85 (4.19)**	−0.01 (−5.42)**		−0.27 (−2.30)*					8.53 (4.80)**	0.652

Note: The numbers in parentheses are t-statistics. Coefficients significantly different from zero at the .05 confidence level or better are indicated by a (*); at the .01 level or better with a (**), using a two-tailed test.
Source: Takacs (1981, p. 690).

NAFTA. Thus, international conditions can both motivate the use of trade policy for national gain and, at the same time, constrain trade policy through international agreements.

Domestically, the effects of trade policy can be best understood through the effects on goods prices. Protecting an industry increases the domestic price of its goods. This price increase causes changes in employment of labor and capital in that sector (and indirectly in other sectors), as well as changing the wage and rental rates in that sector (and perhaps economy-wide). Therefore, one can think of the domestic effects of trade policy as being primarily redistributive. This raises the question of why trade policy (as opposed to other policies) is used to redistribute domestic income. We come back to this question later.

One additional aspect of protection requiring attention is its revenue implications. For example, tariffs raise revenue while export subsidies use government revenue. For some countries, this source of revenue can be quite important, and this consideration must be taken into account in any analysis of subsidization. Revenue considerations are more likely to be important for less developed countries, because as noted earlier, the governments of these countries use trade taxes as a revenue source to a much larger extent than do wealthier countries.

Let us turn now to a discussion of how political agents behave in this type of economic environment, beginning with the modeling of voter behavior. There are two common approaches in the literature to dealing with voters. One is to suppress the role of voters, as in MBY. Alternatively, one can think of voters deciding on policies directly (Mayer 1984). Neither of these approaches is entirely satisfactory, however. We believe that a middle ground approach is best, in which the voter is modeled as choosing a representative, who will be part of a legislative body. There are different ways to model how voters make such decisions. They could vote retrospectively; that is, they vote based on what a legislator has done in the past. Alternatively, they could choose the legislator that proposes the policies that they most prefer. Both approaches have their strengths and weaknesses, which are extensively discussed in the voting literature. We think that the choice of approach should depend on the particular questions addressed.

Voters are typically not perfectly informed about the policies being proposed, the effects of those policies, or the positions of the relevant candidates. Becoming informed takes real resources, and voters presumably devote differing amounts of resources to becoming informed. Modeling this aspect of voter decision making is important for a couple of reasons. First, recall that we have already questioned why tariffs would be used to redistribute income instead of more direct instruments. One answer, given by MBY, is that tariffs are a less "transparent" policy than direct taxes and subsidies. Therefore, they generate less political opposition. By modeling exactly how voters are imperfectly informed, one can investigate the "transparency" argument. The second reason for modeling imperfectly informed voters is to explain why campaign expenditures are regarded as important. Specifically, these expenditures may be used to inform and persuade voters to support a particular candidate.

Modeling interest groups is more problematic. Interest groups are coalitions of voters who have common interests. An interest group raises money and uses it to try to influence policy in a favorable direction. It might do so by making campaign contributions essentially to buy legislators' votes. Another way is to try to persuade legislators that voting according to the preferences of the interest group is in the electoral interest of the legislator. This assumes that legislators do not know voters' preferences perfectly. By being successful at raising money, the interest group "signals" legislators that many people feel strongly about the issue in question. In this manner, interest groups can provide legislators with information about the voters' strength of preference over different issues. Thus, the relationship between legislators and interest groups has two very different aspects. On the one hand, interest groups provide useful information. On the other, they can act as conduits for payments designed to tilt legislation in their favor.

An important puzzle in the analysis of interest groups is how they get their members to contribute money voluntarily. Why don't individual members "free ride" by letting others contribute? Later, we use a simple model to investigate this question. A related issue is how interest groups form, and which interest groups form. The literature on the political economy of trade policy treats interest groups as exogenous. We feel that interest group formation is an important area for future research.

Modeling legislators is somewhat more straightforward. The main issue here is describing the legislator's objective function. One approach is to assume that a legislator cares only about reelection and, therefore, takes those actions that maximize the probability of reelection. Alternatively, one might assume that a legislator has preferences over policies (the legislator is also a voter) and pushes favored policies subject to the constraints imposed by the need to run for reelection. As with voters, the role of information is crucial here. Legislators want money to inform and persuade voters. They can afford to offer concessions to special interests in exchange for campaign contributions, if voters are imperfectly informed about their activities. As discussed earlier, these campaign contributions also provide legislators with information about voter preferences. Large contributions from an interest group representing a particular set of voters may provide a credible signal that these voters feel strongly about a particular issue.

Politics and trade policy

Modeling legislative organization is complicated. The simplest models of legislative organization assume that legislatures take actions based on majority rule. However, the determination of agendas is important. In addition, the institutional framework can have a large influence. For example, parliamentary systems work differently than U.S. type systems, where presidential vetoes play a role. Although the other aspects of the model have to be in place before one can seriously model legislative organization, it nevertheless remains of central importance.

SPECIFIC TRADE POLICY ISSUES

Abandoning the view of the government as omniscient social planner leads us to reconsider a number of issues involving the analysis of trade policies. In this section we discuss a few of the more interesting trade policy issues that we think are strongly affected by political forces.

Tariff bargaining and economic integration

There is now a substantial literature on cooperative and noncooperative models of tariff bargaining, including some work on trade agreements such as customs unions. In these models, governments maximize an exogenously specified social welfare function. Domestic income-redistribution issues are typically ignored.

In contrast, the recent political economy approach to trade agreements and tariff bargaining deals with a situation in which decisions regarding trade relations reflect the interest of groups within countries, rather than the country as a whole. This approach is quite promising. One noteworthy contribution is Grossman and Helpman's (1992) model of domestic politics and international bargaining. Here governments bargain internationally, trying to get the best deal for their citizens, and at the same time raise an appropriate amount of campaign contributions from special interests. The model is used to characterize the structure of protection under both international cooperation and trade war conditions. Domestic political concerns are found to influence international bargaining significantly.

Recent events suggest that this approach is sensible. Consider the dispute between the United States and Europe over agricultural subsidies, which has adversely affected negotiations on a major GATT treaty. In this instance, it seems that internal politics are of paramount importance. This dispute seems to have been largely fueled by the political power of agricultural interests in Europe. Thus, the key to resolving this dispute involves coming to terms with the political realities in Europe.

125

Similarly, the recently negotiated NAFTA agreement was met with strong opposition from several interest groups. There was very little discussion of the overall merits of the agreement. Possible efficiency gains or benefits to consumers received less attention than possible job losses and adverse effects on wages. This suggests that understanding tariff bargaining and trade agreements requires explicit recognition of the domestic political situations.

There are a number of other interesting issues remaining to be explored. In particular, recent events in the EEC, including the Maasterich Treaty, raise the issue of whether economic union can be attained without political union. This issue also was present in the NAFTA negotiations, albeit beneath the surface.

A political economy approach may also be useful in developing new approaches to existing problems. For example, the question of why most favored nation (MFN) treaties exist and who benefits from them remains largely unanswered. Perhaps the solution can be found by considering the problem from the point of view of interest groups within countries. Which interests within a country would benefit from MFN treaties? Considering customs unions from the interest group point of view should also prove useful.

Level playing fields, U.S.–Japan trade, research and development, and high-tech trade

The usual approach to thinking about whether the government should subsidize research and development (R & D) activities or encourage exports in high-tech industries is to view all governments as benevolent social planners. Given this perspective, one then asks how a government can pick the correct industries, which requires successfully confronting significant information and incentive problems. Foreign reactions to these policies are also an important consideration.

A more useful approach might be to view governments as political organizations. Here the relevant question to ask is, under what conditions will high-tech industries or R & D activities be favored in the political equilibrium? This approach takes the point of view that high-tech interests are like any other special interest. Whether they are able to secure favorable policies from the government depends in part on the benefits to society of such aid, but also on their political effectiveness as interest groups. This suggests a different way to think about U.S.–Japan trade relations (i.e., the level playing field issue) and related issues of fair trade and government subsidies for R & D. It could be that Japan subsidizes high-tech industries not because it is socially optimal, but because high-tech interests are able to exert more influence and obtain favorable government policies in the political equilibrium. An interesting question to then consider is, why do these interests not fare as well in the United States? Two possibilities suggest themselves. First, it could be that the political systems differ in such a way that they tend to produce systematically different outcomes. Second, there could be inherent differences in the interest groups themselves. Perhaps high-tech industries in Japan are more concentrated and hence able to be more effective interest groups than U.S. high-tech firms.

Comparative advantage and trade patterns

Most of the work on political economy in international trade (this essay included) has focused on the effects of politics on trade policy. Another promising research direction is to look at the effects of politics on more traditional trade theories. As an example, traditional theories have stressed explanations of trade patterns based on endowments. Applying the same logic, cross-country differences between political systems could be thought of as a source of comparative advantage and hence part of an explanation of trade patterns. For example, suppose that a country has political institutions that are relatively favorable to pressure group politics. If this country were well endowed with capital, but labor was highly organized and able to maintain high levels of protection on labor-intensive goods, then the country could conceivably be a net importer of capital-intensive goods.

Clarida and Findlay (1992) have managed to place government activities squarely in a model of comparative advantage by incorporating public goods into utility functions and public inputs into the production functions for private goods. For two countries that are identical in all respects except for the relative valuations of a public good, Clarida and Findlay identify the pattern of trade that results from this difference. In a related paper (1991), they discuss the possibility that these valuations of the public good result from political economy factors. For example, a high-valuation government may be controlled by public employees, who seek to expand the scope of the public-goods sector. In contrast, the low-valuation government may be controlled by a "power-seeking mercantilist bureaucracy," which places resources in public inputs that enhance productivity in the traded-goods sector. Thus, it is possible for politics to alter the pattern and terms of trade through the provision of productive government resources, rather than through trade restrictions alone.

Comparative politics

An interesting paper by Findlay (1990) addresses the issue of whether the new political economy approach to trade policy is applicable to econ-

127

omies with different political systems. He considers the problem of a government allocating labor to the public sector. Four types of non-democratic governments are identified: traditional monarchies, traditional dictatorships, right-wing authoritarian states, and left-wing authoritarian states. Findlay argues that the first two types of governments will tend to employ less than the optimal amount of labor in the public sector. The basic explanation is that these two governments are able to keep for themselves the surplus generated by public employment. They essentially behave like monopolists and restrict public employment to maximize their revenues. The result is underemployment in the public sector.

Authoritarian states, on the other hand, need to justify and maintain their existence by large public expenditures, since they do not have public acceptance. These expenditures may be in the form of social programs, entitlement programs, or military expenditures. This results in over-employment in the public sector, rather than underemployment. In these regimes, officials and other "friends" of the government tend to be paid through "perks," rather than graft. Democratic regimes would make decisions via the mechanisms discussed earlier in this essay, resulting in an equilibrium somewhere between the extremes of the nondemocratic regimes.

Findlay goes on to add more structure to the model and discuss particular applications. The interested reader can consult his paper for further details. For our purposes, the essential point is that political economy models can be suitably modified to analyze nondemocratic political entities. The views and preferences of the population must be taken into account by politicians in both democratic and nondemocratic regimes. How seriously these views are taken will differ among regimes, but in all cases they still play an important role in determining outcomes.

Factor mobility

The discussion so far has ignored issues related to factor mobility. In doing so, it follows the traditional concern of the international trade literature with goods trade. There is now a sizable trade-theoretic literature on factor mobility (particularly capital mobility), but it is in the local public economics literature that factor mobility (particularly labor mobility) takes center stage. According to the Tiebout hypothesis, the ability of individuals to "vote with their feet" by choosing their most-preferred communities will produce an equilibrium in which each community's local public expenditures are efficiently "tailored" to the preferences of its residents. Indeed, it is possible to construct models in which the assumption of perfect mobility constrains the policy choices of individual communities to such a large extent that there is no role for political conflicts (see, for example, Berglas 1976 and Stiglitz 1983). Introducing labor mobility costs into the model, however, limits the voting with one's feet option and thereby lessens the constraints on government behavior. In fact, this reasoning lies behind the sizable literature that seeks to test empirically Brennan and Buchanan's (1980) "Leviathan" model, which posits that government officials seek to maximize the excess of tax revenue over productive government spending. See Oates (1989) for a discussion of the mixed empirical results in this area.

With regard to the political economy of trade literature, the local public economics literature suggests the need to examine alternative assumptions about labor and factor mobility carefully. Some type of factor immobility assumption lies behind all of the models on lobbying and trade policy. Some papers, such as Findlay-Wellisz (1982), posit a specific-factors model in which industries lobby because doing so increases the returns to factors that cannot move to other industries. These models may be interpreted as applying mainly to the "short run." In MBY, labor and capital are intersectorally mobile, but their international immobility creates an incentive to lobby. This framework applies more to the long run, except that the assumption of no international mobility of capital is increasingly problematic as the world economy becomes more integrated. With greater capital mobility, the ability of restrictions on goods trade alone to help a nation's capitalists should diminish; these restrictions must be supplemented by restrictions on capital movements. Even international labor movements are becoming increasingly important in the short run. For example, Mexican migration into the United States severely limits the extent to which U.S. farm workers can obtain higher wages through export-promotion policies. Future research on the political economy of trade policy should recognize the increasingly important roles of labor and capital mobility in the world economy.

Why tariffs?

The literature reported in the section: "Why Is There Trade Protection?" assumes that governments employ only tariffs as a method of redistributing income across different groups of citizens. But traditional trade theory teaches us that production subsidies should be preferred to tariffs, at least for the case of sufficiently small countries, which is both the case considered by this literature and the case thought to reasonably approximate most countries and product markets. The basic idea is that, for every tariff rate, there is a production subsidy rate that raises an industry's product price by the same amount, but without the cost of a distorted consumption pattern. Mayer and Riezman (1987, 1989, 1990) go beyond this standard argument to consider preferences among voters over tariffs and production subsidies when additional considerations are present. These considerations include the value of the revenue generated by tariffs and significant differences in consumption preferences across voters. Even with a "neutral" distribution of tariff revenue that favors no particular group, the latter consideration by itself may make some voters prefer a tariff over a production subsidy as a means of obtaining what they view as a favorable change in the relative prices of consumption goods.

These papers follow Mayer's (1984) strategy of basing a theory of policy choice on electoral politics, where voter preferences play the central role. At the other extreme, where only pressure group politics appear explicitly, we have the paper by Rodrik (1986). The politics there are even simpler than the Findlay–Wellisz and Wilson type, in that only one import-competing industry lobbies for tariffs or production subsidies, with tariff and subsidy formation functions specifying the relation between policy instruments and lobbying effort. But the Rodrick (1986) paper does make a valuable point. Given the choice between industry-wide tariffs and firm-specific production subsidies, social welfare may be higher (i.e., deadweight loss lower) under the tariff equilibrium. The basic idea is that the industry must overcome the free-rider problem associated with lobbying for tariffs. One firm can benefit from the lobbying efforts of another firm without itself engaging in any such effort. As a result, total lobbying effort in the regime may be lower than in the subsidy regime, implying lower equilibrium tariff rates than subsidy rates. Thus, total deadweight loss may be lower under tariffs, even though a given tariff rate is more distortionary than the same rate for a production subsidy.

As a positive theory of instrument choice, Rodrik's study is incomplete for two reasons. First, it cannot address the issue of how likely deadweight loss is to be lower under the tariff regime, since the answer will depend on the forms of the tariff and subsidy formation functions, which are exogenous in the model. Second, the paper does not address the issue of whether politicians might actually prefer tariffs over production subsidies. In fact, the free-rider problem identified by Rodrik can easily be viewed as implying that politicians would have a preference for subsidies over tariffs. This problem should make tariffs a more costly means of obtaining campaign contributions, in that the tariff rate needed to obtain a given level of contributions exceeds the required subsidy rate, implying greater deadweight loss and therefore more losses in support from general voters.

On the other hand, the very fact that contributions are more costly under tariffs may represent an advantage to politicians as a group, if they tend to engage in "wasteful competition" by expending too much time and effort obtaining contributions. Wilson (1990) examines this possibility in a model in which two candidates offer to support tariff or subsidy policies in exchange for campaign contributions. The equilibrium contribution levels are found to be lower under tariffs, due to their added cost to politicians in terms of higher deadweight losses, even though Rodrik's free-rider problem is absent from the analysis. In fact, tariff rates are so much lower than subsidy rates would be under the subsidy regime that total deadweight loss is also lower under the tariff regime, despite the added consumption distortions. Since politicians are assumed to bear part of the burden from these deadweight losses (through increased efforts needed to gain support for the distortionary trade policies, or future losses in voter support), this means that the two candidates would be better off if they agreed to provide tariffs, rather than production subsidies, in return for contributions.

Missing from this literature are potentially important elements of incomplete information. As discussed earlier, the popular "transparency argument" supposes that the public can more easily be persuaded to accept a tariff than production subsidy because the harmful allocative effects of the latter are more transparent. This reasoning is the basis for MBY's theory of "optimal obfuscation," in which tariffs may be chosen over production subsidies, and quotas may be chosen over tariffs. (Hillman 1989 discusses other considerations involving quotas, including the relative ease of assigning quota rents to particular beneficiaries) Both Mayer and Riezman (1990) and Austen-Smith (1991) find fault with this reasoning, however, for it seems to rest on voters' irrationality with respect to how they process information.

On the other hand, by not recognizing the many forms of uncertainty and asymmetric information that confront politicians, voters, and interest groups, the existing literature may be missing central elements in the equilibrium choice of policy instruments. The critical role of uncertainty in the choice between quotas and tariffs or subsidies has by now been identified in trade models without politics (see Anderson 1988, Cooper and Riezman 1989, and Shivakumar 1993). The exploration of this role should remain high on the list of research priorities for the political economy of trade research.

ILLUSTRATIVE MODEL

In this section we develop a simple political economy model that we use to discuss some of the issues raised earlier. The basic setup of our model consists of an election game played between two candidates "1" and "2." Each candidate collects "political contributions" from a large number of competitive import-competing industries and provides trade protection in return. There are fixed numbers of two types of import-competing industries, those that contribute to candidate 1 ("type 1") and those that contribute to candidate 2 ("type 2"). We do not model the determination of the candidate with which an industry becomes aligned. This allows us to later analyze political reforms that restrict the number of contributors that are aligned with a specific candidate, and it also reflects the common practice of PACs to target their contributions toward one candidate, not both. For simplicity, we also assume that a candidate's contributors are identical in all respects (differences in a fixed-cost variable are added later).

Each import-competing industry uses mobile labor and an industry-specific factor (e.g., a type of capital) to produce its output. The wage is determined by the exogenously given productivity of labor in the economy's export sector. The return on capital in a type-i industry is then a function of the domestic product price: $R_i(w_i + t_i)$, where w_i is the world price facing a type-i industry and t_i is its tariff rate. Candidate i offers this tariff rate to all type-i industries that provide a contribution level c_i, which is also specified by the candidate. Competition among contributors drives profits to zero. Specifically, the expected increase in specific-factor income R_i equals the level of contributions c_i:

$$\pi_i \cdot \{R_i[w_i + t_i] - R_i[w_i]\} = c_i, \tag{1}$$

where the probability of a candidate's election, π_i, is treated as fixed by each of the many contributors.

Each candidate is assumed to maximize the probability of being elected. Following the framework of Baron (1991), this probability is determined by the voting behavior of "uninformed voters," who are influenced solely by political contributions, and "informed voters," who vote according to their assessments of the actual policies of the candidates. In symbols, candidate i's probability of election is expressed,

$$\pi_i = u_i + (1 - \kappa) v_i, \tag{2}$$

where u_i denotes the expected proportion of uninformed voters who vote for i, v_i is the expected proportion of informed voters voting for i, and κ is proportion of voters who are uninformed. As in Baron, the expected number of votes is assumed to be a good measure of the probability of winning. For the determination of u_i, we borrow the following specification from the work of both Baron (1989, 1991) and Hillman and Ursprung (1988):

$$u_i(C_i, C_j) = \frac{(e_i C_i)}{e_1 C_1 + e_2 C_2}, \tag{3}$$

where $C_i = c_i n_i$, parameters e_1 and e_2 reflect differences in the relative efficiencies of the two candidates' contributions, and subscripts identify the candidate $(i, j = 1, 2)$. The support level from informed voters is assumed to depend on the deadweight losses created by both candidates' tariffs:

$$v_i(B_i, B_j) = a_i + a_2[B_j - B_i], \tag{4}$$

for positive constants a_1 and a_2, and deadweight loss levels B_i and B_j associated with i and j's trade policies, respectively. This specification may be justified by assuming that each voter assigns some value s_i to candidate i's "platform" on nontrade issues, and supports candidate i when the difference in excess burdens, $B_i - B_j$ is no greater than the difference in $s_i - s_j$. Assuming the s_i and s_j values are uniformly distributed across voters, the proportion of voters supporting candidate i can be written in the form given by (4). Under the simplifying assumption of linear demand and supply curves for each product, each of these deadweight losses is given by the familiar "Harberger formula,"

$$B_i = n_i(0.5)[t_i]^2[X_i' - D_i'], \tag{5}$$

where the supply and demand derivatives, X_i' and D_i', are both included because a tariff creates both production and consumption distortions.

The two candidates play a Nash game, in which the payoff functions are the probabilities of election, and the strategy variables are c_1 and c_2. The tariff t_i, on which the deadweight loss depends, is then determined by zero-profit condition (1). Reaction curves in $(C_1, C_2) =$ space are represented by the thicker lines in Figure 4.1, and the equilibrium is located where they cross. A notable feature of the reaction curves is that their slopes differ in sign. It is possible to show that the reaction curve for the candidate receiving more support from the uninformed voters (candidate 2 here) slopes up, while the other candidate's curve slopes down.

A comparison of approaches

Comparing this last approach with the others outlined earlier, we see that one major advantage over the exogenous tariff formation function approach is that we may investigate how equilibrium contributions and tariffs are affected by changes in those institutional features that lie behind the relation between tariffs and contributions. For example, Brecher (1982), in his comment on the Findlay–Wellisz essay (1982), argues that greater "government resistance to lobbying" generally has an ambiguous effect on the equilibrium tariff rate. "Greater resistance" in our model occurs when more voters are informed (a decrease in κ), in which case

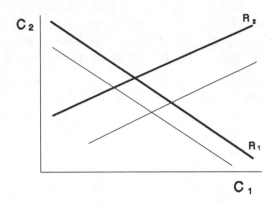

Figure 4.1. Reaction curves in contribution space.

candidates are influenced to a greater extent by the informed voters' opposition to trade policies. If the candidates are identical, a decrease in κ does lower total contributions and the level of protection. It does so by lowering the reaction curves in (C_1, C_2) space for each candidate. However, differences between candidates complicate the story, because the reaction curves then possess slopes with different signs where they cross. Even if both curves decline, as represented by the thinner lines in Figure 4.1, one candidate's total contributions may be higher in the new equilibrium, in which case that candidate's protection level may rise. Thus, the ambiguity identified by Brecher appears to persist.

Note that the distinction being raised here – protection offered by candidate 2 versus the protection offered by 1 – does not arise in Grossman and Helpman (1994), where government is represented by only one agent, not two. Furthermore, no parameter representing support among informed voters appears in MBY, where there is no explicit modeling of why a candidate's trade protection reduces the probability of election at given contribution levels.

Model improvements

We now discuss useful possibilities for future research that are suggested by the limitations of our model. In much of the literature surveyed earlier, there is no distinction made between campaign contributions and other lobbying activities. Our model explicitly considers campaign contributions by assuming that some voters are uninformed and can therefore be influenced by these expenditures. However, our assumption of "uninformed" and "informed" voters can be improved by including a process by which voters become informed. In fact, one would expect this to be one of the roles that campaign contributions might play. Furthermore, while the dichotomy of informed and uninformed voters may serve as a fruitful framework for initial attempts at formal theoretical models, in reality there are various degrees to which voters are imperfectly informed. Future research should address the issue of how both candidate platforms and lobbying efforts affect the preferences of imperfectly informed voters.

More generally, one theme of our essay, which seems to be shared by Austen-Smith, is that the manner in which voters and politicians rationally process incomplete and imperfect information is central to advances in our understanding of the political economy of trade policy. Whereas candidates may use the campaign contributions that they receive to alter voter beliefs, the lobbies providing these contributions may try to alter candidate beliefs. As discussed in our section on the optimal model, a useful task for future research is to model the use of contributions by lobbies as a "signal" to politicians of the strength of voter preferences.

Another important issue that our model does not address is: Why do politicians deliver the promised protection? One obvious answer is that doing so has desirable reputational effects. It would be useful to examine this possibility explicitly in a repeated-game framework. Another possibility is that it is the lobby groups that promise contributions in return for protection, rather than politicians promising protection. As we have already discussed, Grossman and Helpman (1994) take this alternative approach. Suffice it to say that future research should investigate more fully the types of commitments, implicit or explicit, that arise from politician–lobby interactions.

Also ignored in our model and all of the literature surveyed earlier is the issue of how lobbies account for the fact that a legislator has only one vote in an involved process. Investigating this issue will involve explicit models of the decision-making processes used by the types of legislatures under consideration.

Finally, modeling how lobbies form is also an important task. Recent work on lobbying by Austen-Smith and Wright (1990) should be useful in helping to develop a theory of endogenous pressure group formation that would generate new insights and, hopefully, better explanations of protection.

Who gets protection?

The question addressed in this section is: Which pressure groups are most successful in their lobbying activities? The two criteria determining success are (1) how much a group lobbies, and (2) how receptive the government is to these lobbying activities. Our model could be modified to study (2) by allowing different groups of industries to receive different levels of protection. The setup of the model would then suggest that those industries with high import-demand or export-supply elasticities would be less likely to receive protection, since a given tariff rate would create a relatively large deadweight loss, thereby lessening support among informed voters. This type of consideration explicitly falls out of the Grossman–Helpman (1994) model, where a modified Ramsey rule is derived. However, they note that all sectors that actively lobby in their model receive some form of import tariff or export subsidy in the political equilibrium. In our view, the first criteria – how much a group lobbies – is the key to understanding who gets protection. The Wellisz–Wilson (1986) analysis provides one answer – namely, that small groups tend to lobby more, because they are better able to free ride on other members of society by making them shoulder the deadweight losses from the actions of the small groups. However, probably the more important free-rider problem is the one discussed by Rodrik (1986). Specifically, each firm in an industry "underlobbies" for industry-wide protection, because much of the benefits of this lobbying are received by other members of the industry. The industries that receive protection can be expected to be those that most successfully solve the free-rider problem.

We believe, as does Austen-Smith (1991, p. 77), that this free-rider problem is a critical area for future research on the political economy of trade protection. The almost complete absence of research on this issue is evidenced by the lack of discussion it receives in Hillman's (1989) monograph. There is the presumption that small groups are better able to organize and lobby. However, this has not prevented the analysis of highly aggregative models, such as the two-factor model used by MBY, where the lobbying group representing each factor is able to elicit the optimal level of lobbying effort from its members. Clearly, future work should focus on how free-rider problems might be solved.

One direction of work toward this end might be to borrow from models of collusion in the industrial organization literature. Let us illustrate the potential value of doing so by considering the following simple model, using the well-known "trigger strategy" to maintain collusion. Consider the first type of industry described by Rodrik (1986), where there are a fixed number of firms, N, each of which uses both a specific factor and mobile labor to produce output. As we discussed earlier, the return to the fixed factor, say "capital," may then be written as a function of price of output, equal to the world price w plus tariff rate t:

$$R_i = R_i(w + t), \tag{6}$$

where this function is defined for an exogenously fixed wage rate. The tariff is a function of each firm's level of lobbying effort:

$$t = t(L_1, L_2, \ldots). \tag{7}$$

In the static Nash equilibrium, each firm treat's the lobbying of other firms as fixed and chooses its lobbying effort, L_i, to solve:

$$Max \ R_i \ (w, \ 1 + t \ (L_1, L_2, \ldots)) - L_i, \tag{8}$$

where the price of labor is set equal to one. Let Π^n denote the resulting profits for a given firm. As reported by Rodrik, Π^n falls short of the maximum possible profits, due to the free-rider problem.

The way in which the free-rider problem may be solved is to first suppose that the firms collude by increasing lobbying efforts beyond their static Nash levels, thereby producing individual profits equal to Π^c. Under the collusive policy, any individual firm can earn single period Nash profits $\Pi^{ch} > \Pi^c$ by unilaterally lowering its lobbying effort to the lower level that is optimal, given the existing lobbying efforts of all other firms. In other words, a single firm can "cheat" by free-riding on the lobbying efforts of other firms. We assume, however, that Π^{ch} can be earned for at most one period, after which the other firms "punish" the cheater by reverting to their static Nash lobbying levels, sending profits back down to $\Pi^n < \Pi^c$. There will be no incentive to cheat if the single-period gains from doing so, $\Pi^{ch} - \Pi^c$, are no greater than the loss in future discounted profits, $(\Pi^c - \Pi^n)/r$ for discount rate r. As long as r is not too high, this trigger strategy will support lobbying levels that maximize industry profits. In this case, the free-rider problem is fully solved.

This simple example illustrates that the free-rider problem need not be as severe as portrayed by Rodrik and others. Despite the well-known limitations of trigger strategies, the example suggests that thinking about lobbying as a repeated game might lead to insights into how interest groups solve free-rider problems. One potentially interesting direction for future research is to use a repeated-game framework to investigate whether industries with many firms are less likely to be able to solve the free-rider problem than industries with few firms.

Let us now introduce entry considerations into this simple model. The usual way to model entry is to suppose (ignoring integer problems) that firms enter the industry until profits equal zero. Letting C denote a cost of entry, this produces the following condition for the equilibrium number of firms in the case where the static Nash equilibrium game involving tariffs is played in each period:

$$\frac{\pi^n}{r} = C. \tag{9}$$

Let N^t denote the number of firms under which this condition is satisfied. One way for this condition to be obtained is for the entry of additional firms to lower the tariff rate by worsening free-rider problems. We could suppose, for instance, that the tariff formation function takes the form, $t = t(L_1, \ldots, L_n, 0, \ldots, 0)$, where the zeros represent the lobbying efforts of potential entrants. When one more firm enters, a zero is replaced by a positive L_i, but the L_i's for all firms decline because of the worsening free-rider problem. For the appropriately specified function of this type, there would then be a finite N^t under which profits are zero. A limitation of this specification is that in the absence of trade protection, the industry is not viable. Introducing imperfect competition (downward-sloping demands) would eliminate this problem, while producing other opportunities for collusion, but for the current illustrative purposes we stay with the perfect competition case.

While maintaining the assumption of free entry, return now to the case where the trigger strategies are played, thereby raising profits above Π^n to some Π^c. One might argue that new entry occurs, driving Π^c back down. However, entry may be stopped through a second type of trigger strategy. Specifically, once N^t firms have entered, suppose that any further entry will induce all firms to revert immediately to their static Nash strategies. Such a strategy has been analyzed in a different context by Davidson and Martin (1991), who show that it too is subgame perfect. By using this strategy, incumbent firms may deter entry to the level where (9) is satisfied, while earning positive profits $\Pi^c/r - C > \Pi^n/r - C = 0$.

Compare this equilibrium to the equilibrium in the case of firm-specific subsidies. In this case, there is no potential for collusion, in the sense that industry profits are maximized for a given number of firms when each plays its static Nash strategy. In other words, the static Nash strategies are dominant strategies in the sense that they are individually optimal for each firm regardless of the actions of other firms. However, without any recourse to trigger strategies, entry must now drive profits to zero: $\Pi^n/r = C$. One can argue, assuming "similar" tariff and subsidy formation functions, that the absence of free-rider problems drives Nash profits above those that would prevail under a tariff for the same number of incumbent firms, implying that the equilibrium number of firms, N^s, exceeds N^t. Thus, we get the paradoxical result that free-rider problems associated with lobbying for industry-wide tariffs may actually benefit the industry because it gives them an additional way to punish potential entrants; profits are positive in the tariff regime with trigger strategies and free entry, but they equal zero in the subsidy regime. Furthermore, free entry leads to more firms when subsidies are used than when tariffs are. If these are competitive firms with fixed costs, this increased number of firms may be a source of inefficiency.

Return now to the comparison of welfare (deadweight loss) between the tariff and subsidy regimes. The Rodrik argument for tariffs being superior to subsidies is considerably weakened, because the use of trigger strategies allows firms to collude and raise tariff rates close or equal to the equilibrium subsidy rates. However, the entry encouraged by the use of subsidies ($N^s > N^t$) is itself socially wasteful, since the socially optimal number of firms under our simplifying assumptions is zero.

While rich in results, one limitation of this approach is the well-known fact that a trigger strategy equilibria is only one of many subgame-perfect equilibrium. Others, with more severe "punishments" and therefore possibly higher levels of protection, may exist. Ultimately, the manner in which pressure groups solve free-rider problems among their members will depend to a large extent on the particular political institutions that exist in the economy under consideration. Important tasks for future research include an examination of other types of subgame-perfect equilibria in which free-rider problems are affected by the presence of important forms of incomplete information among the members of pressure groups.

Reducing protection by political reform

There is now a sizable literature on the welfare gains from reducing the levels of trade protection, either by one country alone or by many countries. Since political considerations appear to be responsible for the existence of protection, this literature will necessarily be incomplete until it is supplemented by an analysis of the political reforms that lead to reduced protection. Basically, we now have a good idea of how changes in various trade policy instruments affect welfare, but we now have to take one step back and look at changes in the institutions that determine these policy instruments. This difficult problem should be a central task for future research. We next provide an example of this type of analysis by extending our model so that it can be used to examine the effects of partial restrictions on pressure group politics. By "partial," we mean that there exist ways to partially circumvent constraints on the abilities of politicians to obtain contributions in return for trade protection. This seems to us to be a common feature of practical institutional reforms. We conclude this section by discussing the type of reforms known as "delegation."

Returning to the model, recall that the two candidates play a Nash game in the contribution level per industry c_i for an industry contributing to candidate i. Let us now endogenize the number of active contributors of each type, n_1 and n_2, by allowing them to also represent strategy variables for the two candidates. To do this, suppose that the potential contributors to candidate i ("type-i industries") possess different levels of a fixed cost, k_i, which is required to operate the political organization needed to collect and transfer contributions. The existence of this cost may be viewed as resulting from the free-rider problems associated with collecting campaign contributions. Given the contribution level c_i and tariff rate t_i, each type-i industry now chooses whether or not to contribute, taking into account this fixed cost. The "marginal contributor" is the one that earns zero profits from contributing. Specifically, the expected increase in specific-factor income R_i equals the level of contributions c_i, plus the fixed cost k_i:

$$\pi_i\{R_i[w_i + t_i] - R_i[w_i]\} = c_i + k_i. \tag{10}$$

By assuming that k_i varies across industries, we may write the marginal entrant's cost as an increasing function of the number of contributors, $k_i = k_i(n_i)$, in which case the candidate faces an upward-sloping supply curve for contributors; that is, a higher expected increase in specific-factor incomes net of contributions implies a greater number of contributors. Once candidate i chooses contribution level c_i and number of contributors n_i, he or she is forced to offer the tariff rate t_i that induces this number of industries to contribute, that is, the rate that satisfies (10).

With the model thus extended, two types of restrictions on political competition naturally arise: "contribution ceilings" on c_1 and/or c_2, and "entry restrictions" that constrain n_1 and/or n_2. Basically, the analysis in Riezman and Wilson (1993) shows that "small restrictions" of this type are generally desirable. For example, a reduction in c_i lowers deadweight loss B_i, because the politician responds by reducing total contributions C_i, even though he or she is free to take contributions from additional contributors (a rise in n_i). There do exist qualifications to this conclusion. A fall in c_i may lead to a rise in C_i, for example. But one can say that appropriately targeted reductions in both c_1 and c_2, or in n_1 and n_2, lower deadweight losses.

However, these gains may disappear for sufficiently large entry restrictions or contribution ceilings. The elasticity of contributors with respect to the net return on contributions plays a critical role here. If this elasticity is sufficiently high, then it is possible to identify reasonable cases where a sizable reduction in c_i leads to increases in both B_1 and B_2, even when C_1 and C_2 both fall. The basic problem here is that the candidate is being required to raise a given amount of contributions in an inefficient manner, with too few contributions per contributor and too many contributors. This induced inefficiency may defeat the purpose of contribution ceilings as a means of lowering deadweight losses, even when these ceilings do lower total contributions. The assumption of a large contributor elasticity means that C_1 and C_2 do not fall enough to offset this type of inefficiency. The basic idea is that the candidate i finds it easy to replace the contribution ceiling on c_i with a higher number of contributors.

We have also been able to identify cases where a large reduction in the number of contributors, n_i, actually leads to increases in both B_1 and B_2. It is the candidate's ability to respond to the fall in n_i with a higher contribution level c_i that makes this possible. And the possibility arises even when total contribution levels fall, since these contributions are now obtained using an inefficient mix of number of contributors and contributions per contributor. We see, then, that partial restrictions on "political competition" can be self-defeating in political equilibrium.

An important next step in this research will be to endogenize the "partialness" of restrictions on political competition. This will require the identification and successful modeling of the ways in which some participation by special interest groups improves the functioning of representative government. In the model we have been using, special interest groups serve no welfare-improving role. This may be a useful first approach to the problem, but it should not represent the final approach.

Another type of political reform is delegation. Starting in 1934, Congress delegated substantial powers to make trade policy to the executive branch. This has continued in the post-WWII era with fast-track authority. This commits Congress to vote treaties negotiated by the executive branch up or down as presented, with no opportunity to amend the agreement. This fast-track authority is widely believed to have been crucial in getting the U.S. Congress to agree to the Kennedy and Tokyo rounds of tariff cuts, and it is seen as being critical to approval of NAFTA.

These sets of facts present an awkward problem for many theories of the political economy of trade policy. Typically these theories posit that legislators provide protective legislation for special interest groups in exchange for campaign contributions or other forms of support. If this view is correct, then why does the U.S. Congress voluntarily give away the power over trade policy, which means that it is no longer able to provide protection for these special interest groups? There has been some work exploring this issue (Lohmann and O'Halloran 1992, Martin 1992, and Riezman and Wilson 1993).

It still remains to show why delegation is an equilibrium. One might want to look at delegation of other congressional powers and also compare the degree of delegation across countries. A similar idea would be to examine fast-track authority across different political regimes.

CONCLUSION

We began by considering the origins of the international political economy of trade. This literature grew out of an inability to explain the existence of tariffs and other impediments to international trade. We discussed the approaches that have been taken. We feel that a major shortcoming of this literature is that political decision making is modeled

141

using a reduced form or "black box" approach. While this approach is a reasonable starting point, we think that it is important to move on and consider more carefully the political decision-making process. In particular, we feel that imperfect information and uncertainty in political decision making play a key role in understanding how politics and economics interact. Also, if one believes that politics is central to the existence of protection, then trade reform requires political reform. Without understanding how political decisions of this type are made, reforming trade policy will be impossible.

NOTES

1. The variable MF/GDP is manufacturing's share of GDP, XINST is a measure of export instability, and RGGDP is the growth rate of GDP.

REFERENCES

Aizenman, J. 1987. "Inflation, Tariffs, and Tax Enforcement Costs," *Journal of International Economic Integration,* 2: 12–28.

Austen-Smith, D. (1991). "Rational Consumers and Irrational Voters: A Review Essay on Black Hole Tariffs and Endogenous Policy Theory by Magee, Brock and Young," *Economics and Politics,* 3 (1): 73–92.

Austen-Smith, D., and J. Wright. 1990. "Competitive Lobbying for Legislators' Votes," March, mimeo.

Baldwin, R. 1948. "Equilibrium in International Trade: A Diagrammatic Analysis," *Quarterly Journal of Economics,* 62: 748–62.

Baldwin, R. 1992. "Are Economists' Traditional Trade Policy Views Still Valid?" *Journal of Economic Literature,* 30 (2): 804–29.

Baron, D. 1989. "Service-Induced Campaign Contributions and the Electoral Equilibrium," *Quarterly Journal of Economics,* 104: 45–72.

Baron, D. 1991. "Spatial Electoral Competition and Campaign Contributions with Informed and Uninformed Voters," Stanford University, Graduate School of Business Research Paper No. 1174, November.

Berglas, E. 1976. "Distribution of Tastes and Skills and the Provision of Local Public Goods," *Journal of Public Economics,* 6: 409–23.

Bhagwati, J. N. 1982. "Directly Unproductive Profit-Seeking (DUP) Activities," *Journal of Political Economy,* 90: 988–1002.

Bhagwati, J. N., and T. N. Srinivasan. 1980. "Revenue Seeking; A Generalization of the Theory of Tariffs," *Journal of Political Economy,* 88: 1069–87.

Brander, J. A., and B. J. Spencer. 1985. "Export Subsidies and International Market Share Rivalry," *Journal of International Economics,* 18: 83–100.

Brecher, R. 1982. "Comment on 'Endogenous Tariffs, the Political Economy of Trade Restrictions, and Welfare,' by R. Findlay and S. Wellisz," in J. N. Bhagwati, ed., *Import Competition and Response,* University of Chicago Press, Chicago, pp. 234–8.

Brennan, G., and J. M. Buchanan. 1980. *The Power to Tax: Analytical Foundations of a Fiscal Constitution,* Cambridge University Press.

Brock, W., and S. Magee. 1978. "The Economics of Special Interest Politics: The Case of Tariffs," *American Economic Review,* 68: 246–50.

Clarida, R. H., and R. Findlay. 1992. "Government, Trade, and Comparative Advantage," *American Economic Review,* 82: 122–7.

Clarida, R. H., and R. Findlay. 1991. "Endogenous Comparative Advantage, Government, and the Pattern of Trade," National Bureau of Economic Research Working Paper No. 3813.

Conybeare, J. 1983. "Tariff Protection in Developed and Developing Countries: A Cross-Sectional and Longitudinal Analysis," *International Organization,* 37 (3): 441–67.

Cooper, R., and R. Riezman. 1989. "Uncertainty and the Choice of Trade Policy in Oligopolistic Industries," *Review of Economic Studies,* 56: 129–40.

Courant, P. N., and D. L. Rubinfeld. 1981. "On the Welfare Effects of Tax Limitation," *Journal of Public Economics,* 16: 289–316.

Davidson, C., and L. Martin. 1991. "Tax Incidence in a Simple General Equilibrium Model with Collusion and Entry, *Journal of Public Economics,* 45: 161–90.

Deardorff, A., and R. Stern. 1983. "The Economic Effects of Complete Elimination of Post–Tokyo Round Tariffs," in W. Cline, ed., *Trade Policy in the 1980s,* Cambridge, MA: MIT Press, pp. 673–710.

Eaton, J., and G. Grossman. 1986. "Optimal Trade and Industrial Policy Under Oligopoly," *Quarterly Journal of Economics,* 101: 383–406.

Ethier, W. 1982. "Decreasing Costs in International Trade and Frank Graham's Argument for Protection," *Econometrica,* 50 (5): 1243–68.

Feenstra, R., and J. N. Bhagwati. 1982. "Tariff Seeking and the Efficient Tariff," in J. N. Bhagwati, ed., *Import Competition and Response,* University of Chicago Press, Chicago, pp. 245–58.

Findlay, R. 1990. "The New Political Economy: Its Explanatory Power for LDCs," *Economics and Politics,* 2 (2): 193–221.

Findlay, R., and S. Wellisz. 1982. "Endogenous Tarriffs, the Political Economy of Trade Restrictions, and Welfare," in J. N. Bhagwati, ed., *Import Competition and Response,* University of Chicago Press, Chicago, pp. 223–34.

Gardner, G. W., and K. P. Kimbrough. 1992. "Tax Regimes, Tariff Revenues and Government Spending," *Economica,* 59: 75–92.

Graham, F. 1923. "Some Aspects of Protection Further Considered," *Quarterly Journal of Economics,* 37: 199–227.

Grossman, G., and E. Helpman. 1994. "Protection for Sale," *American Economic Review,* 84: 833–50.

Grossman, G., and E. Helpman. 1992. "Trade Wars and Trade Talks," October, Princeton University, mimeo.

Hillman, A. 1989. *The Political Economy of Protection,* Chur: Harwood.

Hillman, A., and H. Ursprung. 1988. "Domestic Politics, Foreign Interests, and International Trade Policy," *American Economic Review,* 78: 729–45.

Husted, S. and M. Melvin, 1993. *International Economics,* Second Edition. New York: Harper/Collins.

Johnson, H. 1954. "Optimum Tariffs and Retaliation," *Review of Economic Studies,* 21: 142–53.

Kennan, J., and R. Riezman. 1988. "Do Big Countries Win Tariff Wars?" *International Economic Review,* 29 (1): 81–5.

Krueger, A. 1974. "The Political Economy in the Rent Seeking Society," *American Economic Review,* 64: 291–303.

Laird, S. and A. Yeats. 1990. "Trends in Nontariff Barriers of Developed Countries, 1966–1986," *Weltwirtschaftliches Archiv* 126 (2): 299–325

Laird, S., and A. Yeats. 1990. *Quantatative Methods for Trade Barrier Analysis,* New York: New York University Press.

Lohmann, S. and S. O'Halloran. 1992. "Delegation and Accomodation in U.S. Trade Policy," Stanford University, mimeo.

Magee, S., W. Brock, and L. Young. 1989. *Black Hole Tariffs and Endogenous Policy Theory,* Cambridge University Press.

Martin, E. 1991. "Free Trade and Fast Track: Why Does Congress Delegate?" University of Iowa, mimeo, November.

Mayer, W. 1984. "Endogenous Tariff Formation," *American Economic Review,* 74: 970–985.

Mayer, W., and R. Riezman. 1987. "Endogenous Choice of Trade Policy Instruments," *Journal of International Economics,* 23 (3–4): 377–81.

Mayer, W., and R. Riezman. 1989. "Tariff Formation in a Multidimensional Voting Model," *Economics and Politics,* 1 (1): 61–79.

Mayer, W., and R. Reizman. 1990. "Voter Preferences for Trade Policy Instruments," *Economics and Politics,* 2 (3): 259–73.

Nelson, D. 1988. "Endogenous Tariff Theory: A Critical Survey," *American Journal of Political Science,* 32: 796–837.

Oates, W. E. 1989. "Searching for Leviathan: A Reply and Some Further Reflections," *American Economic Review,* 79: 578–85.

Ray, E. J. 1974. "The Optimum Commodity Tariff and Tariff Rates in Developed and Less Developed Countries," *Review of Economics and Statistics,* 56: 369–77.

Ray, E. J. 1981. "Tariff and Nontariff Barriers in the United States and Abroad," *Review of Economics and Statistics,* 63: 161–8.

Riezman, R., and J. Slemrod. 1987. "Tariffs and Collection Costs," *Weltwirtschaftliches Archiv,* 123, (3): 545–9.

Riezman, R., and J. Wilson. 1993. "Political Reform and Trade Policy," University of Iowa Working Paper No. 93–09, March.

Rodrik, D. 1986. "Tariffs, Subsidies, and Welfare with Endogenous Policy," *Journal of International Economics,* 21 (3–4): 285–300.

Schattschneider, E. E. 1935. *Politics, Pressures and the Tariff,* New York: Prentice-Hall.

Shivakumar, R. 1993. "Strategic Trade Policy: Choosing Between Export Subsidies and Export Quotas under Uncertainty," *Journal of International Economics.* 35, 1–2: 169–83.

Smith, A. 1981. *An Inquiry into the Nature and Causes of the Wealth of Nations,* Indianapolis: Liberty Classics.

Stiglitz, J. E. 1983. "Public Goods in Open Economies with Heterogeneous Individuals," in J-F. Thisse and H. G. Zoller, eds., *Locational Analysis of Public Facilities,* Amsterdam: North Holland, pp. 55–78.

Takacs, W. E. 1981. "Pressures for Protectionism: An Empirical Analysis," *Economic Inquiry* 19: 687–93.

Taussig, F. W. 1964. *The Tariff History of the United States,* New York: Capricorn.

Wellisz, S., and J. D. Wilson. 1986. "Lobbying and Tariff Formation: A Deadweight Loss Consideration," *Journal of International Economics,* 20: 367–75.

Wilson, J. D. 1990. "Are Efficiency Improvements in Government Transfer Policies Self-Defeating in Political Equilibrium?" *Economics and Politics,* 2: 241–58.

5

Elections, party structure, and the economy

ALBERTO ALESINA

INTRODUCTION

In 1987 I wrote an article entitled "Macroeconomics and politics" (Alesina 1988a), which highlighted new research in "political macroeconomics." At that time, this literature was still relatively small: It had developed from applications of game theory to problems of monetary policy. Since then, this field has literally exploded: The "new political economics" is one of the most active areas of research in economics. A major contribution to the development of this field comes from a closer interaction between economists and political scientists.

Recent research in political macroeconomics has covered a large number of topics: political business cycles, the politics of the government budget, the political economy of growth, the politics of inflation and stabilization policies, problems of external debt and capital flight in less developed countries, the effect of institutions (such as the degree of Central Bank independence) and different electoral systems on economic policy, the performance of coalition and minority governments relative to single-party governments, the relationship between domestic political competition and international policy coordination, and the politics of international agreements such as the European monetary system, just to name a few.

Even this incomplete list makes it quite clear that it is impossible to assess the progress and shortcomings of all of this body of research in one essay. Therefore, here I concentrate on two broad issues: the economic and political cycle; the effect of electoral systems and party structure on the economy, with particular reference to the issue of "divided government."

I thank William Keech, the conference organizers, and several other conference participants for their useful comments.

Alberto Alesina

The literature on political business cycles developed in two distinctive phases. In the mid-seventies, Nordhaus (1975) and Hibbs (1977) identified two different types of cycles. Nordhaus emphasized the "opportunistic" cycle of politicians interested only in their reappointment. Hibbs identified a "partisan" cycle in which different parties, when in office, follow systematically different policies: The Left fights unemployment even at the cost of increasing inflation, while the Right fights inflation even at the cost of higher unemployment. Both of these opportunistic and partisan models were based upon a traditional, prerational expectations approach.

The second phase took off in the mid-eighties as a branch of the game-theoretic approach to the positive theory of macroeconomic policy, pioneered by Hamada (1976), Kydland and Prescott (1977), and Barro and Gordon (1983). Cukierman and Meltzer (1986), Rogoff and Sibert (1988), Rogoff (1990), and Persson and Tabellini (1990) developed rational opportunistic models; Alesina (1987, 1988a, b) proposed a rational partisan model. This second generation of models departs from its predecessors in two important dimensions. First, the assumption of rational expectations makes real economic activity less directly and predictably influenced by economic policy in general, and monetary policy in particular. Second, rationality implies that the voters cannot be systematically fooled in equilibrium: A repeated, openly opportunistic behavior is punished by the electorate. In the next section I review the theory and the empirical evidence on these models of political cycles.

The third section addresses the other half of the story, namely, the effects of macroeconomic conditions on voting behavior. A discussion of several open issues in this area of research and a call for models in which the economy and the polity are jointly endogenous conclude this section. The fourth section illustrates recent work by Alesina, Londregan, and Rosenthal (1993) and Alesina and Rosenthal (1995), which builds a general equilibrium model of the political economy of the United States. This section leads to a discussion of the effects of "divided government" on the economy; a topic which is tackled directly in the fifth section. I shall take a "comparative" approach, by emphasizing the similarities between divided government in the United States and coalition governments in parliamentary democracies.

MODELS OF POLITICAL-ECONOMIC CYCLES[1]

Traditional opportunistic models

This is probably the most well-known model of political cycles and is due to Nordhaus (1975). The assumptions underlying Nordhaus's "political business cycle" (henceforth, PBC) can be characterized as follows:

146

Elections, party structure, and the economy

A.1. A stable Phillips curve, according to which growth (and unemployment) depend upon unexpected inflation, describes the economy.

A.2. Inflation expectations are adaptive; that is, current and expected inflation depends only upon past inflation.

A.1 and A.2 imply that an increase in inflation *always* leads to a reduction of unemployment (and an increase in growth); in fact, since expectations are adaptive, they catch up with a lag to actual inflation.

A.3. The policy maker controls the level of aggregate demand by means of monetary and fiscal instruments.

A.4. Politicians are "opportunistic": They only care about holding office, and they do not have "partisan" objectives.

A.5. Voters are "retrospective." They judge the incumbent's performance based upon economic performance during the incumbent's term of office, and heavily discount past observations. Also the voters cannot distinguish between good economic conditions caused by "luck" or by skilled policies.

Under these assumptions, Nordhaus derives the following testable implications: (i) Every government follows the same policy; (ii) toward the end of his term of office, the incumbent stimulates the economy, to take advantage of the "short-run," more favorable Phillips curve; (iii) the rate of inflation increases around election time as a result of the preelectoral economic expansion; after the election, inflation is reduced with contractionary policies.[2] Thus one should observe high growth and low unemployment before each election and a recession after each election.

Rational opportunistic models

Cukierman and Meltzer (1986), Rogoff and Sibert (1988), Rogoff (1990), and Persson and Tabellini (1990) have developed the PBC model with "rational behavior." In a nutshell, this line of research removes assumption A.2 and substitutes it with the following two:

A.2'. Economic agents have rational expectations concerning all the relevant economic variables.

A.2". Voters cannot perfectly assess the level of "competence" of the incumbent; that is, they can only imperfectly distinguish between the effects of "unlucky shocks" to the economy from the effect of the government's lack of competence in handling the economy.

Assumption A.5, which implies naive retrospective voting behavior, is substituted by the following:

147

A.5'. Each voter chooses the candidate who is expected to deliver the highest utility, given his or her rational expectations of postelectoral economic outcomes. In particular, the voters try, as best as they can, to disentangle the effects of exogenous shocks on the economy from the effects of government's competence in policy making.

The competence of the policy makers is defined as their ability in reducing waste in the budget process (Rogoff and Sibert 1988 and Rogoff 1990), in promoting growth without inflation (Persson and Tabellini 1990), or in insulating the economy from random shocks (Cukierman and Meltzer 1986).

The critical assumption of all these models is that the policy makers are more informed than the citizens about their own competence. By taking advantage of this informational asymmetry, and by trying to appear as competent as possible, politicians behave in ways leading to a Nordhaus-type PBC. However, given voters' rationality and awareness of politicians' incentives, the latter are limited in their "opportunistic" behavior. In fact, if politicians appear too openly as opportunistic, they are punished by the electorate. Thus, the political cycles in these "rational" models are more short lived, smaller in magnitude, and less regular than in Nordhaus's model.

For example, Rogoff and Sibert (1988) and Rogoff (1990) consider a budget problem and predict short-lived opportunistic cycles on monetary and fiscal variables, rather than four-year cycles and output growth as in Nordhaus' model. Specifically, these essays suggest that monetary and fiscal policies should be relatively loose in election years; for example, fiscal stabilization with tax increases are postponed until *after* the election, while spending program and transfer payments are implemented *before* the election. However, these short-run budget manipulations have no significant effect on GNP growth and unemployment.

Some of these models are based upon rather stringent informational assumptions. This is particularly true for the model by Persson and Tabellini (1990), which is the effort more directly devoted to a "resurrection" of the traditional PBC on growth and unemployment, since this model predicts that the rate of growth should be higher than average in election years. This result relies on the assumption that the voters first observe growth and then, after a significant delay, inflation (or monetary policy). The election has to take place after the voters have observed growth but before they have observed inflation. In fact, suppose that the voters observe a high rate of growth in the election year. Since they do not observe inflation (or monetary policy), they do not know whether the high growth is due to a burst of inflation, which will be observed after the election, or to a particularly competent government that manages to keep growth high without inflation.

These assumptions are not very plausible: It is not at all clear why GNP growth is more readily observable than the rate of inflation. The same criticism does not apply to the model by Rogoff (1990). In fact, in that model the asymmetry of information emerges because the voters observe more easily and promptly government current expenditures and transfers, relative to government investment. Rogoff's model is quite realistic; different government programs certainly have different degrees of visibility. While a "check in the mail" is easily observable, the effects of long-run projects on public investments are much less evident.

An interesting result of all of these essays based on the idea of competence is "rational retrospection." Rational voters have to be retrospective because by observing the preelectoral state of the economy they can gather information on the incumbent's competence, and, therefore, on future economic policies and outcomes. However, the constraint of rationality imposes conditions on "how' and "how much" a rational voter should be retrospective.

Alesina, Londregan, and Rosenthal (1993) note, however, that "rational retrospection" and "rational opportunistic cycles" do not necessarily go together: You can have the former and not the latter. In fact, if one removes the artificial assumption about when the voters observe growth and inflation in the Persson and Tabellini model, one obtains a model with retrospective voting but no opportunistic cycles. This is one of those rare cases in which, by removing an unrealistic assumption, one obtains a similar model, which, as we will see later, is also more consistent with the empirical evidence.

Suppose that competence is not directly observable and economic outcomes are influenced by both administrative skills and random shocks out of the politicians' control. If the voters cannot distinguish between competence and random shocks, they rationally acquire information on the former by observing the state of the economy. In technical terms, the voters, by observing the economy, gather a "noisy" signal of competence. Rational retrospection emerges from a so-called signal extraction problem: The voters attempt, as well as they can, to "extract" from the observation of, say, GNP growth, an indication of how competent the incumbent administration really is. Rational retrospection occurs even if the voters observe at the same time all the relevant economic outcomes, namely, even if they observe inflation and growth at the same time. No artificial asymmetric information between elected politicians and voters is necessary. Therefore, one can have rational retrospection without opportunistic cycles: This result is important, because it appears consistent with the empirical evidence discussed later.

Finally, Boylan, Ledyard, and McKelvey (1990) generate PBCs in income and private consumption in a growth model that is not based upon asymmetries of information. In their model the voters differ in their discount factors, and the growth path is chosen by majority rule. The results differ depending upon whether the candidates can make multiperiod commitments or not: PBCs are obtained only in the case of multiperiod commitments. This result on PBCs is, in my view, sort of a by-product in a rich and original essay that deals mainly with the feasibility of optimal growth paths with majority voting.

The traditional partisan model

A strong version of the partisan theory (Hibbs 1977, 1987), based upon a nonrational expectation mechanism, adopts assumptions A.1, A.2, and A.3. Assumptions A.4 and A.5 are substituted by the following:

A.4'. Politicians are "partisan," in the sense that different parties maximize different objective functions. Left-wing parties attribute a higher cost to unemployment relative to inflation than do right-wing parties.

A.5'''. Each voter is aware of the partisan differences and votes for the party that offers the policy closer to his or her most preferred outcome.

The assumption of partisanship is justified by the distributional consequences of unemployment. Hibbs (1987) shows that, in the United States, in periods of high unemployment, low growth, and low inflation, the relative share of income of the upper middle class increases and vice versa. Obviously, since both inflation and unemployment are undesirable economic outcomes, both political parties will proclaim that, if elected, they will fight both evils. The partisan model does not require that, say, the right-wing party actually *prefers* high unemployment to low unemployment. It simply requires that the Right is willing to bear higher costs in terms of unemployment in order to achieve a reduction of inflation.

Hibbs (1987) discusses at length, how, in the United States, the official electoral platforms of the two major parties reveal differences of emphasis on the costs of unemployment and inflation. Kiewiet (1983) shows that, in fact, the American voters are aware of party differences on this point and vote accordingly. Havrilesky (1987) develops a partisan model in which the distributional consequences of partisan monetary policies are explicitly taken into account.

In summary, this model implies that different parties choose different points on the Phillips curve: Output growth and inflation should be permanently higher and unemployment permanently lower with the left-wing than with the right-wing governments.

The rational partisan theory

Alesina (1987, 1988a,b) developed a model that became known as the "rational partisan theory," by adopting assumptions A.1, A.2′, A.3, A.4′ and A.5‴. It should also be noted that Chapell and Keech (1988) had independently developed an empirical model with some of the same features.

This model generates a political cycle if nominal wage contracts are signed at discrete intervals (which do not coincide with the political terms of office) and electoral outcomes are *ex ante* uncertain. The basic idea of the model is that, given the sluggishness in wage adjustments, changes in the inflation rate associated with changes in governments create temporary deviations of real economic activity from its natural level.

More specifically, the following testable implications can be derived from the model: (i) At the beginning of a right-wing (left-wing) government, output growth is below (above) its natural level, and unemployment is above (below) its natural level; (ii) after expectations, prices and wages adjust, and output and unemployment return to their natural level; after this adjustment period, which lasts for no more than a couple of years, the level of economic activity is independent of the party in office; (iii) the rate of inflation should remain higher throughout the term of a left-wing government. That is, the time-consistent (but suboptimal) inflation rate remains higher when the Left is in office even after the level of economic activity returns to its natural level because of a credibility problem. The public knows that the Left has a strong incentive to follow expansionary policies to reduce unemployment: Thus, expected inflation remains high. In particular, because of rational expectations, after the initial adjustment to the new regime, expected inflation is high enough so that the government does not have an incentive to inflate more. Thus, actual inflation is equal to the "high" expected inflation, and unemployment is at its natural level.[3]

In summary, this rational partisan model differs from the traditional one because it emphasizes how differences in growth and unemployment associated with changes of government are only temporary. For example, a left-wing government, committed to reducing unemployment by means of expansionary aggregate demand policies is bound to "succeed" only in the short run. After a brief period in which unemployment may actually fall, this government will find itself trapped in a high-inflation equilibrium with no benefit on the unemployment side. According to Hibbs's model, instead, a left-wing government can permanently lower the rate of unemployment by permanently increasing the rate of inflation.

Waller (1992) relates the preferences over inflation and unemployment that underlie the partisan theory to the existence of two sectors in the economy. In one sector, wages are sticky, as in the rational partisan model; in the other, wages and prices adjust with no delays or frictions, as in a classical model of the economy. Agents in the two different sectors of the economy have different preferences over the conduct of monetary policy because of these structural cross-sector differences. This essay moves a step toward explaining within the model itself the difference in party preferences, which, instead, is assumed as given in the previous literature. This is indeed a major item in the research agenda of this field: how to derive endogenously the number of objective functions of the parties, starting with a distribution of voters' preferences, distribution of resources, and mechanisms of market behavior.

The rational partisan theory has been recently criticized by Hibbs (1992), who raises several important points. The first issue is why rational agents would lock themselves into nominal wage contracts lasting one or two years. The identical criticism has been repeatedly raised against this entire "neo-Keynesian" research that assumes wage and/or price rigidities. Neo-Keynesians have responded to this objection in several ways (see, e.g., Mankiw and Romer 1991). The first answer has to do with the complexity of writing state-contingent wage contracts. In Alesina (1987) the contracts would have to be made contingent only on the election result: Even a simple indexation clause would be enough. In reality, however, wages would have to account for several additional contingencies, such as various demands and supply shocks on the economy; nevertheless, one rarely observes very complicated wage contracts. Even full indexation is not observed often and is not even optimal in a world with several demand and supply shocks. Gray (1976) shows that if the nature of the economic shocks cannot be identified with certainty, full indexation may be worse than no indexation, and it is certainly worse than partial indexation. Miles–Ferretti (forthcoming) extends the study of optimal indexation schemes to the case of electoral uncertainty. He shows that in the presence of electoral uncertainty, coupled with other forms of economic shocks, full indexation is not optimal.

A second argument, originally suggested by Mankiw (1985) in a different context, has to do with the effects of "small" costs of changing prices in an imperfectly competitive market. In our context, the same idea can be applied to nominal wages. Suppose that a monopolistic union sets the real wage, given union members' preferences, market conditions, union "power," and so forth. We can think of a union having an objective function that reaches a maximum at the real wage chosen. Because of the concavity of the objective function, the loss in utility for union members is relatively small – in technical terms "second order" – relative to the size of the fall in real wages. Thus, even a small cost of recontracting the wage to account for a shock would be enough to not make it worthwhile for the union to change the wage. These "small" costs could be the time and effort spent in organizing meetings and bargaining with the employers. However, even though the effect of union members' utitlity of the inflation shock may be small, the aggregate effects on employment may be large.

A second, related criticism is why contracts are not signed *after,* rather than before, elections, thus eliminating the electoral uncertainty. Clearly, the assumption that all the contracts are signed just an instant before the elections is a simplification needed to facilitate exposition. In reality, contract terms are staggered and overlapping, as in models by Taylor (1979, 1980). At least a fraction of staggered contracts will "go over" the election date. This neo-Keynesian approach embodied in the rational partisan theory has been criticized on both sides: by rational expectation purists who do not believe in price rigidities and by traditional Keynesians (like Hibbs) who believe in a long-run exploitable trade-off. Later, I will argue that the middle-ground neo-Keynesian approach is, in fact, empirically more successful than either one of its extreme alternatives.

However, even though all these specific criticisms can be answered, their basic thrust is well taken. The Achilles' heel of the "rational partisan theory" is that the mechanism of wage formation is postulated exogenously rather than derived from optimal individual behavior.

Finally, partisan and opportunistic PBC models are not incompatible; a more elaborate model could encompass both features in a unified framework. As early as 1978, Frey and Schneider suggested that partisan politicians become opportunistic when the election time approaches and they are in danger of losing, while they "go for" their partisan goals when they are electorally confident. However, they do not develop this insight in a model based on rational behavior.[4]

The opportunistic behavior of politicians belonging to different parties might be different: A "run toward the middle" is the most effective opportunistic policy for a partisan politician. For example, a high-inflation Democratic administration (such as President Carter's) should not expand the economy even more, creating even more inflation, before an election. If this type of administration wants to appeal to the middle of the road voters, it needs to turn to a more anti-inflationary policy. A low-inflation administration (say the first Reagan one) faces the opposite problem. Thus, a run toward the middle implies different preelectoral macroeconomic policies for different administrations.

The incorporation of both partisan and opportunistic incentives in a fully specified rational model of the PBC, is an important topic of future research.

Empirical evidence

Soon after the publication of Nordhaus's article, McCallum (1978) rejected the implication of the PBC model on post-war U.S. unemployment data. Several others studies later confirmed McCallum's negative results.[5] This sequence of rejections led Alt and Chrystal (1983) to wonder how a theory could survive so many empirical failures and still retain a wide appeal.

On the other hand, Tufte (1978) provides support for this theory by looking at a handful of U.S. elections. He disregards on a priori (and somewhat questionable) grounds the Eisenhower era, which provides no support for the theory, and he is left with only a few presidential elections in the post-World War II period, considering that he was writing in the mid-seventies.

Tufte's most convincing and widely cited evidence is on fiscal transfers, rather than on macroeconomic variables such as unemployment and growth. The most famous example of opportunistic fiscal manipulations is the 1972 election. The possibility of short-run manipulations of the budget and of monetary policy is also consistent with the evidence presented by Grier (1987, 1989) on monetary policy, Alesina (1988) on fiscal transfers, Keech and Pak (1989) on veteran benefits, Beck (1992) on monetary policy, and Hibbs (1987) on disposable income, that is, income net of taxes. This body of research suggests that some opportunistic manipulations of monetary and fiscal policy instruments occur, but they do not take place before every election and they are rather small in magnitude. For instance, Alesina (1988) shows, in accordance with Tufte (1978), that the evidence on fiscal transfers is much weakened if the fifties are included in the sample. Keech and Pak (1989) also show that Tufte's evidence is much weakened if the post-1978 period is included in the sample. The evidence by Grier (1989) on monetary policy is much weakened if the eighties are included (Alesina, Cohen, and Roubini 1992, 1993).

Probably the best way of finding evidence on opportunistic cycles is by looking at specific programs targeted to key constituencies, rather than macro variables, as Keech and Pak (1989) have done. Rogoff (1990), in fact, emphasizes the opportunistic manipulation of the composition of the budget, rather than its size. Empirical work on the composition of the budget, rather than its size, might be a promising avenue to explore more expansively both at the federal and at the state level.[6]

In summary, while there is no evidence of a regular four-year cycle on

Table 5.1. *Rate of growth of GNP in real terms*

	Year			
	First	Second	Third	Fourth
Democratic administrations				
Truman	0.0	8.5	10.3	3.9
Kennedy/Johnson	2.6	5.3	4.1	5.3
Johnson	5.8	5.8	2.9	4.1
Carter	4.7	5.3	2.5	−0.2[a]
Average	3.3	6.2	5.0	3.3
Average first/second halves		4.8		4.1
Republican administrations				
Eisenhower I	4.0	−1.3	5.6	2.1
Eisenhower II	1.7	−0.8	5.8	2.2
Nixon	2.4	−0.3	2.8	5.0
Nixon/Ford	5.2	−0.5	−1.3[a]	4.9
Reagan I	1.9	−2.5	3.6	6.8
Reagan II	3.4	2.7	3.4	4.5
Bush	2.5	0.9	−0.7	—
Average	3.0	−0.3	2.7	4.3
Average first/second halves		1.4		3.5

[a] Oil shocks
Source: *Economic Report of the President 1992*

unemployment and growth as predicted by the PBC model, one can find signs of relatively "loose" monetary and fiscal policies before elections.

The rational partisan theory has received much stronger empirical support on growth, unemployment, and inflation. Alesina and Sachs (1988a), Chapell and Keech (1988), Alesina (1988), and Beck (1992) find that the rational partisan theory performs better than its alternatives for the United States. In particular, the partisan effects on growth unemployment are much more short lived than the traditional partisan model by Hibbs (1987) implies.

Every Republican administration in the post-World War II period except Reagan's second one has started with a recession. No recessions have occurred at the beginning of Democratic administrations. These partisan differences are, however, short lived: The second halves of the two types of administrations show a rather similar average growth. Finally, the election year does not show, on average, the opportunistic upward jump. Table 5.1 highlights these basic observations.[7]

One problem of these empirical studies on the post-World War II period in the United States is their scarcity of degrees of freedom. The sample size can be expanded in two ways. One is to go back in time. This strategy presents several problems, such as the deterioration of the quality of the economic data, the need to include major war periods and the Great Depression, and the diminished plausibility of the assumption of stability of the parameters of the model. Despite these problems, the gain in degrees of freedom may be worth the cost, and Alesina, Londregan, and Rosenthal (1993) present favorable evidence for the rational partisan theory on U.S. GNP growth in a sample that begins in 1915 and ends in 1988. (Several arguments discussed in the essay justify the choice of 1915). They take into account the effects of military mobilizations and demobilizations, which, as expected, have a major impact on GNP growth.

The degrees of freedom can also be increased by a cross section/time series analysis on a sample of industrial democracies. The problem here is that one has to assume that evidence drawn from different countries can be pooled together. This is the approach followed by Alt (1985), Alesina (1989), Paldam (1989, 1991), Alesina and Roubini (1992), and Alesina, Cohen, and Roubini (1992, 1993). The conclusions of this literature are remarkably similar to those summarized earlier for the United States.

The traditional PBC model by Nordhaus is generally rejected quite strongly and unambiguously on growth and unemployment. On the other hand, one can find some evidence of opportunistic budget and monetary electoral cycles. For instance, monetary growth tends to be slightly higher than average in the six to twelve months before an election, and budget deficits tend to increase in election years. These effects are, however, not very large in magnitude, and these policy manipulations do not occur systematically before each election. These findings are consistent with the rational opportunistic models, which emphasize the constraints that limit the latitude available to the policy makers when they wish to systematically fool the voters by appropriately timing recessions and expansions.

The data also are much better explained by a rational version of the partisan theory rather than the traditional Hibbs partisan model. In fact, differences in growth rates and unemployment have a partisan connotation, but are observable only in the short run, for about eighteen to twenty-four months after a change of government. Partisan effects on growth and unemployment completely disappear about two years after the change of government.

Alesina and Roubini (1992) also find that the partisan theory of macro-economic policy with rational expectations is much more successful in countries with either a two-party system or, at least, two clearly identifia-

156

ble "Right" and "Left" coalitions, with clearly marked shifts from one to the other. For instance, the countries that provide a better fit for the theory include the United States, the United Kingdom, Canada, Germany, France, Australia, New Zealand, and Sweden. On the contrary, this approach is not very successful in describing countries with large middle-of-the-road coalition governments, such as Italy or Belgium. These empirical results are consistent with the spirit of the theory, which, in fact, was developed for a two-party political environment.

The partisan effects are short lived but are *not* small in magnitude; on the contrary, they are rather large. For instance, Alesina and Roubini (1992) calculate that in the group of countries just mentioned, the rate of GNP growth eighteen months after a change of government to the left is 2.5 percent higher than it would be eighteen months after a change of government to the right. Unemployment shows a similar pattern; the same comparison reveals that unemployment is 1.5 percentage points lower eighteen months after a left- to right-wing change of government relative to what it would be after a right- to left-wing change. As for inflation, they report that for the same group of countries, the difference between left- and right-wing governments is about 1.5 percent per year in the sample 1960 to 1988 and 2.5 percent per year in the sample 1971 to 1988, namely, for the period with flexible exchange rates. Even when the entire sample of eighteen countries is used, the results do not change substantially.

In summary, two general conclusions can be drawn from this empirical literature. First, the recent rational approaches to modeling opportunistic and partisan cycles are much more successful empirically than their predecessors. This is a clear endorsement of modeling choices that emphasize rationality. Second, partisan effects are quite strong on macroeconomic outcomes, such as growth, unemployment, and inflation. Opportunistic effects are, overall, rather small in magnitude and appear only in policy instruments, in particular, fiscal variables.

An important avenue for empirical research is a study of how partisan forces interact with other institutional features likely to influence unemployment, inflation, and growth. Alvarez, Garret, and Lange (1991) examine how labor market institutions and union behavior influence the nature of the partisan cycle. Grilli, Masciandaro, and Tabellini (1990), Cukierman (1992), and Alesina and Summers (1993) study the macroeconomic effect of Central Bank political independence. The feasibility and nature of partisan monetary policy is clearly influenced by the institutional role of the Central Bank. International constraints on domestic macroeconomic policies are also likely to influence the extent of partisan cycles. These cycles were smaller in magnitude during the Bretton Woods system than in the following decades. The European monetary system may also have reduced the flexibility of partisan politicians to pursue their macroeconomic goals.

Finally, the empirical research just summarized involves only industrial democracies. PBCs, are, however, not necessarily a prerogative of these countries. On the contrary, PBCs are possible and perhaps even more likely in countries and dictatorships: Even dictators need to please the public, at least to a certain degree, in order to reduce the likelihood of insurrections.[8]

THE EFFECT OF ECONOMIC CONDITIONS ON VOTING BEHAVIOR

The traditional PBC model by Nordhaus (1975) has two major implications: Politicians stimulate the economy before each election, and the electorate reward the incumbent if the economy is "doing well" in the period immediately preceding the election.

In the preceding section, we argued that the first implication is rejected by the data. There is virtually no evidence that growth is systematically high and unemployment low in election years. On the contrary, one can find much evidence that the state of the economy in the preelectoral period strongly influences electoral results: Incumbents do well, ceteris paribus, when the economy is in good shape.

For the United States, Kramer (1971) and Fair (1978, 1988) among many others, have shown that the rate of growth of income (or GNP) strongly influences the results of presidential elections. Other macro economic variables such as unemployment and inflation may also have an influence, but, overall, the strongest impact comes from growth. A second important determinant of presidential elections is the incumbency advantage.

The effects of the economy on congressional elections are more subtle. A crucial observation on this point (Erikson 1988, 1990; Alesina and Rosenthal 1989) is the following: The first half of Democratic administrations typically exhibit above average growth, as shown in Table 5.1 and discussed earlier. According to a simple retrospective voting model, the Democratic party should do well in midterm elections. On the contrary, the Democratic party loses in midterm when it holds the White House. The rate of growth in the first half of Republican administrations is low, and this party also loses votes in midterm elections: This is the well known "midterm cycle."[9]

Even in on-year elections, the effect of the economy in congressional elections is dubious. Alesina, Londregan and Rosenthal (1993) show that the economy has no direct effects on congressional elections, beyond its indirect effect through presidential coattails.[10] The general point here is that the relationship between the state of the economy and presidential and congressional elections is more complex than the simple idea that when growth is high the party of the incumbent president does well in every election.

The evidence drawn from other industrial democracies is, "mutatis mutandis," not dissimilar from that of the United States. Lewis-Beck (1988) concludes, after carefully reviewing a vast literature and providing many novel results, that good economic conditions help incumbent governments in several industrial democracies. However, as argued earlier, there is virtually no evidence of a systematic opportunistic electoral cycle. That is, while high growth in the election year helps the incumbent, the rate of growth in election years is not higher than average.

If one considers the empirical research on elections and the economy in the United States and other industrial democracies, one is really struck by the similarities of the results, much more than by the differences: The United States is not an exception.[11]

The theoretical and empirical results reviewed thus far leave open several questions. First, how can we reconcile the apparent lack of opportunistic behavior of politicians with the finding that the voters reward the incumbent when the economy is in good shape? Second, are the voters rational when they vote by looking at the state of the economy in the period immediately preceding an election? In particular, is the evidence of "short memories" sufficient to rule out rational voter behavior? Third, how are presidential and congressional elections influenced by the economy in on-year and midterm elections? Fourth, can we reconcile a partisan model with the observation that, regardless of party affiliation, incumbent governments do well at the polls when growth is high immediately prior to elections?

Alesina and Rosenthal (1995) address these questions, amongst others, by constructing and testing a model of the political economy of the United States. The next section illustrates this model.

A GENERAL MODEL OF THE POLITICAL ECONOMY OF THE UNITED STATES

The most important aspect of this approach is that both the economy and the polity are jointly determined. The empirical research reviewed thus far either takes electoral results as given and studies the effects of elections on the economy, or takes the economy as predetermined and studies the

159

effects of the economy on elections. In Alesina and Rosenthal (1995), both the effects of elections on the economy and the effects of the economy on elections are jointly modeled and tested. The only exogenous variables are the party ideological positions, the institutional structure that leads to policy formation by virtue of a compromise between the president and Congress, and the degree of administrative competence, which may vary over time.

Seven key ingredients underlie this model. First, the two parties are policy motivated. Second, the economy is modeled as in the rational partisan theory described earlier. Third, administrative competence influences the rate of GNP growth. The voters prefer more to less competent administrations, and for the reasons also described earlier, this model of competence gives rise to rational retrospective voting on the economy. Fourth, everybody, including the voters and the economic agents, are rational. No asymmetry of information between the policy makers and the voters is postulated. Consequently, opportunistic preelectoral manipulations of economic policy are ruled out.

Fifth, policy outcomes depend upon which party holds the presidency and the composition of Congress. With a Republican president, for instance, the larger the share of the Democratic party in Congress, the more the policy outcome is pulled toward the ideal policy of the Democratic party, and vice versa. Moderation does not occur only with divided governments (namely, when one party has a majority in Congress and the other party has the White House); the degree of moderation is a "continuous" variable, which depends on relative shares in the legislature.

Sixth, middle of the road voters use institutional balancing to bring about moderate policies. Since policy must reflect a compromise between the president and Congress, moderate voters (i.e., those with preferences in between those of the two parties) balance the president of one party by turning to the opponent in congressional elections. Alternatively, if the voters perceive that because of the incumbency advantage, one party controls Congress, they turn to the opponent party in presidential elections. The model does not predict that the U.S. government should *always* be divided: It provides conditions under which one should observe divided or unified government.

Seventh, the midterm cycle is part of this institutional balancing. Part of the balancing occurs in presidential election years. However, in these elections there might be uncertainty about the identity of the future president. Under uncertainty, balancing is incomplete. Moderation is completed in midterm when the uncertainty about the presidency has been removed.

The model is rather involved. Given the space constraint here, I shall illustrate with an example.[12] Suppose that a Democratic president, who was a slight favorite according to the polls, is elected. This presidential result is accompanied by a relatively strong show of Republican candidates in congressional elections. In fact, the electorate tilts in favor of the Republican party in House electorate elections in order to moderate the favorite Democratic candidate in the White House. The Democratic administration follows expansionary policies, which lead to an upsurge of growth in the first two years of the term and to an increase inflation. In midterm, the electorate further balances the Democratic administration by turning toward the Republican party: The voters want to insure themselves against excessive inflation. This voting behavior implies a nonobvious correlation: Strong economic growth in the first half of the Democratic administration is accompanied by a poor show of this party at midterm.[13]

In the second half of the term, growth returns to its average level, because of adjustment of expectations and in the wage price system, while inflation remains relatively high. In addition, negative shocks hit the economy in the fourth year, reducing growth below average. The electorate cannot perfectly distinguish whether the low growth is caused by these adverse shocks or by administrative incompetence. Even if the Democratic administration were relatively competent, the negative shocks would lead the electorate to be skeptical. Therefore, the voters turn to the Republican party in the following presidential election. The Republican administration fights inflation and causes a recession. In midterm, the voters balance the president by reinforcing the Democratic contingent in Congress. In the second half of the term, growth returns to its average level, and inflation remains relatively low. In addition, a combination of luck and (perhaps) competence leads to a particularly favorable growth in the election year. As a result, the Republican adminstration is reappointed.

This story reads as a rather accurate description of the period 1976–84, with the Carter and first Reagan administrations. The empirical work by Alesina, Londregan, and Rosenthal (1993), and Alesina and Rosenthal (1989, 1995) shows that this model performs remarkably well in the sample 1915 to 1989 in the United States. More specifically, the model is consistent with the following regularities of U.S. political economy:

i. The vote share of the incumbent president party's presidential candidate increases with the rate of GNP growth in the election year.

ii. Congressional elections are less sensitive to economic conditions; the economy influences these elections only through its effect on presidential votes.

iii. There is a midterm cycle where the party holding the White House loses votes in midterm.

iv. GNP growth exhibits a partisan cycle with short-run postelectoral deviations from average growth.

v. The rate of GNP growth in election years is not systematically different from average.

In confronting the model with the data, Alesina and Rosenthal (1995) also develop a test of rationality of retrospective voting. They test whether, given their assumptions about the dynamic behavior of the economy, and, in particular, of administrative competence, the voters rationally use all the available information when voting. Rationality is rejected. That is, they find that the voters punish the incumbent when growth is low, without trying to disentangle the effect of competence from the effect of luck. To put it more bluntly, the American voters care *too much* about the rate of economic growth in the election year when voting in presidential elections.

The reasons for this negative result could be many. First, the voters may know much less about the economy and its shocks than the model assumes. Thus, what is rejected is not rationality per se, but specific assumptions about the distribution of information. Second, the model of competence might be misspecified, even though it seems unlikely that a more sophisticated dynamic structure for this variable would lead to very different results.[14] Third, the voters may not know or learn anything about competence and simply vote against the incumbent when growth is low in order to encourage administrative effort. As a consequence, the politicians will show the maximum amount of effort if they know that they are always punished if the economy is not doing well. This simple strategy on the part of the voters is optimal (Austen-Smith, and Banks 1989). The problem is that this strategy is consistent with the same empirical implications of naive retrspection; thus, empirical tests are impossible.

A related question is how far back rational voters should look when voting on the economy. The answer is not obvious: It depends on the dynamic structure of the economy and on the dynamic behavior and persistence of competence. There is no presumption whatsoever that short memories are synonymous with lack of rationality. For instance, if competence does not persist for more than one period, it is perfectly rational for the voters not to look back more than one period.

The question of how to reconcile retrospective voting with standard notions of rationality is an important topic for future research. The highest payoffs on this point are likely to come from empirical work. We now have several models that predict rational retrospective voting. The next question is empirical: How do these models do when faced with reality?

Are rational models of retrospective voting a solid guide for empirical research?

DIVIDED GOVERNMENT: MODERATION OR GRIDLOCK?

The previous section has emphasized the role of divided government as a balancing device against excessive polarization of partisan policies. A similar argument on moderation has also been put forward by Fiorina (1988, 1990a,b). A commonly heard argument holds, instead, that divided government leads to a legislative gridlock.

The resolution of this controversy is to a large extent, an empirical issue; however, one has to be clear what is meant by "moderation" and "gridlock." In fact, the two concepts are indistinguishable in some cases. Suppose, for instance, that the status quo is a middle-of-the-road policy. If, because of the division of government, the status quo cannot be changed with either a left-wing or a right-wing policy, should we call this situation "balancing" or "gridlock"? A so-called "gridlock" that does not change a middle of the road status quo might be the essence of institutional balancing. It may be precisely what the middle of the road voters, who split their ticket, want. Therefore, the amount of legislative production is hardly a statistic for the amoung of gridlock.

A more useful definition of gridlock should focus instead on delays in the adoption of efficient policies, which sooner or later will have to be adopted in situations where delays are costly. For instance, since large peacetime budget deficits are generally suboptimal,[15] a prolonged period of large deficits typically is a departure from efficiency. The same argument applies to a runaway inflation, to the delay in dealing with the savings and loan crisis, and the like.

The evidence discussed in Fiorina (1990b) and the literature reviewed therein (particularly if one takes into account the previous discussion on the possible overlap between balancing and gridlock) leads me to be rather skeptical on the magnitude of the alleged gridlock caused by divided government in the United States.

One of the most widely cited examples of legislative gridlock is on budget deficits. At the federal level, McCubbins (1991) argues that when the legislature is divided, budget deficits increase. This result occurs because the House and the Senate reconcile their differences on spending priorities by spending more on everything and financing these spending programs with debt.[16] In my view, the biggest problem of McCubbins's results is that they are driven to a very large extent by one observation:

the early eighties. Furthermore, the roots of the deficits in the eighties have to be found in the 1981–82 period. These are the two years with the most unified Republican control of the decade. If divided government is truly the problem, the deficits should have increased at increasing rates throughout the decade. On the other hand, McCubbins' point appears a priori quite plausible.

An alternative view on the politics of the budget that may explain the budget deficits observed during the Reagan era is put forward by Alesina and Tabellini (1990), Tabellini and Alesina (1990), and Persson and Svensson (1989). They show how, in a model with partisan politicians, government debt can be used as a strategic variable, which influences the choices available to future governments. For example, a unified Republican government could choose to leave a large deficit to future administrations. If the latter are Democratic, they are constrained by the size of the inherited debt when choosing the size of their favorite spending programs. Thus, a Republican adminstration can prevent a future expansion of the welfare state by committing future tax revenues to debt service. According to this model, a unified partisan government is more likely to create deficits than a divided one: The dynamic interaction of polarized governments, rather than divided governments, create deficits.

An interesting topic for future research is to integrate these two insights into a unified model. That is, one could have a model in which both mechanisms are in operation: debt as a commitment device in a game between current and future governments, and debt as a result of a game between different parties controlling different branches of government at the same time.

Poterba (1994) and Alt and Lowry (forthcoming) report evidence of the gridlock effect of divided government in American states. These authors find that the adjustment to budget shocks is slower in states with divided control of the institutions than in states with unified control. To put it differently, divided government does not generate deficits, but when deficits appear for some exogenous reason, they last longer with divided government.

In summary, the American electorate faces a trade-off between moderation and gridlock. By splitting control of the institutions, the electorate avoids excessive partisan swings in policy making. On the other hand, the same split may delay the adoption of necessary reforms. It should be possible to incorporate this trade-off in a formal model of elections, by extending the framework of Alesina and Rosenthal (1995) to allow for inefficiencies and delays in policy formation under split control.

As noted by Fiorina (1991), Leaver and Shepsle (1991) and Alesina and Rosenthal (1995), divided government can be interpreted as the U.S. version of coalition governments in parliamentary democracies. The same question can then be asked: Do coalition governments lead to moderation of policies or to legislative deadlocks?

Spolaore (1992) addresses this question in a model that produces intuitive and plausible results. He shows that in majoritarian systems with one-party governments, one observes "too much" policy action and an excessive partisan variability of policies. In coalition governments, instead, one observes costly delays in policy making. A comparison of Great Britain and Italy in the past thirty years is a splendid illustration of this result.

The deadlock of coalition governments stems from the veto power that each member has, a power that generates a war of attrition (Alesina and Drazen 1991) between coalition members: Policies are not implemented until this conflict is resolved. Costly delays in coalition government can occur under a variety of different assumptions concerning the nature of the game between coalition members or social groups. For instance, Spolaore (1992) shows that the delays in policy making are increasing as the number of coalition members increase.

The empirical results by Roubini and Sachs (1989a,b) and by Grilli, Masciandaro, and Tabellini (1991), are consistent with these ideas. They show that countries with large coalition governments have had much trouble in adjusting their budget after the adverse shocks of the early seventies. The large deficits that have emerged in the mid-seventies have persisted under coalition governments, leading to extremely high debt level. Belgium and Italy have the two largest debt/GNP ratios in the industrial countries, and they have two of the most proportional electoral systems. Both countries have had large and unstable coalition governments. On the contrary, Great Britain may not be in great shape economically, but it does not have a significant debt problem.

Once again one is struck by the similarity of these results on industrial democracies with results on American states obtained by Alt and Lowry (forthcoming) and Poterba (1994) and reviewed earlier. In both the American states and in European countries, divided governments do not create deficits, but they perpetuate them and aggravate them when deficits appear.

The results by Alesina and Roubini (1992) discussed earlier are also consistent with this contrast between coalition governments and unified governments. They find that while partisan differences in policy making emerge clearly in two-party systems (or two-block systems), policy differences are not evident in countries with large coalition governments: Economic policies are less partisan in coalition governments.

In summary, different electoral systems imply different choices in the trade-off between moderation and gridlock. An English system is probably at the extreme of the "no moderation but no gridlock" scale. The current Italian system is at the opposite end.[17] Perhaps the U.S. system is a "happy medium."

NOTES

1. This section is largely based upon Alesina (1992). For a survey that takes a rather different view from mine, see Nordhaus (1989).
2. Whether inflation begins to increase before or immediately after the election date depends upon the specification of the model, and in particular upon the postulated leg structures in the Phillips curve. See Linkbeck (1976) for a discussion of this point.
3. See Cukierman (1992) for a recent survey of these credibility models.
4. Alt and Chrystal (1983) criticize Frey and Schneider's empirical results.
5. Paldam (1979), Golden and Poterba (1980), Hibbs (1987), Alesina (1988a), Beck (1992).
6. For state level evidence related to this point, see Poterba (1994) and Alt and Lowry (forthcoming).
7. Recently, Hibbs (1993) has proposed a model with learning as an alternative to the rational partisan theory to explain the short duration of partisan effects shown in Table 5.1.
8. See the survey by Alesina (1992) and the references cited therein.
9. For a discussion of how the midterm cycle interacts with the incumbency advantage, see Alesina and Rosenthal (1995).
10. However, for somewhat dissenting opinions see Chapell and Suzuki (1990) and Jacobson (1990).
11. An interesting question that is particularly relevant for parliamentary democracies with coalition governments is how the voters share the blame for a bad economy (or the praise for a good one) between different parties' members of the same coalition government. The answer may vary across countries and time periods but may be important for a theory coalition formation (Austin-Smith and Banks 1988; Laver and Shepsle 1990, 1991).
12. The same example is given in more detail in Alesina and Rosenthal (1995).
13. This chapter was written in 1993: this example was chosen *before* the 1994 midterm election.
14. Technical reasons for this view are given in the work cited.
15. See Barro (1979) and Lucas and Stokey (1983) for a discussion of optimal fiscal policies.
16. Barro (1991) sharply criticizes McCubbins' results, on both theoretical and empirical grounds.
17. Italy has recently implemented an electoral reform that made the system less proportional.

REFERENCES

Alesina, A. 1987. Macroeconomic policy in a two-party system as a repeated game. *Quarterly Journal of Economics*, 101: 651–78.
———. 1988a. Macroeconomics and politics. *NBER Macroeconomic Annual*. Cambridge: MIT Press, 13–52.

———. 1988b. Credibility and policy convergence in a two-party system with rational voters. *American Economic Review,* 78: 796–805.

———. 1992. Political models of macroeconomic policy and fiscal reforms. World Bank working paper.

Alesina, A., G. Cohen, and N. Roubini. 1992. Macroeconomic policy and elections in OECD economies. *Economics and Politics,* 4 (March): 1–30.

———. Forthcoming. Electoral business cycles in industrial democracies. *European Journal of Political Economy.*

Alesina, A., and A. Drazen. 1991. Why are stabilizations delayed? *American Economic Review,* 82 (December): 1170–88.

Alesina, A., J. Londregan, and H. Rosenthal. 1993. A model of the political economy of the United States. *American Political Science Review,* 87 (March): 12–35.

Alesina, A., and N. Roubini. 1992. Political cycles in OECD economies. *Review of Economic Studies,* 59: 663–88.

Alesina, A., and H. Rosenthal. 1989. Partisan cycles in congressional elections and the macroeconomy. *American Political Science Review,* 83:373–98.

———. 1995. *Partisan politics, divided government and the economy.* Cambridge University Press.

Alesina, A., and L. Summers. 1993. Central Bank independence and economic performance: Some comparative evidence. *Journal of Money Credit and Banking,* 25 (May): 151–62.

Alesina, A., and G. Tabellini. 1990. A positive theory of fiscal deficit and government debt. *Review of Economic Studies,* (July): 403–14.

Alt, J. 1985. Political parties, world demand, and unemployment: Domestic and international sources of economic activity. *American Political Science Review,* 79 (December): 1016–40.

Alt, J., and Alec Chrystal. 1983. *Political Economics.* Berkeley: University of California Press.

Alt, J., and R. Lowry. Forthcoming. Divided government and budget deficits: Evidence for the states. *American Political Science Review.*

Alvarez, M., J. Garret, and P. Lange. 1991. Government partisanship, labor organizations and macroeconomic performance. *American Political Science Review,* 85: 539–56.

Austen-Smith, D., and J. Banks. 1988. Elections, coalitions and legislative outcomes. *American Political Science Review,* 82 (June): 407–22.

———. 1989. Electoral accountability and incumbency. In P. Ordeshook (ed.), *Models of Strategic Choice in Politics,* Ann Arbor: University of Michigan Press, pp. 155–77.

Barro, R. 1979. On the determination of public debt. *Journal of Political Economy,* 87: 940–7.

Barro, R., and D. Gordon. 1983. Rules, discretion and reputation in a model of monetary policy. *Journal of Monetary Economics, 31: 589–610.*

Beck, N. 1987. Elections and the Fed: Is there a political monetary cycle? *American Journal of Political Science,* 31 (February): 194–216.

———. 1992. The shape of the electoral cycle. Unpublished.

Boylan, R., J. Ledyard, and R. McKelvey. 1990. Political competition in a model of economic growth. Unpublished.

Calvo, G. 1978. On the time consistency of optimal policy in a monetary economy. *Econometrica,* 46 (November): 1411–28.

Chapell, H., and M. Suzuki. 1990. Aggregate fluctuations for the U.S. presidency, Senate and House. Unpublished.

Chapell, H., and W. Keech. 1988. The unemployment consequences of partisan monetary policy. *Southern Economic Journal,* 55: 107–22.

Cukierman, A. 1992. *Central Bank Strategy, Credibility and Independence.* Cambridge, MA: MIT Press.

Cukierman, A., and A. Meltzer. 1986. A positive theory of discretionary policy, the cost of a democratic government and the benefits of a constitution. *Economic Inquiry,* 24 (July): 367–88.

Erikson, R. 1988. The puzzle of midterm loss. *Journal of Politics,* 50: 1012–29.

_____. 1990. Economic conditions and the congressional vote: A review of the macrolevel evidence. *American Journal of Political Science,* 34: 373–99.

Fair, R. 1978. The effects of economic events on votes for president. *Review of Economics and Statistics,* 64: 327–62.

_____. 1988. The effect of economic events on votes for president: 1984 update. *Political Behavior,* 10: 168–79.

Fiorina, M. 1988. The Reagan years: Turning to the right or groping toward the middle, in B. Cooper et al. (eds.), *The Resurgence of Conservatism in Anglo-American Democracies,* Durham, NC: Duke University Press, pp. 430–59.

_____. 1990a. An era of divided government, in B. Cain and G. Peele (eds.), *Developments in American Politics,* Oxford: Oxford University Press, pp. 324–54.

_____. 1990b. *Divided Government.* New York: Macmillan. pp. 235–59.

_____. 1991. Coalition government, divided government and electoral theory. *Governance,* 4: 236–49.

Frey, B., and F. Schneider. 1978. An empirical study of politico–economic interaction in the United States. *Review of Economics and Statistics,* 60 (May): 174–83.

Golden, D., and J. Poterba. 1980. The price of popularity: The political business cycle reexamined. *American Journal of Political Science,* 24: 696–714.

Gray, J. 1976. Wage indexation: A macroeconomic approach. *Journal of Monetary Economics,* 2: 221–35.

Grier, K. 1987. Presidential elections and the Federal Reserve policy: An empirical test. *Southern Economic Journal,* 54 (October): 475–86.

_____. 1989. On the existence of a political monetary cycle. *American Journal of Political Science,* 33 (May): 376–89.

Grilli, V., D. Masciandaro, and G. Tabellini. 1991. Political and monetary institutions and public finance policies in the industrial democracies. *Economic Policy,* no. 13: 57–91.

Hamada, K. 1976. A strategic analysis of monetary interdependence. *Journal of Political Economy* 84: 677–700.

Havrilesky, T. 1987. A partisan theory of fiscal and monetary regimes. *Journal of Money, Credit and Banking,* 19: 677–700.

Hibbs, D. 1977. Political parties and macroeconomic policy. *American Political Science Review,* 7 (December): 1467–87.

_____. 1987. *The American Political Economy.* Cambridge, MA: Harvard University Press.

_____. 1992. Partisan theory after fifteen years. *European Journal of Political Economics,* 8: 361–74.

_____. 1993. The partisan theory of macroeconomic cycles: More theory and evidence for the United States. Unpublished.

Jacobson, G. 1990. Does the economy matter in midterm elections? *American Journal of Political Science*, 34: 400–404.

Keech, W., and K. Pak. 1989. Electoral cycles and budgetary growth in veterans' benefit programs. *American Journal of Political Science*, 33: 901–12.

Kiewiet, R. 1983. *Macroeconomics and Micro Politics: The Electoral Effects of Economic Issues*, Chicago: University of Chicago Press.

Kramer, G. 1971. Short-term fluctuations in the U.S. voting behavior, 1896–1964. *American Political Science Review*, 65: 131–43.

Kydland, F., and E. Prescott. 1977. Rules rather than discretion: The inconsistency of optimal plans. *Journal of Political Economy*, 85: 473–90.

Laver, M., and K. Shepsle. 1990. Coalitions and cabinet government. *American Political Science Review*, 84: 843–90.

———. 1991. Divided government: America is not exceptional. *Governance*, 4: 250–69.

Lewis-Beck, M. 1988. *Economics and Elections: The Major Western Democracies*. Ann Arbor: University of Michigan Press.

Lindbeck, A. 1976. Stabilization policies in open economies with endogenous politicians. *American Economic Review. Papers and Proceedings*, 1–19.

Lucas, R., and N. Stokey. 1983. Optimal monetary and fiscal policy in an economy without capital. *Journal of Monetary Economics*, 12: 55–94.

Mankiw, G. 1985. Small menu costs and large business cycles: A macroeconomic model of monopoly. *Quarterly Journal of Economics*, 100: 529–39.

Mankiw, G., and D. Romer (eds.). 1991. *New Keynesian Macroeconomics*. Cambridge, MA: MIT Press.

McCallum, B. 1978. The political business cycle: An empirical test. *Southern Economic Journal*, 44 (January): 504–15.

McCubbins, M. 1991. Party governance and U.S. budget deficits: Divided government and fiscal stalemate, in A. Alesina and G. Carliner (eds.), *Politics and Economics in the 1980s*, Chicago: University of Chicago Press, pp. 83–122.

Milesi-Ferretti, G. Forthcoming. "Wage Indexation and Time Consistency," *Journal of Money Credit and Banking*.

Nordhaus, W. 1975. The political business cycle. *Review of Economic Studies*, 42 (April): 169–90.

Paldam, M. 1979. Is there an electoral cycle. *Scandinavian Journal of Economics*, 85: 452–61.

———. 1989. Alternative models to political business cycles. *Brookings Papers on Economic Activity* no. 2.

———. 1989. Politics matter after all: Testing Hibbs' theory of partisan cycles. Aarhus University Working Paper.

———. 1991. Politics matter after all: Testing Alesina's theory of RE partisan cycles, in Thygesen, K. Velupillai, and H. Zombelli (eds.), *Business Cycles: Theories, Evidence and Analysis*, London: Macmillan, pp. 154–73.

Peltzman, S. 1992. Voters as fiscal conservatives. *Quarterly Journal of Economics*, 107: 327–62.

Persson, T., and L. Svensson. 1989. Checks and balances on the government budget. *Quarterly Journal of Economics*, 104: 325–46.

Persson, T., and G. Tabellini. 1990. *Macroeconomic Policy, Credibility and Politics*. London: Harwood Academic.

Poterba, J. 1992. State responses to fiscal crises: "Natural experiments" for studying the effects of budgetary institutions. Unpublished.

Rogoff, K. 1987. Reputational constraints on monetary policy. *Carnegie-Rochester Conference Series on Public Policy,* 24.

_____. 1990. Political budget cycles. *American Economic Review,* 80 (March): 1–16.

Rogoff, K., and A. Sibert. 1988. Equilibrium political business cycles. *Review of Economic Studies,* 55 (January): 1–16.

Roubini, N., and J. Sachs. 1989a. Political and economic determinants of budget deficits in the industrial democracies. *European Economic Review,* 33 (May): 903–33.

_____. 1989b. Government spending and budget deficits in the industrialized countries. *Economic Policy* 8 (Spring): 55–91.

Spolaore, E. 1992. Policy making systems and economic efficiency: Coalition governments versus majority governments. Unpublished.

Tabellini, G., and A. Alesina. 1990. Voting on the budget deficit. *American Economic Review,* 80 (March): 17–32.

Taylor, J. 1979. Staggered wage setting in a macro model. *American Economic Review,* 69: 108–13.

_____. 1980. Aggregate dynamics and staggered contracts. *Journal of Political Economy,* 88: 1–23.

Tufte, E. 1978. *Political Control of the Economy.* Princeton, NJ: Princeton University Press.

Waller, C. 1992. The choice of a conservative central banker in a multi-sector economy. *American Economic Review,* 82 (September): 1006–12.

6

The politics and economics of budget deficit control: policy questions and research questions

EDWARD M. GRAMLICH

An important area where political and economic considerations intersect involves government fiscal policy. Most economists feel that government budget deficits reduce national saving, which in turn reduces the long-term capital intensity of an economy and its standard of living.[1] Hence, controlling budget deficits is one way, perhaps the best way, for present generations to protect the economic interests of future generations. At the same time, to control budget deficits politicians must vote for either tax increases or spending reductions, both of which are politically unpopular and increase politicians' chances of being voted out of office. Hence, the deficit control issue sets up an immediate tension between the policies that might be necessary for long-term economic expansion and the votes that might be necessary for political survival.

Given this tension, one might ask why real-world governments would ever balance their budgets. Part of the answer is that there are natural economic costs to letting budget deficits get out of control. If governments try to finance deficits by printing money, inflation will rise. If governments try to finance deficits by borrowing, interest costs will rise and, indeed, beyond some level, borrowers will not hold the government securities at any interest rate. To the extent that these natural outcomes can be linked to fiscal performance, it becomes harder for politicians to win reelection and will at least force them to internalize the costs of budget deficits. Another part of the answer is that in recognition of this tension, most governments have legislative or constitutional balanced budget ammendments (BBA) that enforce fiscal responsibility.

This tension has always existed, but it has suddenly become much more important for the U.S. government in recent years. Despite the fact that the federal government has never had any legislative or constitutional

I thank Henry Aaron, Paul Courant, Eric Hanushek, Rudolph Penner, and Charles Schultze for comments on earlier drafts.

BBA and has always faced a relatively loose set of economic constraints, U.S. fiscal policy has generally been reasonably responsible, with federal budget deficits averaging less than 1 percent of GDP through the 1960s and 1970s. But budget deficits abruptly shot up to more than 4 percent of GDP in the 1980s and 1990s. These budget deficits went along with a sharp fall in net national saving rates, from 8 percent of GDP in the 1960s to 3 percent in the 1980s and 1990s, just the sort of intergenerational transfer that might have been feared, and also presaging a continuation of the low rates of economic growth that have plagued the U.S. economy lately.

The budget situation looks even more worrisome when one looks ahead. The 1980s budget deficits raised the ratio of outstanding public debt to GDP from 27 percent and falling at the start of the decade to 48 percent and rising at the end. This rise has built in a permanently higher interest burden. Partly because of this rise in interest payments, the long-term baseline budget projections of the Congressional Budget Office (CBO), which have always shown declining deficits no matter how much the base year budget was out of balance, have changed too. The 1992 CBO long-term forecasts show deficits rising over the last half of the 1990s (CBPO, 1992). Economic growth is slower than in earlier times, and the continuing rise in health care costs adds to interest payments to raise spending disproportionately. The upshot is that one can no longer anticipate that the United States will slowly work its way out of its deficits by simply forswearing new tax reductions or government spending pro-grams. From now on, deficit problems are likely to get worse and harder to correct the longer the country waits, even without new tax reductions or spending programs.

Where were the natural economic constraints when all this was hap-pening? Since the Federal Reserve did not permit the massive federal borrowing of the 1980s to lead to excessive money creation, inflation was quiescent, even dropping over the decade of the 1980s. The implied bor-rowing should have raised interest rates, but increasingly the U.S. econ-omy should be treated as an open economy with interest rates set by world funds markets. The United States was generally able to borrow without much rise in interest rates, implying that the dollar would appre-ciate against foreign currencies and that U.S. net exports would fall, as indeed happened. The natural economic checks then became very subtle, mainly involving a change in the U.S. international asset position. As long as the foreign loans were forthcoming, it became difficult to activate the natural political checks to budget deficits, and the deficits went on and on. The already-weak political checks were weakened further by the di-vided government where Republicans controlled the presidency and the Democrats generally controlled Congress. Just who was it that voters were supposed to throw out? For better or worse, deficits persisted and the politicians in office while these deficits were created were generally reelected.

Because of the apparent failure of the natural economic and political checks, there has been a clamor to impose an external check on U.S. budget deficits. In 1985 Congress passed the Gramm–Rudman–Hollings Deficit Reduction Act (GRH), which purported to bring deficits down to zero over a five-year period. Purported to but did not – since GRH was a legislative limit, when it became binding on the Congress, it was simply amended to become less binding. Because of the frustration with this performance, in 1992 the Congress nearly passed a constitutional BBA – nearly passed, but did not pass. Right now there is no legislative or constitutional limit to deficits, though the clamor for one continues.

In this essay I take a careful look at this important question in the intersection of politics and economics. I first write about the problem from an economic and political point of view, and then I identify the main research questions that arise, especially those lying in the intersection of economics and politics.

The first section analyses the economics of budget deficits: How damaging are they really? Are they really getting worse? Is it really getting harder to turn fiscal policy around? The next section focuses on the politics of deficit reduction – what role was played by divided government; did constraining legislation such as GRH and the Budget Enforcement Act of 1990 work; are more drastic institutional restrictions necessary? Then I examine the experience of American state governments, more than forty of which presently have BBAs in their own constitutions – cannot something be learned from the states' experience? Then I consider the pros and cons of a federal BBA from a policy advice point of view. While there are serious problems with a version of the BBA proposal voted down by Congress in 1992, there may also be versions that could work and should be taken more seriously. The last section collects the various arguments and hypotheses in the essay into a list of underlying economic-political research questions involving budget deficit control.

THE ECONOMICS OF DEFICIT CONTROL

Analyzing budget deficits is complicated by the fact that one component of spending, interest payments, is dynamically endogenous. Higher budget deficits raise the outstanding public debt, which raises future interest payments, future deficits, and future levels of outstanding debt. Hence, it is easier to understand dynamic patterns and to identify the influence of

173

discretionary budget policies by splitting off interest payments and focusing on what is known as the primary deficit, the true driving variable in budgetary analysis. This is done through the following nominal identity for the budget deficit, or change in the outstanding debt(ΔD):

$$\Delta D = E - T + (r + p)D, \qquad (1)$$

where E refers to program spending, T to taxes, $(E - T)$ to the primary deficit, r to the real interest rate, p to the inflation rate, $(r + p)$ to the nominal interest rate, and D to the start-of-period level of debt. Now let Y refer to nominal GDP, n to the growth rate of real GDP, and $(n + p)$ to the growth of nominal GDP. The formula for the derivative of a quotient gives:

$$\Delta(D/Y) = \Delta D/Y - (\Delta Y/Y)(D/Y). \qquad (2)$$

Substituting (1) into (2) for the ΔD term and replacing $(\Delta Y/Y)$ with $(n + p)$ yields:

$$\Delta(D/Y) = (E - T)/Y + (r - n)D/Y. \qquad (3)$$

The dependent variable here is the change in the debt burden ratio, the change in the stock of outstanding debt to GDP. The variable $(E - T)/Y$ is called the primary deficit ratio.

Table 6.1 gives numbers by decade for the 1962–2002 period. Using decade averages abstracts from cyclical movements and other transitory forces such as deposit insurance bailouts, giving a better picture of long-term trends. The numbers after 1991 are forecasts, the baseline forecasts of CBO (1992). These assume no changes in tax law, no changes in entitlement provisions, and no changes in real appropriations.

The story of the table is as follows. In the 1960s the United States ran primary surpluses of 0.5 percent of GDP, had interest payments of 1.3 percent of GDP and deficits of 0.8 percent of GDP (see equation(1)), and saw its debt burden ratio fall by 16.0 points over the decade (equation (3)), from 45 percent of GDP to 29 percent. Net national saving (NSS), the sum of private and state and local saving less the federal deficit, was 7.8 percent of GDP. In the 1970s primary deficits rose to 0.8 percent of GDP, the interest burden rose slightly because of higher interest rates, total deficits rose to 2.4 percent of GDP, and the debt burden ratio fell only 1.9 percent of GDP, to 27 percent. NNS was down to 6.8 percent of GDP. Hence, the 1.6 point rise in the deficit ratio (2.4 less 0.8) corresponded to a fall of 1 point (7.8 less 6.8) in NNS: here there was some increase in private saving (0.6) to offset higher deficits.

The 1980s then saw the great fiscal experiment. Primary deficits actually only rose slightly, to 1.2 percent of GDP. Interest payments were up, mainly because of still higher interest rates, so that the overall deficit ratio

The politics of budget deficit control

Table 6.1. *Past and future deficits (percent)*

Years	Primary	Interest	Deficit[a]	Debt[b]	Net national saving
1962–70	−0.5	1.3	0.8	−16.0	7.8
1971–80	0.8	1.6	2.4	−1.9	6.8
1981–90	1.2	3.0	4.2	17.4	3.3
1991–2002	0.3	3.6	3.9	14.9	

Note: Unless noted, all numbers are annual percents of GDP. Components may not add to totals because of rounding.
[a]The sum of primary deficits and interest.
[b]Change in the debt burden ratio over the decade.

was now 4.2 percent of GDP, a rise of 3.4 points from the 1960s (4.2 less 0.8). This rise in deficits turned the debt burden ration around; now it climbed by 17.4 points back up to 44 percent. NNS dropped further, now down to 3.3 percent of GDP, 4.5 points below rates in the 1960s (7.8 less 3.3). So the deficit rise of 3.4 points triggered a drop in NNS of 4.5 points, as if a drop in private saving compounded the drop in public saving. Not only was there not a private saving offset, but rather private saving moved in the same direction, a matter I speculated on earlier (Gramlich, 1989). Given this sustained fall in NNS, there seems little doubt that federal deficits were indeed transferring consumption power from the future to the present on a rather massive scale, as most economists had feared.[2]

The fiscal experiment effectively continues in the forecast period of the 1990s. Primary deficits are now reduced from the 1980s, but the damage has been done: Rising interest burdens mean that total deficits are little changed. Again the debt burden ratio is slated to rise sharply. The CBO makes no explicit forecast of the NNS, but it is realistic to expect that as long as federal deficits remain high, NNS will remain low.

This simple decomposition illustrates the dramatic erosion in the U.S. fiscal position. Back in the 1960s, the interest burden added only 1.3 percentage points to the deficit ratio; for the 1990s it is 3.6 points and rising. This makes it much harder to control future deficits and to raise future NNS rates. Indeed, the link would be even stronger in a full Solow growth model, because then the drop in NNS would lower the capital intensity of the economy, raise r above n, and increase the rise in the debt burden ratio through both components of the last term in equation (3)(Tobin, 1986).

Suppose now that some fiscal variable were constrained by a constitutional or legislative provision – what are the options? The weakest standard would be to constrain primary deficits to be zero. Were that done, Table 6.1 shows that the debt burden ratio would still be growing exponentially, by about 1 percent a year by the start of the next century. This standard is so weak it does not even stop the upward drift in the share of interest payments.

The next standard might be to arrest the rise in the debt burden ratio. To do this, a solution of equation (3) finds that the primary surplus must equal 0.9 percent of GDP for the decade. That would amount to a discretionary shift in fiscal policy of 1.2 percentage points of GDP relative to CBO's baseline scenario shown in Table 6.1. Total deficits would still be large, just under 3 percent of GDP, NNS rates would still be low, but at least the interest drift would be arrested.

A more ambitious standard, the only one that gives promise of significantly raising NNS, would be simply to eliminate federal budget deficits. To do this, a solution of equation (1) finds that the primary surplus must equal just the interest burden, 3.6 percent of GDP for the decade, a discretionary shift in fiscal policy of 3.9 percentage points of GDP relative to CBO's baseline scenario. This implies a very large fiscal contraction indeed. Had the interest burden not grown so much over the past three decades, this standard might be attainable: The primary surplus would then only need to be 1.3 percent of GDP, a discretionary shift of only 1.6 percentage points of GDP relative to CBO's baseline scenario. But those days are unfortunately gone forever, or at least until the debt burden ratio is cut substantially, and now the no deficit standard implies very austere fiscal policy.

Primary deficits

The preceding analysis shows why it is important to focus on primary deficits. These drive the system, and the other results fall out from a series of accounting identities.

Table 6.2 gives a decomposition of past and future primary deficits for the same 1962–2002 period, from the same CBO projection. The table shows primary deficits rising up to the 1980s, and then falling back down, just as in Table 6.1. It shows that revenues and one component of spending, "other," are not responsible for any significant changes in primary deficits over the whole period. On the other hand, it shows that the interplay between two important components of spending – for national defense and for entitlements (social security, health programs, and some other transfer programs) – is responsible.

Defense spending followed a path that is reasonably well understood historically. In the Vietnam decade of the 1960s, defense spending ab-

Table 6.2. *Primary deficits (percent)*

Years	Defense	Entitlements	Other	Spending[a]	Revenue	Deficit[b]
1962–70	8.8	6.0	3.2	18.0	18.4	−0.5
1971–80	5.7	9.9	3.6	19.2	18.5	0.8
1981–90	6.0	11.1	3.0	20.1	18.9	1.2
1991–2002	3.8	12.5	3.1	19.3	19.0	0.3

Note: All numbers are annual percents of GDP. Components may not add to totals because of rounding.

[a] The sum of defense spending, entitlements, and other spending.

[b] Total spending less revenues. The same numbers as are shown in Table 6.1.

sorbed 8.8 percent of GDP. This share dropped to 5.7 percent in the 1970s, and only rose to 6.0 percent through the Reagan defense buildup of the 1980s. With the dissolution of the Cold War and under the Budget Enforcement Act of 1990 (BEA), defense spending is now expected to trend down through the 1990s. One measure of the so-called peace dividend is 2.2 percent of GDP (6.0 less 3.8). But note that this measure is unfortunately the *already spent* portion of the peace dividend. It is incorporated in a forecast that still shows a rising debt burden. This is the opposite of a sports team that wins even when it is not playing well. In this case the country has had the good fortune of a sizable peace dividend, and *still* cannot manage to reduce its debt burden.

The true villain in this budgetary drama is the steady growth in entitlement spending. The entitlement spending share of GDP rose 3.9 percentage points in the 1970s and from 1.2 to 1.4 percentage points a decade since. The sharp rise in the 1970s was due to liberalizing changes in social security, but the more recent changes were not due to discretionary policy changes. The main recent influence is the sharp rise in relative prices for health care – these relative price increases are driving up the share of GDP devoted to health care, the share of GDP devoted to public spending on health care, and even the share of GDP devoted to private spending on health care.

The previous analysis showed that primary deficits must be cut by 1.2 percent of GDP to stabilize the debt ratio and by 3.9 percent of GDP to eliminate deficits altogether. Where would such cuts come from? The table shows that the possibilities from defense and other spending are actually rather modest. Both are slated to be at historic lows relative to GDP in the 1990s already, so further reductions must come from these already depressed totals. Among other things, these limited prospects make irrelevant much of the literature on budget control (Fiorina, 1981;

Shepsle and Weingast, 1981) – aggrandizing bureaucrats, high-wage civil servants, and pork barrel projects are all confined to this narrow slice of the federal budget. Of course, efficiency savings can always be made in any component of government spending, but if one's target is 3.9 percent of GDP, one almost inevitably must focus on entitlements and/or taxes. Policy measures that do not affect these items have limited prospects for controlling deficits.

THE POLITICS OF DEFICIT CONTROL

The economics of deficit control in the United States set up the worst sort of political challenge for a democratic government. If the economic costs of budget deficits were visible and short run, it would be apparent to all that deficits must be stopped, there would be political retribution if they were not stopped, and they would be stopped. But if, as seems to be the case, these economic costs are difficult to perceive and long run, these checks disappear. Politicians and voters have clear incentives to let the tangible short-term benefits of high spending or low taxes outweigh the uncertain long-term benefits of deficit reduction.

A particular facet, in this case, weakness, of the U.S. political system complicates this intrinsic problem. Most democratic governments have parliamentary systems where the executive and legislative branches are controlled by the same party, elected in four- or five-year intervals. If large deficits persist, the party in power is at least forced to answer for these deficits. The U.S. democratic system is different, with a multiparty arrangement where the Republican party controls the presidency most of the time and the democratic party controls Congress most of the time. Who should be blamed for the large deficits? The president points to Congress, the Congress points to the president, and both get reelected more often than not. The election of 1992 might at last herald an end to this blameless political system, or it may be just a blip in the trend. If there is a new period of unified government, at some point it may be possible to conduct more powerful tests of the hypothesis that divided governments lead to higher deficits (McCubbins, 1991; Alt and Lowry, 1992; Poterba, 1992)[3]

It may also be possible to test another hypothesis that is generally asserted around Capital Hill, though not so much by academic political scientists. Up to the mid-1970s at least, the Congress was somewhat organized. Until a series of "democratic" reforms at that time, the Speaker of the House met with entrenched committee chairs and this leadership group worked out the position of the House. But this system too broke down in the 1970s, and now it is much more nearly true that each member of Congress is a free agent. If some legislative measure has to be altered to help somebody in the local district, so be it. While the hypothesis sounds reasonable, the difficulty in testing it is that the hypothesis refers only to the U.S. government, and a before–after design is hamstrung by the fact that so many other things were going on at the same time. Among other things, the first budget act came roughly at the same time as these reforms. But perhaps it would be possible to examine the experience in states to test the hypothesis.

Beginning in the mid 1980s, there were attempts to control these political forces in voting on deficits. The first was the Gramm–Rudman–Hollings Deficit Reduction Act of 1985 (GRH). This act laid out a series of deficit targets that had deficits dropping slowly to zero over the space of five years. In any year that the deficit did not hit this target, there was to be an automatic sequester, or equal cut in defense and nondefense appropriations, to hit the target. It might seem that GRH put the entire burden of deficit reduction on the expenditure side, but in fact things were more complicated than that. The idea of GRH was that the president, at the time Reagan, who was wedded to a rapid defense buildup, would negotiate with the Democratic Congress. Reagan would want to negotiate a budget deal to avoid a defense sequester and the Congress would want to negotiate a budget deal to avoid a nondefense sequester, and the result would be a negotiated deal that would imply phased reductions of deficits.

Did it happen? The triumphs were modest, but they could have been positive on balance. There were only modest sequestrations under GRH, but there were budget negotiations that entailed some true deficit reduction in all GRH years. An analysis of year-to-year fiscal changes does find some evidence of overall deficit reduction in the mid-1980s (Gramlich, 1990; Hahn, Kamlet, Mowery, and Su, 1992), though these efforts were later swamped by the savings and loan bailouts and the recession of 1991. GRH started a valuable tradition of voting on tax bills in a balanced budget manner – any amendment to raise some tax preference had to contain its own financing. The Tax Reform Act of 1986, debated under these new rules, had a very modest impact on the long-run fiscal position of the federal government, while the Economic Recovery and Tax Act of 1981, not so debated, had an enormously negative impact on the long-run fiscal position of the federal government. Subsequent tax legislation has also protected the government's fiscal position better because of this balanced budget voting.

But there were also problems created by GRH. There were various creative accounting devices used to meet budget targets. The most common of these was the sales of assets, sales that should have had no impact on a properly measured flow budget.[4] And whenever the deficit targets got really binding, as they did first in 1987 and later in 1990, the Congress simply passed a new law or new version of GRH to modify the targets.

The second modification of the GRH target path was an entirely new piece of legislation, the Budget Enforcement Act of 1990 (BEA). This act did not have any formal deficit targets, though it did contain caps on appropriated discretionary spending (all of the defense spending and some of the other spending in Table 6.2). These caps were adhered to and they do seem to be keeping discretionary spending under control (CBO, 1992). The BEA also stopped the practice of selling loans to meet budget targets, by the simple device of counting all transactions by their present value of budgetary savings: If an action did not make any present value saving, it did not count as budget reduction. The combination of GRH and BEA have also almost entirely ended the practice of adding to spending after the budget was adopted (CBO, 1992).

But while the combination of GRH and the BEA have curbed some of the most egregious problems in the way budgets are proposed by the president and voted on by Congress, the plain fact of the matter is that deficits are still excessive. Table 6.2 shows that the primary deficit problem is more and more a problem of entitlements and taxes, and neither GRH nor BEA did anything explicit about either of these items. Most entitlement spending was exempt from sequester under both GRH and the BEA caps. On the tax side, while politicians are not free to vote deficit-increasing measures, there is also nothing to force them to vote deficit-reducing tax measures. It is not surprising that there continues to be discussion of a more radical approach for controlling deficits, such as a BBA.

THE STATES' EXPERIENCE

All states but Vermont have BBAs, either in their state constitutions (41 states) or in legislation (8 states). These provisions seem to work reasonably well (Gold, 1992; Poterba, 1992), and certainly the public saving experience of state and local governments is far better than for the national government (Gramlich, 1991). Does this state experience suggest that a similar measure could work at the national level?

There is one similarity and two alleged differences. The similarity is that all real-world BBAs have significant enforcement problems – what is to prevent states (or the federal government) from selling assets, changing paydays, moving items off-budget, and all the rest of the activities that now go under the heading "smoke and mirrors"? These activities are widespread for the states, but at least Poterba still finds that even with the "leakages," constrained state fiscal policy is more responsible than unconstrained state fiscal policy.

The first of the two alleged differences is that states, unlike the federal government, have capital budgets where public investment is generally exempt from the budget balance requirements. If a government is to have a BBA, it makes sense to confine it to the operating budget, permitting long-lived capital to be bond-financed and paid off over the life of the capital stock.

The federal government does not have a capital budget. In the past, this has not mattered much, because the federal government does surprisingly little physical investment. In Table 6.2, all spending for interest and entitlements would be considered as current spending and subject to a BBA in a proper budget system. The only capital spending there is in the federal budget occurs in defense and the "other" category, with tangible physical investment being a tiny fraction of that. Most other spending is for research (0.8 of the 3.0 percent for the 1980s), income security and veterans (0.7 percent), and grants to state and local governments (1.0 percent), all of which would normally be considered current spending.[5]

At the same time, the point of a BBA is to raise national saving, and it certainly makes sense to exempt federal tangible investment in enforcing fiscal discipline. The federal government does not now invest much, but it always could. If there were a BBA, one would not want to see farsighted public investment behavior curbed by a BBA. Hence, it would seem that this part of the states' provisions should be carried over to a federal BBA. But that unfortunately is easier said than done. There are a number of measurement problems in defining federal investment, and a number of political problems in enforcing *any* definition, however sensible. The accountants' preferred approach might be to define investment quite narrowly, counting only spending on tangible items by the federal government. This approach would consider grants to state and local governments, even grants for capital purposes, as consumption, on the grounds that closed-ended grants probably operate more like income subsidies than price subsidies. It would also consider spending for health care, education, and even research and development as consumption – most of this spending is also in the form of grants, and even if the spending were direct, the assets created are not tangible and it is very difficult to prove that human capital spending raises future output. And this narrow approach might even consider defense capital spending as consumption because, again, defense capital cannot be shown to increase future output (though it may increase future security).

Each of these treatments is controversial, both from an economic and

181

political standpoint. The economic question is whether the item should be treated as current consumption or investment, and if investment, how depreciation should be measured, because even in a capital budget depreciation of the capital must be charged to current consumption. The political question is much knottier. *However* investment and consumption are defined and depreciation measured, how will these difficult economic concepts be translated into convincing political realities? What is to stop appropriations committees from having a field day defining consumption, investment, and depreciation in ever more arbitrary and less meaningful ways?

The second alleged difference between the states and the national government is that states are alleged not to have cyclical responsibilities. But when cyclical shocks are uneven across the country, it is hard to see how the states' cyclical problem is qualitatively any different from that faced by the national government. On one side, in an open economy, state governments operating under fixed exchange rates are likely to have higher fiscal multipliers than the national government operating under flexible exchange rates. On the other side, by altering their funds balances and their borrowing from the national unemployment trust funds, states already do operate countercyclical policies (Burtless and Vroman, 1984; Gramlich, 1987).

A better way to view state governments and the national government would seem to be that both could be confronted with cyclical stabilization problems, and both would have to balance the benefits of the stabilization against the long-run interest costs. In this sense there would be no intrinsic difference between governmental responsibilities at the two levels.

This cyclical issue is an important one for a BBA, because taken literally, a BBA would seem to prevent the automatic fiscal stabilizers from dampening cyclical swings. But this is just the point where the state experience *can be* relevant, because most states have developed a nice way to deal with the problem. Most state BBAs do not require a balanced flow budget at all, simply that some designated stock of balances not run below zero. Hence, if a state wants to run deficits in recessions, all it has to do is to build up its assets in its good years. It can run down these assets, run deficits, and approach the macro textbook dream – short-term fiscal stabilizaion consistent with long-term fiscal responsibility.

The upshot is that on all counts the states' experience seems highly relevant to the federal government. If there is to be a federal BBA, it could be written much like similar provisions at the state level.

The politics of budget deficit control

THE POLICY QUESTION: A FEDERAL BALANCED BUDGET AMENDMENT?

Turning now to the question of whether there should be a federal BBA, the issue is an old one. There has always been some interest in a BBA to the U.S. Constitution. Constitutional amendments can be proposed either by two-thirds of both houses of Congress or by a convention called by two-thirds of the states. Whichever procedure is used to propose amendments, these amendments must then be ratified by three-fourths of the states. The first unsuccessful attempt to add a BBA in the 1970s went through the states; the second unsuccessful attempt in 1992 went through Congress. Since most states have already shown themselves in favor of the federal BBA and almost all actually have their own BBA, if the proposed amendment ever does pass two-thirds of both houses, it may well be adopted.

But from a normative perspective, the version of the BBA voted down by the House of Representatives in June 1992 (shown in Appendix A) had one desireable property and three questionable properties. On the positive side, it did go into effect gradually. The proposal was for a zero deficit, the most ambitious of the three standards listed earlier but the only one with a realistic chance to improve NNS rates. This means that compared with the present CBO baseline budget scenario, the proposal involves fiscal tightening of 3.9 percent of GDP, an enormous amount. Negative fiscal shocks of this magnitude, if placed on the economy abruptly, would very likely create recession and cyclical unemployment, and be self-defeating in lowering revenues automatically. Most macroeconomists figure that the negative fiscal shocks must be much more gradual.

This of course leaves open the economic question of just what is the optimal path back to responsible fiscal policy: How much fiscal austerity can a country bear in a year? Can fiscal austerity be compensated by monetary policy changes? Should the pace of austerity be varied according to cyclical phenomena? Can flexible austerity plans be written into overall deficit constraint legislation? Each of these issues raises a host of economic and political issues.

On the negative side, there were at least three problems with the 1992 proposal. First, the measure omitted taxes (Section 4). As said earlier, cutting fiscal policy by 3.9 percent of GDP represents an enormous cut in government spending. Why overconstrain the system by leaving some valuable fiscal responses off the table? Tax increases are likely to be necessary to bring budgets into balance. Certain tax increases (perhaps a gas tax or taxation of social security as if it were a private pension) might

183

be among the most economically efficient or equitable ways to correct deficits; they should be studied carefully, and it would certainly seem unwise to prevent tax increases constitutionally.

The tax question has come to be of almost religious political importance in the United States. The rule of thumb is that no politician can get elected swearing anything but rigid adherence to a no-tax pledge. This is in the face of poll results suggesting that most voters expect tax increases to be necessary to balance the budget, and experiential results that tax increases usually have been part of budget-balance packages at both the state and federal level. Why the disjoint? Why can taxes be so unimportant in Barro's (1989) economic theory and so important in practical politics? Is it true that taxes control expenditures, so that tax changes do not result in deficit changes (von Furstenberg, Green, and Jeong, 1986)?

Second, the measure did not exempt tangible federal investment. Present low levels of tangible federal investment are relevant, because some day this type of investment may loom larger. If so, it directly adds to the nation's capital stock and should in principle be exempted from a BBA.

But this investment question raises all the economic and political issues discussed earlier: How can investment be defined economically? What political constraints should be imposed on voting on investment? What checks are there on politicians' ability to avoid budget constraints by changing definitions of intrinsically arbitrary concepts?

Third, the measure constrained flows instead of stocks (Section 1). As said earlier, the genius of many state BBAs is that they do not in fact constrain flows. They let flows respond to and stabilize business cycles, while constraining fiscal policy in the long run through a limitation on stocks. Why not do likewise at the national level?

States enforce their stock limitation both by borrowing from their unemployment trust funds and by creating rainy day funds and allowing governments to draw these down. Given the large stock of outstanding federal debt, at the national level it would make more sense to enforce stock constraints through the existing federal debt limit. If low NNS rates are adjudged to be the key problem, and since NNS rates depend on budget deficits, the BBA should be written according to the maximum standard referred to earlier – that is, to prevent the outstanding debt from rising beyond some definite level once the amendment takes effect. If on the other hand, the country were only interested in constraining the interest drift, not NNS rates, the BBA could be written in terms of debt burden ratios, raising a whole new set of issues on how national output should be measured.

The politics of budget deficit control

RESEARCH QUESTIONS

This journey through the politics and economics of deficit control raises a number of research questions for both disciplines. For economists the prominent issues involve the most effective way to alter NNS, by added public or private saving, along with the general role of national saving and capital accumulation in the growth process. For political scientists the prominent issues involve the role of natural checks and different political structures in the deficit-control process.

I will not elaborate on these disciplinary questions, but instead focus on a list of prominent research questions that have clear policy relevance and that involve *both* economics and politics.

• The politics and economics of Ricardian equivalence. The basic economic question is reasonable well known – do private households in fact offset movements in government fiscal policy by changes in private saving (Bernheim, 1987; Barro, 1989)? There is an equally important, but much less commonly discussed, political question. If households do offset fiscal changes by changes in private saving, indicating that current taxes do not matter much to them, why do taxes seem to be so important politically? Why are there antitax candidates? Why are taxes viewed as death-wish political issues? Why is there so much fuss about the T-word?

• The causality of Ricardian equivalence. The standard economist's view is that households respond to government fiscal policy. But why should that be? Why should people vote for politicians who do one thing, and then be forced to respond to that thing? Why don't they make their private saving decisions and choices of representatives to set public saving simultaneously? Perhaps the answer is that households are entirely in control of their personal finances and only remotely in control of their representatives and the political behavior of those representatives. But that supposition is testable, and it and other such suppositions should be tested.

• How can spending be controlled? Past research (Fiorina, 1981; Shepsle and Weingast, 1981) has focused on appropriated spending, spending that benefits a small group of users where logrolling is possible. Nowadays, entitlement spending is much more important, and this type of spending has very different characteristics. The spending benefits very large groups of users, and any logrolling would have to be of a very different sort. Is there a new form of middle-class logrolling theory that becomes relevant in today's world?

• Where were the political checks against deficits in the 1980s? Throughout history U.S. fiscal policy was reasonably responsible; in the 1980s politicians threw budgetary caution to the wind. What changed? Is this a

185

particular phenomenon of the Reagan years, or does it represent the dawn of a new era of fiscal profligacy? Is there any feasible way to return to the older politics of deficit reduction now that the country has experienced the enormous costs of a decade of large-scale deficit spending? Will the country naturally return to the older politics of deficit reduction now that it has experienced these costs?

• What role has divided government played in the process? Both political scientists (Crain and Ekelund, 1978; Alt and Lowry, 1992) and economists (Poterba, 1992) find divided government to be a significant factor determining budget policy. Why? Does this imply that the congressional or bicameral form of government is not as effective in controlling fiscal policy? Will President Clinton be able to succeed where Republican presidents have failed because the control of both the executive and legislative branches rests in the hands of one party. Is the foreign experience with parliamentary forms of government all that much better?

• Was there a role for the democratizing House of Representatives reforms of the 1970s? Did democratization mean that the natural leaders of the House, such as the Speaker, had their power diluted so much that they could not control the troops and stamp out logrolling or the growth of middle-class entitlements?

• Have deficit constraints worked? How did GRH and the BEA fare and why? Would stronger or different provisions have the desired effect of forcing deficit-cutting negotiations or the undesireable effect of encouraging cheating and gimmicks? Would a constitutional limit on the stock of outstanding public debt, similar to that advocated by Buchanan and Wagner (1977) and Niskanen (1992), work at the national level when the present legislative limit is so notoriously unsuccessful?

• Are the state constitutional restrictions really that significant, or do they work because bond-rating agencies stand behind ready to lower credit ratings when state fiscal policy becomes less responsible? What is the historical record of the states? Are there examples of state constitutional changes that led to fiscal policy changes, hence, giving more direct evidence from the states?

• Will official federal capital budgets help or hurt the deficit control process? On the plus side, if deficit constraints really lower public investment, perhaps a more precise set of constraints would permit more government investment and less government consumption. On the minus side, perhaps capital budgets just introduce one more possibility for political mischief, this time undermining attempts to bring all public spending under more effective political controls.

• How can the transition path be managed? Federal deficits are so large now that few macroeconomists want to eliminate them abruptly. But gradual elimination of deficits takes time and may be more difficult because there has to be a nonconstitutional transition stage. Designing rules for this stage will preoccupy lawyers, economists, accountants, and perhaps others as well. Can research offer any guidance on transitional policies or restrictions?

• What about carrots and sticks? President Clinton is being beseiged with advice for a two-part fiscal package – the first part is fiscal stimulus followed by the hard medicine of deficit reduction. For contemporaneous tax changes, that approach has often worked well. But for long-term budget strategies, there is a potentially serious timing problem. The Congress may be happy to give out carrots now, recognizing that they may never have to bring out the sticks. Precisely this happened with GRH – difficult deficit targets were either eliminated or delayed – and it is hard to imagine what will change this most basic political impulse. Is there any feasible way to combine carrots and sticks in a phased deficit-reduction strategy?

This list could go on and on. Perhaps the deepest mystery about U.S. fiscal policy is why the country has not always had a serious deficit problem. The U.S. government can apparently borrow almost endlessly without short-run economic costs and short- or long-run political costs. It took policy makers many years to wake up to this anomaly, but once they finally did in the 1980s, interest burdens accumulated rapidly and made it ever harder to change course. In contrast to previous budgetary discussions, the future is beginning to look frightening, and there are real costs to further delay in solving the nation's budget problems. The election of President Clinton ended the divided government, but it remains to be seen whether unified government can significantly alter fiscal policy. Research on the economics and politics of deficit control would easily pay for itself if it could help illuminate the situation – and pay for itself many times over if it could help change the situation.

APPENDIX A:
TEXT OF THE PROPOSAL ON A BALANCED BUDGET

Resolved by the Senate and House of Representatives of the United States of America in Congress assembled (two-thirds of each House concurring therein), that the following article is proposed as an amendment to the Constitution of the United States, which shall be valid to all intents and purposes as part of the Constitution if ratified by the legislatures of three-fourths of the several States within seven years after its submission to the States for ratification:

SECTION 1. Total outlays for any fiscal year shall not exceed total receipts for that fiscal year, unless three-fifths of the whole number of each House of Congress shall provide by law for a specific excess of outlays over receipts by a rollcall vote.

SECTION 2. The limit on the debt of the United States held by the public shall not be increased, unless three-fifths of the whole number of each House shall provide by law for such an increase by a roll-call vote.

SECTION 3. Prior to each fiscal year, the President shall transmit to the Congress a proposed budget for the United States Government for that fiscal year, in which total outlays do not exceed total receipts.

SECTION 4. No bill to increase revenue shall become law unless approved by a majority of the whole number of each House by a roll-call vote.

SECTION 5. The Congress may waive the provisions of this article for any fiscal year in which a declaration of war is in effect. The provisions of this article may be waived for any fiscal year in which the United States is engaged in military conflict which causes an imminent and serious military threat to national security and is so declared by a joint resolution, adopted by a majority of the whole number of each House, which becomes law.

SECTION 6. The Congress shall enforce and implement this article by appropriate legislation, which may rely on estimates of outlays and receipts.

SECTION 7. Total receipts shall include all receipts of the United States Government except those derived from borrowing. Total outlays shall include all outlays of the United States Government except for those for repayment of debt principal.

SECTION 8. This article shall take effect beginning with fiscal year 1998 or with the second fiscal year beginning after its ratification, whichever is later.

The above is the text of the proposed constitutional amendment on a balanced budget, sponsored by Representative Charles W. Stenholm, Democrat of Texas, and cosponsored by 277 of his House colleagues.

NOTES

1. Most but not all. One school of thought led by Barro (1989) argues the Ricardian equivalence point that whatever the level of deficits, private saving will offset the budget changes and there will be no change in national saving. Another school led by Eisner (1989) argues that once one corrects for public capital formation and inflation, deficits are not dangerously high (though they did rise in the 1980s). Another school led by Kotlikoff (1992) argues that deficits are so meaningless they should be ignored and replaced by calculations of fiscal flows for people of different ages. But while Kotlikoff does not take deficits seriously, he does take the drop in national saving seriously. Previously (1989) I have taken on all of these dissenting views.

2. On a more technical level, Summers (1986) and Boskin (1988) give evidence that the long-run private saving offset is from 20 to 40 percent of the deficit change. See also Bernheim (1991).
3. Fitts and Inman (1992) also analyze the role of presidential leadership in the process, and Keech (1985) provides a good literature survey.
4. It is commonly felt that asset sales improve this year's budgetary picture at the expense of the future. In fact, their impact on the future is approximately neutral, because the proceeds of asset sales can be used to pay off the government's outstanding debt and save on interest payments, while the sales themselves cut interest repayments by about the same amount.
5. Grants to states and localities for capital purposes might seem like capital grants, but in general they do not work that way. These grants only subsidize spending up to some limit: hence, at the margin they are not price subsidies, they are not likely to encourage much added capital spending, and the grants themselves should not be treated as capital outlays.

REFERENCES

Alt, James E., and Robert C. Lowry, 1992. "Divided Government and Budget Deficits: Evidence from the States," Harvard University mimeo.

Aranson, Peter A. 1983. "Public Deficits in Normative Economic and Positive Political Theory," In L. H. Meyer (ed.), *The Economic Consequences of Government Deficits.* Boston: Kluwer-Nijhoff, pp. 157–82.

Barro, Robert J. 1989. "The Ricardian Approach to Budget Deficits," *Journal of Economic Perspectives,* vol. 3, no. 2, pp. 37–54.

Bernheim, B. Douglas. 1989. "A Neoclassical Perspective on Budget Deficits," *Journal of Economic Perspectives,* vol. 3, no. 2, pp. 55–74.

———. 1991. *The Vanishing Nest Egg: Reflections on Saving in America.* New York: Twentieth Century Fund.

Boskin, Michael J. 1988. "Alternative Measures of Government Deficits and Debt and Their Impact on Economic Activity," in K. J. Arrow and M. J. Boskin (eds.), *Economics of Public Debt.* New York: Macmillan, pp. 72–112.

Buchanan, James, and Richard E. Wagner. 1977. *Democracy in Deficit.* New York: Academic Press.

Burtless, Gary, and Wayne Vroman. 1984. "The Performance of Unemployment Insurance Since 1979," *Industrial Relations Research Association Series,* December.

Congressional Budget Office. 1992. *The Economic and Budget Outlook: Fiscal Years 1993–1997.* Washington.

Crain, W. M., and R. B. Ekelund Jr. 1978. "Deficits and Democracy," *Southern Economic Journal,* vol. 44, pp. 813–28.

Eisner, Robert. 1989. "Budget Deficits: Rhetoric and Reality," *Journal of Economic Perspectives,* vol. 3, no. 2, pp. 73–93.

Fiorina, Morris P. 1981. "Universalism, Reciprocity, and Disruptive Policymaking in Majority Rule Institutions," *Research in Public Policy Analysis and Management,* vol 1, pp. 197–221.

Fitts, Michael, and Robert Inman. 1992. "Controlling Congress: Presidential Influence in Domestic Fiscal Policy," *Georgetown Law Journal,* vol. 80, no. 5, pp. 1737–85.

Gold, Steven D. 1992. "State Government Experience with Balanced Budget

Requirements: Relevance to Federal Proposals," Testimony before the U.S. House Budget Committee, May 13.

Gramlich, Edward M. 1987. "Subnational Fiscal Policy," in J. E. Quigley (ed.), *Perspectives on Local Public Finance and Public Policy.* Greenwich, Ct: JAI, vol. 3, pp. 3–28.

———. 1989. "Budget Deficits and National Saving: Are Politicians Exogenous?" *Journal of Economic Perspectives,* vol. 3, no. 2, pp. 23–36.

———. 1990. "U.S. Federal Budget Deficits and Gramm–Rudman–Hollings,'/ *American Economic Review,* vol. 80, no. 2, pp. 75–80.

———. 1991. "The 1991 State and Local Fiscal Crisis," *Brookings Papers on Economic Activity,* no. 2, pp. 249–75.

Hahm, Sung Deuk, Mark S. Kamlet, David C. Mowery, and Tsai-Tsu Su. 1992. "The Influence of the Gramm–Rudman–Hollings Act on Federal Budgetary Outcomes, 1986–1989," *Journal of Policy Analysis and Management,* vol. 11, no. 2, pp. 207–34.

Keech, William R. 1985. "A Theoretical Analysis of the Case for a Balanced Budget Amendment," *Policy Sciences,* vol. 18, pp. 157–68.

Kotlikoff, Laurence J. 1992. *Generational Accounting: Knowing Who Pays, and When, for What We Spend.* New York: Free Press.

McCubbins, Matthew. 1991. "Party Governance and U.S. Budget Deficits: Divided Government and Fiscal Stalemate," in A. Alesina and G. Carliner (eds.), *Economics and Politics in the 1980s.* Chicago: University of Chicago Press, pp. 83–111.

Niskanen, William A. 1992. "The Case for a New Fiscal Constitution," *Journal of Economic Perspectives,* vol. 6, no. 2, pp. 13–24.

Poterba, James M. 1992. "State Responses to Fiscal Crises: Natural Experiments for Studying the Effects of Budgetary Institutions," Natural Bureau of Economic Research mimeo.

Shepsle, Kenneth A., and Barry R. Weingast. 1981. "Political Preferences for Pork Barrel: A Generalization," *American Journal of Political Science,* vol. 25, pp. 96–111.

Summers, Lawrence H. 1986. "Issues in National Saving Policy," in G. F. Adams and S. M. Wachter (eds.), *Savings and Capital Formation.* Lexington, MA: Lexington Books, Health, pp. 65–88.

Tobin, James. 1986. "The Monetary-Fiscal Mix: Long Run Implications," *American Economic Review,* vol. 76, no. 2, pp. 213–18.

Von Furstenberg, George R., Jeffrey Green, and Jin-Ho Jeong. 1986. "Tax and Spend, or Spend and Tax," *Review of Economics and Statistics,* vol. 68, pp. 179–88.

7

Law, legislation, and positive political theory

JOHN FEREJOHN

INTRODUCTION: LEGISLATION AND LAW

The study of politics is dominated by what might be called a "legislative" view of government. In this view government proceeds largely through enacting general rules to channel social and economic conduct and then using more mundane administrative means to enforce them. This emphasis on legislation encourages us to see other institutions and practices in terms of their connection to or similarity to the legislature. Thus, electoral studies are frequently justified or motivated by their consequences for selecting lawmakers or expressing "mandates" for new laws; presidents are often seen and judged in terms of their role in the legislative process; and administrative agencies and courts are seen as quasi-legislative bodies, promulgating general rules and regulations. If the Founding Fathers were wrong to fear congressional dominance of other national institutions, they were perhaps prescient in foreseeing how the legislative model would dominate the way we have come to understand government.

This focus on legislation while, perhaps, natural enough in a democratic nation − statutes are, after all, the principal normatively sanctioned route by which public opinion is translated into public action − produces a distorted description of governmental activity. The centrality of legislative studies suggests that there is a simple relationship between statutes and the law by which we live. This premise is both unexamined and misleading and causes us to ignore the ways in which the law actually evolves, to undervalue other sources of law, and to pay very little attention to the distinctive ways in which nonlegislative institutions operate to create law as well as to enforce it.

The consequence of this ignorance is very great for the study of politics − it has led not only to the separation of legal studies from political science, but also to the fragmentation of political science itself into dis-

191

tinct positive and normative components. I think that these developments are linked. Positive theories of legislation seek to explain the passage of laws in terms of their consequences for citizens, interest groups, or legislators. This consequentialist focus tends to obscure the role of deliberation and debate in legislation.[1] Normative theorizing, whether done by law professors or political theorists, tends to ignore actual legislative processes altogether and instead evaluates legal rules either in terms of external moral standards or in terms of the internal integrity of the system of legal rules themselves. Thus, in this scholarly division of labor, positive theory concerns itself with describing and explaining the process by which legislation is produced; normative theory focuses on evaluating, criticizing, and advising the substance and practice of law.

Whatever else might be said in favor of this division, it seems impossible to engage in meaningful normative discourse – to criticize practices or give advice – without some conception of how political institutions either do or could be made to work. Without some conception of the politically possible, normative advice is inherently vulnerable to utopian impulses. Conversely, positive theorists trying to understand the behavior of political actors, who are themselves often engaged in normative deliberation, need to take some account of substantive aspects of normative reasoning, in order to understand the objectives and beliefs of the political actors whose behavior they hope to explain. Legislators, judges, and bureaucrats are all engaged in a normative enterprise – deciding how best to deploy the state's coercive authority for public purposes – and it seems not only possible but likely that their actions are sometimes explained by what they think is right or just, as well as by beliefs that contain normative elements.

I argue that we can and should reintegrate the study of law and legal reasoning with more analytic and explanatory approaches to the study of politics. I shall argue that we can begin to do this in two ways: first, by transferring some of the elements that have proved useful in legislative studies to judicial contexts. Such a transfer would permit us to see the political context within which courts operate and to identify operating characteristics of judicial institutions that parallel those of legislatures as well as those that do not. At the same time, we should consider transfers in the opposite direction, by developing models that see legislatures as engaged in deliberation and persuasion as much as in preference aggregation. I shall not pursue this line of thinking very much here because I think that recent work by Austen-Smith, Riker, Krehbiel and Gilligan, and others has already begun this vital task.

I shall argue that by identifying institutional incentive structures within which legal actors find themselves, we can learn something important about the traditional areas of law and legal reasoning. By imagining that judges have preferences both as to policies and procedures, we do not thereby commit ourselves to any particular theory as to their source and content. Such preferences may be induced by attachments to substantive or procedural public values, or they might be traceable to narrowly defined material interests. Preferences, however they are constructed, may have mathematical properties that arise from the processes that give rise to them,[2] but there is no a priori reason to think that they cannot be tractable elements of analytical models.

I argue, therefore, that we can begin to "get behind" judicial preferences by using to advantage what we can know about the institutional structures that surround them as well as by taking seriously their normative substance.[3] This activity will involve paying attention to and even doing some of the things that normative theorists and law professors do, which are themselves sometimes pretty close to what judges do as well.

SOURCES OF LAW

Legislative statutes are an important part of the law, but they are not coextensive with it.[4] Many nonstatutory legal materials – agency rules, and executive orders, for example – bear a formulaic resemblance to statutory commands, while having a different pedigree. Others, such as judicial rulings, common law doctrines, and interpretive principles appear to be more inchoate and difficult to see as general rules. The diversity of legal "texts" not only is characteristic of the pluralistic historical and geographical origins of U.S. law, but is a feature of any legal system, and especially any that recognize legislative commands as a source of law.

It is no surprise that the body of legal commands, emerging as it does from so many diverse sources, is both incomplete and contradictory, as well as of uncertain relevance to any particular dispute.[5] This is why interpretation is central to law. In approaching a dispute, a court must interpret the available legal materials to determine if it has the authority to attempt to resolve the question and, if legal authority exists, to determine what the law requires. The resolution of a dispute therefore requires a court to find ways of filling in gaps and resolving contradictions in received legal materials. Courts engaged in gap filling typically employ canons, methodologies, and doctrines for orchestrating legal sources and applying them to the facts of particular disputes. Because legal materials are so disparate, these "interpretive conventions" can exercise a powerful effect on the substantive content of law and for that reason can be deeply controversial.

We may distinguish two main lines of theoretical controversy regarding the role of interpretive practices in law. Some legal scholars regard interpretive methods as potentially binding on outcomes and object that some of the interpretive canons and methodologies are impermissibly biased for or against certain outcomes. For example, the ancient canon that "statutes in derogation of the common law should be narrowly construed" might be thought to limit the power of democratically elected legislatures. Indeed, one could claim the main effect of the "revolution" of 1937 – a series of rulings in which the Supreme Court abandoned its view that constitutional protection of private property precluded many New Deal regulatory statutes – was to force the court to discard this canon, at least in broad areas of economic regulatory legislation, and perhaps replace it with another: "remedial statutes are to be broadly construed."

Other commentators argue that the canons and other metarules are themselves internally contradictory and cannot be binding on outcomes at all. These scholars regard such canons as (mere) rhetorical devices that are used to justify decisions reached on other grounds.[6] Indeed, many of the most influential strands of twentieth-century legal scholarship argue that judges can reach any decision they want using extant doctrinal materials and methods. These "legal realists" – so called because they trace judicial decisions to exogenous (real) sources outside of the body of legal materials – differ in their conceptions of what shapes judicial preferences. The various schools of legal realists see judges as acting on a range of motivations from personal policy preferences, class interests, internally held moral views, and community interests to reflective views of the good life.

While the many forms of legal realism differ greatly in their accounts of judicial preferences, all are reacting to what we shall call "legal formalism," the view that judges are constrained both in how they decide and in what outcomes they can reach by legal materials and interpretive doctrines. Legal formalists see judges as trying to find out what the law requires in the particular disputes that they must decide. They see judicial deliberation as the process by which judges and lawyers try to persuade each other that the law requires this or that particular holding in a case in view of the structure and content of received legal materials.[7] The operative principles of formalist reasoning are consistency, coherence, and stability, rather than any reference to external standards of justice or equity, and certainly without reference to external political or economic forces. It is striking to me that even though it is regularly subjected to the onslaughts of legal realists, legal formalism never seems to die and that each new generation of law professors feels the need to attack it. This leads me to think that there is something true about formalism, that important aspects of law are endogenous to the legal system itself, and that there is something constraining about legal reasoning and doctrine.

If, or insofar as, the formalists are right, legal institutions are not just like any other institutions, but they have some special characteristics that we need to understand.[8] While I cannot confidently enumerate these characteristics, it seems clear that the requirement that judges interpret diverse legal materials in deciding cases is central to their nature and to their method. That courts are engaged in interpreting legal materials and that they have found it useful to develop systematic and communicable methods of interpretation would seem to place limits on the kinds of outcomes that they can achieve. We might call this the "formalist hypothesis."

Whatever special features are shared by legal institutions, however, I think it likely that many of the features of more distinctly political institutions like legislatures will be operative as well. We may call this the "the institutional realist" hypothesis. To say this is not to deny that legal discourse and reasoning is confining, but it is to say that the incentive structures induced by institutional arrangements and policy preferences might carry over to the legal setting as well, even if they may more often be defeated or trumped in that setting. That incentives carry across domains is probably the kernel of truth in any of the realist views of law; that they do not invariably prevail seems the essential insight of formalism; that both views have a fair amount of truth probably accounts for the fact that neither seems to disappear. I shall take it as given, for the purposes of this essay, that the formalists are right to say that doctrine is constraining in some way and that it is our task to begin to find out how this could be so.

INTERPRETATION AND LAW

Legal reasoning is "interpretive" in two fundamental senses: A court confronts a particular dispute with its particular "facts" and must first determine what acts occurred and why. For example, given that someone died, the court must determine whether a homicide occurred (was the victim killed as a result of someone's intentional action or was the death the result of an accident?). Finding some sequence of events to constitute an action entails first finding intentionality – that the event in question was partly brought about by the purposiveful action of an agent – and attributing certain kinds of intentions to an agent: A murder can be said to have occurred only if some agent intended harm to another.

Second, courts must interpret received legal materials issuing from various "authorities" – courts, agencies, legislatures, community morality – in light of a particular dispute to determine what the law permits or requires in the current case. The task of legal interpretation is to construct general legal rules from the texts in such a way that particular disputes

195

can be brought under them. A court decides a case by finding or creating a general rule with an appropriately interpreted scope that covers the instant dispute, and demonstrating that apparently conflicting legal rules have sufficiently narrow scopes that they do not reach this particular dispute. Legal interpretation, therefore, results simultaneously in the construction of rules (including their scopes) and in the resolution of disputes.

It is important to emphasize that, however much the legislature might wish to limit judicial discretion, legal interpretation is unavoidable. This is so for several reasons. First, the particular dispute before the court may not have been explicitly contemplated by the formulators of the legal text: Statutes have "gaps." Statute makers in the early nineteenth century may not have anticipated the invention of the automobile or the telephone. Second, key terms in a statute may have changed "ordinary" meanings since the text was adopted. Third, there may be unresolved conflicts among statutory provisions that come to light when a particular dispute arises. Fourth, constitutional expectations as to what may be done through statutes as opposed to other means may shift over time. Fifth, a statute exists among other statutes and other legal sources, and there will be gaps and conflicts between statutes and other legal materials just as there are within statutes.

Finally, from a more political viewpoint, we must recognize that statutes issuing from a legislative assembly are not simple commands aimed at achieving a particular purpose. Statutes are composed of sets of provisions that could appear for all sorts of distinct, contextually specific reasons whose relation to any particular subsequent dispute is problematic. Various elements of a statute might, for example, have the purposes of expressing condemnation or approval of some behavior, of targeting a payoff on some interest group whose support was needed to enact the legislation, as well as the more mundane purpose of regulating or encouraging some forms of behavior through the application of the state's coercive forces.

INTERPRETING STATUTES

The various approaches to legal interpretation differ primarily in terms of what would count as a good explanation of a statute. Some approaches attempt to explain a legal text by finding or attributing *intentions* to its authors and argue that the meaning of a statute can be found by determining what the authors either intended or would have intended in the particular dispute.[9] We can distinguish two variants of intentionalism. Intentional realists are committed to determining preexisting intentions

196

held by the actors. Intentional instrumentalists attribute intentions to agents to account for the words and structure of the statute (and perhaps other documents as well) without assuming that these intentions were actually held by anyone. Intentional realism sees the words in the statutes as causally determined by the intentions of the drafters. Intentional instrumentalists are agnostic as to causation; they say only that one could explain the statute by attributing intentions of a certain sort to the drafters.

Another approach sees statutes (or major titles) as having *purposes* and proceeds to explain the text (and possibly other materials) by reference to these underlying purposes. Purposivism would claim that a case falls within a statute if it is covered by its purpose.[10] As with intentionalism, we can distinguish realist and instrumentalist forms of purposivism. Both intentional and purposive realist approaches can be seen as intrinsically *originalist* in that the circumstances under which a statute is drafted, the intentions and purposes held by the legislators who enacted it, are considered germane to its interpretation. Origninalism invites the use of techniques of historical reconstruction to help interpret the law. Such techniques often draw extensively on nonstatutory materials – floor debates, committee reports, sponsor statements, and the like – to assist in finding intent or purpose. How these sources are used depends in their evidentiary value in uncovering the actual intents and purposes of the drafters.

Instrumental approaches to interpretation, while they cannot be intrinsically originalist, may adopt a form of conventional originalism. Such a view might employ historical reconstructions of statutes not on the ground that the drafters intentions enjoy any normative privilege, but instead on the ground that having such conventions helps settle actual disputes. Instrumentalists typically rely on what we might call theoretical techniques for attributing intentions or purposes. Some of these theoretical methods are embodied in conventional interpretive practices of the sort that we discuss later. Others involve the explicit use of either philosophical or social scientific theories.

A *textualist* approach to interpretation relies exclusively on the language of statutes in interpreting what the law requires in a particular case. A strict version of textualism is distinguished by a refusal to extend the force of legislative agreements to areas not explicitly dealt with in the particular statute. Strict textualists regard statutes as explicit political settlements that happened to win legislative approval at a particular time, and interpret those statutes as having bearing only on those cases that "clearly" fall under them. Strict textualists refuse to use either historical construction or theoretical attributions to extend the reach of statutes into new domains.[11]

We may identify another textual approach that sees the text of a statute as the most reliable way or perhaps the only reliable way to determine the intentions or purposes of the legislature that enacted the statute. Such an approach would eschew the use of nonstatutory materials for interpreting statutes on the ground that they did not gain the approval of legislative majorities and may have been produced by biased sources (staffs, lobbyists, partisans, etc.). But this kind of textualist might be willing to use other techniques of reasoning and construction (e.g., canons of construction, use of dictionary meanings) to interpret law to cover new cases.

We can illustrate these interpretive approaches by considering a dispute about a contract. One way that a court might try to resolve a contractual dispute is by determining what the parties would have agreed to had the particular problem been anticipated at the time the contract was negotiated. Alternatively, a court might calculate what prudent or rational contractors would agree to in such a contingency (no matter what the particular contractors would have agreed to). Both of these approaches to contractual interpretation might be called intentionalist, but the first is based on a contemplation of the current parties to the bargain and what they intended when the contract was made, whereas the second is based on what might be called a hypothetical or "rational man" construction.[12]

A purposive court might ask what the point or purpose of the contract was and then decide the instant case in terms consistent with this underlying purpose. If courts view the purpose of contracting as allowing the parties to arrange their transaction efficiently, remedies for failures to perform should be set in a way that allows only ex post efficient promises to be performed, even if the actual contracting parties made no explicit agreement of this sort. Courts might, in effect, adopt "default" rules in contractual settings that induce efficient levels of contractual performance. Of course, if the contract explicitly specified inefficient remedies for performance failure, a court might be bound to enforce its terms, but absent such an agreement, the court would set remedies to induce efficiency.

Finally, a strict textualist court might refuse to enforce anything not found within the explicit terms or plain meaning of the contract. An originalist form of textualism might be unwilling to employ materials outside the contract in its interpretation but might be willing to use contractual language to attribute either intentions or purpose to the contractors.

To see how these ideas apply to statutes consider the principal opinions in *Weber v. Kaiser Steel*, in which the Court permitted the adoption of voluntary affirmative plans. In that case Brian Weber, a white steelworker who was denied admission to a training program under Kaiser Steel's affirmative action plan argued that that plan was illegal under Sections 703(a), 703(d), and 703(j) of the 1964 Civil Rights Act. Section 703(a) of

Title VII makes it an unlawful employment practice "to discriminate against any individual" because of his or her "race, color, religion, sex, or national origin."[13] Section 703(d) extends this prohibition to apprenticeship programs. Finally, section 703(j) says that nothing in Title VII "shall be interpreted to require any employer"[14] to prefer one racial group over another in order to correct a racial imbalance in the employer's work force.

Writing for the majority, Justice Brennan argued that the purpose of Title VII was remedial – it was supposed to improve the position of groups that had previously suffered discrimination – and that the specific language of 703(j) could not be read to *prohibit* private employers from voluntarily adopting affirmative action plans to achieve the purposes of the title. Had Congress intended to do that, it could have written 703(j) to prohibit such plans. In his dissent, Justice Rehnquist argued that the purpose of Title VII was to achieve a society in which employment decisions were made in a color-blind manner and that affirmative action plans, whether voluntarily adopted or not, were inconsistent with that purpose.[15] Moreover, he argued from the legislative history (specifically the statement of various senators during the floor debate) that the intent of Congress was to make such plans illegal.

Brennan and Rehnquist each employed purposive methods to justify their conclusions. Both referred extensively to the legislative history to try to establish what the purposes of the act were; in this respect they both would seem committed to a realist conception of purpose. But when all is said and done, they both presented relatively little actual evidence in favor of their perferred purposes: Very few congresspeople actually said anything relevant to the question and those that did didn't all agree with each other. To conclude anything from the spoken record both justices needed to invoke controversial theoretical ideas such as silence implies assent, or that certain things were just understood by everyone. In the end both Brennan and Rehnquist were forced to make heroic interpretive leaps to reach strong conclusions as to the actual purpose of the title. In this sense, in spite of realist appearances, the lack of compelling evidence forced both justices to an instrumentalist conception of purpose: The title and the whole act (together with the legislative history) simply make most sense when read in terms of one or the other imputed purpose.

While both Brennan's and Rehnquist's opinions are purposive – affirmative action plans are either to be permitted or prohibited based on attribution of a purpose to the title – both were also concerned to show that their conclusions are sustainable in light of the specific textual language of the various parts of Title VII. Brennan employed a canon of construction (*inclusio unius:* the inclusion of a thing implies the exclusion of others) to conclude from the fact that 703(j) does not explicitly forbid such plans that Congress must have wished to permit them. Rehnquist concluded from floor colloquys and sponsor statements, which seemed either not to contemplate or actually to oppose affirmative action plans of the sort subsequently adopted by Kaiser, that Congress intended 703(j) to prohibit such plans (in effect, giving a purposive reading to 703(j)). Again, while the historical reconstructions carried out by the justices suggests a realist commitment, the scarcity of relevant evidence leads both to conclusions that can best be justified on instrumentalist grounds.

It is important to see that each of these interpretive approaches attempts to reach normative conclusions based on a construction of the legislative "contract." Each proceeds by giving a positive theory of the contract or statute and showing that its resolution of the particular dispute follows directly from that theory. Judicial action is shown to be automatic and nondiscretionary. Each approach takes the *form* of legal formalism. It is possible to believe – indeed, for many observers it is impossible not to believe – that it was Brennan's liberalism and Rehnquist's conservativism that actually drove their respective views on the case. But, whether that is true or not, both justices felt compelled to adopt a version of formalist reasoning that connected their opinions to the legislative statute. Moreover, the extent to which their arguments were persuasive to others might be partly explained by these appeals.

In a way, judicial attempts to reduce normative commands to factual claims about contracts and statutes are unsurprising. Courts have to make decisions in cases where legal sources are vague, conflicting, or nonexistent, and judges nowadays do not feel able to claim the right to make law. In addition, the political and moral authority of judges within a democratic system are always in question, so perhaps it is not startling that courts go to great lengths to conceal the nonstatutory bases of judicial commands, or at least to show how it is that their commands can be justified in relation to commands issued by institutions with the lawmaking authority.

INTERPRETATION AND THEORIES OF LEGISLATION

We emphasize that each of the prominent interpretive approaches rests on a specific conception of what legal materials are and how and why they were produced. In the case of statutes, each rests on a theory of the legislature. But whereas the originalist variants of the approaches are based on what might be called a realist conception of the legislature – legislative intent and purpose are conceived as genuine properties of the enacting legislature – nonoriginalist versions are grounded in more theoretical or instrumentalist notions.

Law, legislation, and positive political theory

The use of terms such as "purpose" and "intent" predictably triggers reactions by those of us who do positive political theory. How can we speak of the "purpose" of a statute independently of the desires and expectations of those who drafted and enacted it? "What," we ask, "is the intention of a collective body anyway?" and recognizing that any acceptable notion of collective intention may be quite badly behaved, "How could it help us to resolve legal disputes?" Moreover, even if there were an acceptable conception of legislative intent, some theorists question actual interpretive practices, such as the use of legislative history materials to determine what this intent is. Why should we think that committee reports (or sponsor statements, etc.) reflect the intentions of those who drafted, amended (or chose not to amend), or voted for the bill?

These questions, while they may be important from certain viewpoints, have distracted us from understanding the uses of intent and purpose in law and legal reasoning. Social scientists are inclined to see legislative intent in the same way that they see individual intentional states such as preference or belief. Such states are often thought of as actual mental states that can be revealed through action. The theory of social choice tells us that legislative intent, so construed, may have some very strange properties. It may not exist in many cases and exhibit a good deal of incoherence when it does. In either case, such conceptions of intent (and purpose) would not generally be of much assistance in resolving disputes in a lawlike or regular fashion. Rather than assuming that judges and legal scholars are actually using a psychological conception of intent in statutory interpretation, it seems better to pay attention to the way such notions are employed in legal reasoning.

Many sophisticated legal commentators employ what we have called "intentionalist" or "purposivist" methodologies in interpreting statutory texts. We shall take as examples the work of Ronald Dworkin and Frank Easterbrook, two important legal thinkers who otherwise differ greatly in their approach to legal and political issues. Dworkin's view of law emphasizes its "normativity" – that it is a system of obligations that people are expected to fulfill. It is because law makes normative claims on our actions that courts and legislatures should treat "integrity" as a fundamental value of law. "Integrity demands that the public standards of the community be both made and seen, so far as this is possible, to express a single, coherent scheme of justice and fairness in the right relation." Integrity requires of the legislature that it refrain from enacting piecemeal or "checkerboard" patterns of law (which include logrolling and private bargains), but attempt instead (where it does not conflict with other values) to produce a coherent pattern of legislation that could be construed as flowing from a single will. Integrity perhaps requires even more

201

of courts acting as interpreters of legislation. A court guided by integrity will think that litigants "are entitled, in principle, to have their acts and affairs judged in accordance with the best view of what the legal standards of the community required or permitted at the time they acted, and integrity demands that these standards be seen as coherent, as the state speaking with a single voice."[16]

Easterbrook too, while noting that the idea of a genuine collective purpose is incoherent on Arrovian grounds, endorses a form of (instrumental) purposive analysis that he attributes to Oliver Wendell Holmes. For Easterbrook (and Holmes), the question is not what purpose the legislature had but what purpose a user of those (English language) words in the statute, with their ordinary meanings, could be deemed to have meant. He argues against a historical construction of the legislative situation (arguing that it would lead to incoherent readings anyway) and in favor of a "reasonable" or "prudent" person's construction of the statute's provisions.[17]

While they embrace very different methodologies, Dworkin's and Easterbrook's views might both be placed in the legal process tradition of Hart and Sacks (1958), who argued that we (judges and commentators) should "construe" statutes as having purposes and construe their provisions as bearing some relation to this purpose. For Hart and Sacks, legislative intentions and purposes are not located "in" the statute, but are interpretive constructions or attributions made by courts, agencies, and private parties. For example, the constructed purpose of antitrust law (economic efficiency) might have no connection with the intentions held by those who enacted the Sherman or Clayton Acts (who were probably primarily concerned to protect certain small businesses from large firms), but might instead be that of ensuring that markets operate competitively.

You might ask, "By what right do judges make such a construction of a statute?" I think that, ultimately, for these commentators a satisfactory answer has to come from a normative assessment of what "law" is and why it has authority for us. For both Dworkin and Easterbrook, for example, construing the purpose of antitrust statutes as small business protection would make of them mere rent-seeking ordinances unworthy of judicial respect. Seeing antitrust law, instead, as guided by the pursuit of economic efficiency, permits judges to construe it in terms of a genuinely public purpose: that of improving the economic welfare of the community.[18]

POLITICS AND INTERPRETATION

There are several noteworthy aspects to the description of traditional forms of legal interpretation presented here. First, each involves an interpretive "triangle": producer of the text (legislature, common-law courts), text (statute, previous court decisions), reader of the text (courts, agencies, citizens). Second, the reader of the text has information at a level (the facts of the particular case) unavailable to its producer. Third, and this is the point of various literary approaches to law, systematic shifts in context can effectively shape what the "law" is by systematically shifting legal outcomes, without any change in the "text."[19] The effect of this description is to separate the application of law from the making of it and to show that legal reasoning is at least partly autonomous from the production of law.

I think the traditional triangular view of law as interpretation can be distorting in two senses: First, lawmakers can and sometimes do "talk back" authoritatively, in order to correct judicial interpretations. In this sense, law operates in a political context that is richer than that captured by the triangular model of interpretation. Second, authorship of legal texts (which are made of commands and imperatives) is distinguishable from the authorship of literary texts, in that there may be reasons to obey only legitimate statutory commands, where legitimacy issues from their provenance (so that legal reasoning ought to be linked to the production of the text in the way that literary interpretation need not be). Thus, within a democratic society, an acceptable interpretation of a statute might depend on a positive theory of what actually happened in the legislature that produced the text. None of this is to say that the context of application does not matter; but it may not matter as powerfully in the case of legal texts as in the case of artistic ones. We may say, in effect, that the triangular model of interpretation overlooks both the reality of power and the special authority of legislative commands.

The point of these criticisms of the traditional interpretive model is not to reject it but to find a way to place it within a fundamentally political structure. In my view, this amounts to developing a conception of the political constraints within which both courts and legislatures operate, and I shall try to sketch out a primitive way of doing this in the remainder of this section. My construction relies on a very simple sequential model of legislating and judging that has the advantage of illuminating some aspects of legal interpretation that have hitherto remained veiled. It might be thought of as a model of political or institutional realism in that the constraints it places on law depend on the actual structure of political institutions. At the same time, courts are not completely constrained in this kind of model so that formalist influences retain ample scope for shaping the law.

The model employed in this discussion is one that was initially developed by Brian Marks and employed in papers by Gely and Spiller, and by Charles Shipan and myself.[20] In the spirit of these papers we assume that congresspeople and agencies have policy preferences defined in a space of alternatives, that action takes place in time, and that all of the actors attempt fully to anticipate future actions by other agents. Thus, agency actions are chosen in light of anticipated judicial and congressional responses. When Congress enacts a statute empowering an agency to take some action in the policy space, that action will stand unless overturned either in by the court or by Congress. If an agency or a court overturns an agency action, Congress may or may not enact additional legislation.

While congressional and bureaucratic actors are taken to be policy motivated in this way, we may understand judicial preferences in at least two different ways. Judges might be policy motivated like the other actors, in which case the special features of judicial action arise from the place of courts in the sequential policy-making process. Alternatively, judicial preferences might arise from some normative grounding having to do with special "duties" of judges. In a model of this sort, courts are different from other policy-making institutions on account of their preferences as well as their sequential location. It is useful to provide an illustration of this sort of model.

We may distinguish the "enacting" congress, the one that drafted the original legislation, from the "sitting" congress, which is currently in office. Because of intervening elections, these two congresses will generally have conflicting preferences. The conflict of interest between the current legislature and previous ones can be seen as one of the fundamental structures of conflict in government.[21] If either agency or court action has the effect of stimulating a congressional response, the preferences of the sitting legislature, not those of the enacting congress, are what will be reflected in the new law, and these new statutes might be very different from what the earlier legislature would have wished.

Thus, insofar as courts in particular have allegiance to statutes – that is, to the duly encoded preferences of the *enacting* congress – they should be careful to devise interpretive methods that protect statutes from contemporary political responses, and in particular do not provoke congressional responses that are very far from the statutory desires of the enacting congress.[22] Such courts would engage in what might be called "strategic jurisprudence,"[23] in that they would have to take account of the preferences of the sitting congress in interpreting statutes. Only by doing so would such courts be able to act as "sophisticated honest agents" of the enacting congress.[24]

While judges are constrained in these models, they are not directly constrained by doctrine. The constraints on their behavior comes from the preference distribution of other political actors interacting within the sequential structure. Doctrinal effects such as *stare decisis,* arise from the nonpolicy objectives (i.e., wanting law to be reliable and predictable over time) held by the judiciary. There is some striking empirical information bearing on congressional overrides,[25] which shows that in certain areas (especially civil rights) Congress has been quite active in "correcting'" judicial actions. The thrust of this work is to point to the fact that Congress can and sometimes does react to judicial actions and that judges rightly anticipate such reactions in their construction of statutes. The empirical work is useful in showing that Congress can and does react. Its significance is ambiguous in that it shows that the court seems often to make "mistakes" in particular policy areas (and not in others).

In addition to highlighting the temptation for judges, whether motivated by policy or procedural concerns, to engage in strategic interpretation, the empirical efforts in this area bring out the importance of describing judicial techniques in a systematic way. Elsewhere, William Eskridge and I have hypothesized that we may understand judicial construction in terms of what might be called an *interpretive regime* – a relatively unified body of interpretive methods that includes a conception of the appropriate role of government and a theory of the legislature, together with a variety of techniques (canons and methodologies) that are more or less consistent with it.[26]

The notion of an interpretive regime is intended to suggest that the methods of judicial interpretation in use at a particular point in time tend to have some degree of coherence or structure. This coherence might arise from the hierarchical nature of the appellate court system or perhaps from some tendency to systematization in the legal community. Whatever the source, an interpretive regime permits the coordination of legal expectations both within the legal community of judges, lawyers, and commentators, and beyond it to agencies, legislators, and ordinary citizens. This coordinating role suggests that an interpretive regime might be seen as a more or less stable convention in the same way that a language is sometimes understood. To suggest that interpretive regimes serve to stabilize expectations is not to say that there is no dispute over their content. Indeed, because they can have far-reaching political effects, these regimes are contested and, occasionally, undergo substantial change. We present some candidate interpretive regimes from twentieth-century legal history.

What is sometimes called "Lochner era jurisprudence" represents a sharply etched example of an interpretive regime: the Lochner regime regarded public intrusion in private contracting as constitutionally illegitimate,[27] adopted an instrumental intentionalist theory of legislature that treated the legislature as accepting primacy of private ordering[28] and endorsed such canons of construction that protected the common law against all but the most explicit statutory intrusions.[29]

A second candidate for an interpretive regime might be the New Deal regime, which is said to have replaced the Lochner regime after 1937.

That regime endorsed a broader role for public action, an instrumental purposive theory of legislation that treated public statutes as aimed at remedying glaring defects due to private action,[30] together with judicial techniques of statutory and constitutional construction that shielded statutorily created public agencies against judicial intrusions aimed at protecting private ordering.[31]

The interpretive regime of the Warren and Burger courts represents, perhaps, a third example of an interpretive regime. It embraced the New Deal conception of an expansive public sector while limiting state intrusions into private moral life,[32] retained a purposive view of legislation, and developed techniques for making extensive use of nonstatutory sources to establish these purposes.[33] The increasing use of such sources seems to indicate a shift in favor of realist versus instrumentalist interpretation.

More recently, the new textualist jurisprudence articulated by Justice Scalia might be seen as a candidate for a new interpretive regime. New textualists tend to endorse a more limited role for government in the economy and a correspondingly broader governmental role in community moral life,[34] a narrowly intentionalist view of the legislature,[35] and practices of construction that tend to limit the expansiveness of congressional delegations of authority to agencies.[36]

The idea of an interpretive regime highlights the importance of what we might call internal constraints on judicial action. Internal constraints arise from the incapacity of courts, responding to disputes in real time, to commit themselves to future courses of action. Judges might prefer to decide cases by developing interpretive regimes, making them publically known, and then deciding cases through the application of these rules. Such practices would be attractive to courts that desired to instill rule-of-law values since court action would be fairly predictable by other political actors as well as by ordinary citizens.

Courts, however, face a commitment problem that limits the availability of such a strategy. The Supreme Court may very well find it worthwhile to announce a policy that would constrain its future acts – perhaps the *Chevron*[37] decision might be a good example of this – but why would it feel bound by that constraint in future decisions, if alternative courses of aciton were then to seem preferable? Speaking just of *Chevron,* we can certainly find legal scholars who doubt that this decision actually represents a credible constraint on the Court and who can point to cases, like the recent *Aramco* decision, where the defenders of *Chevron* had little trouble evading its principle.[38]

Once we recognize the flexibility of interpretive methods, we must ask if interpretive regimes – formalist doctrinal structures – actually limit court discretion. At this level of thinking, it is hard to find a satisfactory answer. Decisions respecting precedent in the face of powerful reasons to decide otherwise are usually (always) justified on grounds of rule-of-law values such as stability and legitimate reliance. People, it is said, need to plan their lives based on an understanding or prediction of the law, so precedent may be overturned only where it has not evoked much reliance or where there is an overwhelmingly public purpose that would be served by disturbing settled expectations.

Stability in law is taken by courts to be a fundamental value of law and is a reason for upholding even bad laws at times (depending on how bad these laws are). The opinions in the recent *Casey* decision (in which the Court permitted some state regulation of the provision of abortion services) might be a example of this, but my favorite is the *Curt Flood* case in which the court declined to overturn baseball's reserve clause in spite of what were acknowledged to be very powerful but not overwhelming economic reasons for doing so.

But even if courts usually act in ways that maintain legal stability, they are faced frequently with the opportunity and incentive to make opportunistic decisions. This is not to say that they don't try to maintain stability or that they don't often succeed. The point is that doctrinal elements are always vulnerable to "reneging" and that this fact represents what we might call an internal constraint on judicial decision making: Doctrinal principles would seem to vary in how sustainable they can be in the face of incentives to renege and this fact may help explain what kinds of principles could be doctrines.

It seems to me, therefore, that the techniques of positive political theory offer a systematic way to begin to understand both internal and external constraints on judicial action, and, just as importantly, the ways that they interact with one another. We take up some of these issues in the conclusion.

CONCLUSION: COMPARATIVE LAW AND LEGAL HISTORY

The approach taken in this essay might best be called institutional neorealism. It recognizes realist or externalist influences on the structure of law, but those influences are filtered through formal institutional structures. Moreover, such external influences might, in certain circumstances, include the kinds of economic, cultural, or social forces spoken of in other varieties of legal realism. The circumstances under which one or another sort of external influence can exercise a shaping influence on law are themselves endogenous and mediated by institutional structures: the organization of the electoral system, the structure of the legislature, the form of parties and the party system, and the like.

However, while external forces can shape law, institutional neorealism emphasizes that law and legal reasoning can be autonomous under certain quite general conditions. These conditions can be given concrete expression within a model of the sort introduced by Gely and Spiller. That model, however simple it may be for some purposes, allows us to see that the conditions for legal autonomy are variable both historically and comparatively. It is useful, I think, to conclude this essay by pointing out some of the kinds of results that could be anticipated from an approach of this sort.

U.S. law like U.S. politics itself is often thought to be "exceptional." U.S. law is characterized by a complex amalgam of legal sources including common law, statutory law, and constitutional law. To a greater degree than is true in other advanced countries, U.S. courts appear to have great interpretive latitude to draw from these diverse legal sources in deciding cases. Martin Shapiro, contrasting them with continental courts, writes that "Anglo-American judges often construct their opinions as mosaics of excerpts from, citations of, and comments about earlier judicial decisions. Even when the case is one of statutory interpretation, the wording of the statute may be buried in a footnote."[39] The opinions of continental judges are more apt to be framed as direct commentary and elaboration of specific provisions of legal code.

We might think of the U.S. legal tradition as one exemplifying the combination of a relatively great degree of judicial discretion and judicial power to make policy. The English legal tradition, alternatively, might be thought to exhibit interpretive discretion without substantial policy-making power. Continental courts exhibit both limited discretion and limited power. Taking this characterization as fact, how can it be explained?

U.S. exceptionalism is often given a cultural explanation, either by invoking America's inheritance of diverse legal sources and cultures, or, following Louis Hartz and others, pointing to more general aspects of U.S. history or geography.[40] Rather than taking claims of exceptionalism simply as peculiar facts about U.S. culture and historical experience, a comparative approach would try to explain them in terms of other presumably more basic factors. Institutional neorealism would seek an explanation by looking at cross-national institutional differences as a likely locus of forces shaping and maintaining both the structure of law and the practices of courts.

The comparative hypothesis would be stated as follows: nations with traditions and practices of unrestricted parliamentary sovereignty would tend to have judges that are more or less neutral appliers of received law to cases. Conversely, those nations that restrict parliamentary sovereignty, whether constitutionally or in some other way, might be expected to develop traditions of judicial independence and power.

Judges in parliamentary sovereignty systems would not emphasize or even notice the discretionary or interpretive elements of their decisions. They would see themselves, instead, as we see our agency heads: charged with carrying out parliamentary directives. This tendency would be strongest in those nations with pure majoritarian practices (like England, New Zealand, and Canada); one would expect courts to develop as more or less servants of the legislature and not to develop practices of independence. One would also expect this to be true regardless of the history of the legal system. English courts, on this account, even if they exhibited some degree of judicial independence two hundred years ago, would not be central policy-making courts. Even if they cloak their decisions in the interpretive model of common-law adjudication, their decisions take place under the shadow of a parliament able to act quickly and decisively.

U.S. institutions, of course, exemplify an opposing political tradition: one that checks and disperses power, limits the capacity of the legislature to act, and reacts and leaves ample opportunity for judicial action. To the extent that electoral or partisan forces temporarily overcome these constitutional limitations, judicial discretion is correspondingly reduced. While the centrifugal forces in U.S. institutions have indeed been defeated occasionally, such defeats have always turned out to be temporary so that we may hope to explain the long-run configuration of judicial independence and discretion in terms of the underlying constitutional structure.

Institutional neorealism might also help to explain variations in legal institutions and practices within a give constitutional tradition. Bruce Ackerman has recently published an extremely interesting account of U.S. legal history that argues, essentially, that two kinds of politics take place in America: ordinary politics (logrolling, interest group bargaining and compromise, rent seeking, etc.) and constitutional politics (principled, aimed at changing the rules of the game, etc.)[41] He locates the decisive events in U.S. legal history as those in which constitutional politics was ascendant: the founding, the early Jackson years (Bank Crisis), the 1850s and 1860s (abolition movement), the judicial revolution in the New Deal. At these periods, ordinary politics was somehow subsumed or preempted, however temporarily, and momentous constitutional events occurred. Descriptively, I think there is something to this – enough, in any case, to see if a positive theory of law can have anything interesting to say about it.

Consider a simple version of the model introduced in the previous section but now where the actors are embedded in a two-dimensional space. Assume (following a model of Spiller and Gely)[42] that H, S, and P stand for the House, Senate and president, that each has circular preferences, that their ideal points form a triangle, and that each actor has an absolute veto. Thus, the points inside the triagle will be stable, in the sense that the three institutions could not agree to move from any point in the triangle. However a policy position in the triangle arises, whether the result of previous legislation, administrative action, or court decisions, such an outcome is politically stable.

The insight of the Spiller–Gely model is that when this triangle is large – that is, when the actors disagree with each other – the court is unconstrained in using interpretive techniques to set policy. In such periods – perhaps recent periods of divided government are good examples or perhaps the period from the mid-1930s to the mid-1970s, when the Democratic party was deeply divided on racial issues – we would expect courts to be an important institutional location of policy making on big or controversial issues. An even more interesting period from this point of view might be that of the Marshall court, when the absence of party organization may have permitted extraordinary license in the court. During these periods, Congress and the president, being unable to accomplish significant projects, concentrate on delivering goodies to their constituencies.

When the triangle is small, aggressive judicial policy making risks correction by other actors, and these corrections often have constitutional significance. On this account I would think that likely periods of constitutional crisis might be associated with rapid shrinkings of the triangle. Such periods might be the Civil War and Reconstruction period – in which the court refrained from emasculating the reconstruction program (ex parte Macardle) – the New Deal, and perhaps the period after Jackson's election. In all these periods, temporary unity of political actors permitted what Ackerman called constitutional politics to occur.

While constitutional crises of a certain sort might be associated with shrinkings in the triangle, rapid increases in the size of the triangle, by permitting extensive court-centered policy making, might support constitutional politics of a different sort. In such a setting judges would be free to engage in principled argument, relatively unconstrained by external political forces. In such settings, the constitutional dialogue might be expected to result in the elaboration of fairly stable and routinized interpretive regimes. We may look to what electoral historians have termed the relatively disorganized first (pre-Jacksonian), fourth (1896–1932), and post-New Deal party systems for examples. The Marshalls, "Lochner," and Warren courts might exemplify judicial eras of this sort.

The point of this story is that a simple positive political theory that shows how electorally generated phenomena establish the boundaries of judicial action may go far in explaining an important set of phenomena in legal history. This is done by showing how it is that court action could be understood within a larger shifting political context and, in particular, relating events of legal history to more fundamental shifts in electoral outcomes.

Indeed, we can go further. By explaining when the locus of policy making is in the courts – relatively deliberative institutions in which reason and argument are central aspects of policy making – we can help to understand the changing quality of public political discourse. There are times in U.S. history when political outcomes seem heavily influenced by who won an election or a war, and others when normative "ideas" seem especially important as causes of policy evolution. We might see the postwar period as one such era: Ideas of equal treatment for those of various racial, ethnic, and sexual identities took on a kind of urgency that might have been impossible had this period not been one condusive to judicial policy making. Perhaps the reconciliation of legal and political history can help us shed light not only on the shifting institutional foci of policy formation, but also on changes in the kind of public policy that is produced in different political eras.

NOTES

1. Recently a number of positive theorists have developed models within which learning, inference, and persuasion occur. These are central components of deliberation, but there is reason to believe that we will need to develop broader notions of deliberation and reasoning to explain judicial action. See Keith Krehbiel, *Information and Legislative Organization* (Ann Arbor: University of Michigan Press, 1992).
2. I am thinking here of the implications of deontological views that are found in ethics. For an exploration of this and related issues, see Amartya Sen, "Rational Fools," *Philosophy of Public Affairs,* 6 (1977): 31–44. There is no reason to think that preferences that derive from procedural or constitutional values necessarily have such a form, however. Elsewhere, I argue that certain procedural preferences might plausibly have a standard neoclassical form. John Ferejohn and Barry Weingast, "Limitation of Statutes," *Georgetown Law Journal,* 80 (1992): 565–82.
3. See Lewis A. Kornhauser and Lawrence G. Sager, "Unpacking the Court," *Yale Law Journal,* 96 (1986): 82–117.
4. For a much more detailed account of diverse legal sources of U.S. law, see Kermit Hall, *The Magic Mirror* (Oxford: Oxford University Press, 1989).
5. Indeed, even if all legal texts emanated from a single source such as a legislature, there would be good reasons to expect those commands to be contradictory and incomplete. Among these reasons would be the fact that elections, retirements, and deaths cause shifts in legislative preferences, and that legislators face time inconsistency problems, as well as the chronic instability of collective choice. Note that the first two forces would apply as much to a monarch as to a legislature.

211

6. The standard move here is, for a given canon, to point to a "counter-" canon that has more or less the opposite sense: for example, statutes "will be liberally construed if their nature is remedial." As it is a little hard to imagine nonremedial statutes, this canon permits courts to justify very different decisions than the one cited in the text. See Karl Llewellyn, "Remarks on the Theory of Appellate Decision and the Rules or Canons about How Statutes are to be Construed," *Vanderbilt Law Review,* 3 (1950): 395–401. Easterbrook suggests that these two canons may have distinct scopes that can be identified by discerning the "purpose" of the statute: Remedial statutes should be broadly construed, rent-seeking statutes more narrowly (see his "Supreme Court, 1983 Term" *Harvard Law Review,* 98 (1984): 4–60.

7. See Kornhauser and Sager, "Unpacking the Court."

8. I shall leave aside the issue of whether the properties of these other institutions – Congress, the president, bureaucratic agencies – have been adequately understood. A number of scholars would put interpretive practices near the center of congressional, presidential, and bureaucratic activity and argue that lawmaking and application requires interpretation no less than deciding cases does.

9. For the present we do not take account of the ambiguities of the idea of "authorship" in a legislature: the fact that legislatures have many members and that they generally employ nonunanimous decision rules. We consider these issues in the following sections.

10. Attributions of either intent or purpose to authors can be done in many distinct ways and is an area of controversy in (legal) interpretation. Attribution could amount to an assertion that some actual author actually had some specific intention at the time of writing a provision. Alternatively, an attribution of purpose might mean that the purpose of a particular law or legal provision is to prevent x, whether or not any particular author intended to prevent x or not. Attribution of the latter sort is found in common-law interpretation, where the "authorship" is inherently ambiguous, but it is found in other areas of law as well. Witness the effort by some legal scholars to claim that the purpose of some constitutional provisions is to provide a protection for privacy. One common method for constructing hypothetical intentional attributions of this sort is to ask what would a rational agent have intended if he or she were legislating in some sort of "ideal" situation.

11. A sophisticated version of strict textualism is defended in Frank Easterbrook, "Statutes' Domains," *University of Chicago Law Review,* 50 (1983): 533–50.

12. This approach is obviously similar to hypothetical consent notions found in some social contract theories. Rawls's construction of the principles of justice as rules that would be agreed to by rational agents acting in a certain kind of information environment is an example. John Rawls, *Theory of Justice* (Cambridge, MA: Harvard University Press, 1971).

13. 42 U.S. C. 2000e-2(a) (1).

14. 42 U.S.C. 2000e-2(j).

15. Indeed Rehnquist went on to challenge the sense in which Kaiser's plan could be regarded as voluntary since Kaiser was under pressure from federal agencies to ameliorate its employment practices in regard to blacks.

16. The citations in this paragraph are from Ronald Dworkin, *Law's Empire* (Cambridge, MA: Harvard University Press, 1986), pp. 219, 176, 218.

17. This paragraph describes Easterbrook's methodology for those statutes that he would regard as having a public purpose, which he distinguishes from those that are mere interest group bargains. Statutes in the latter category should, on his account, be interpreted very narrowly to cover only those cases that clearly fall within the plain meaning of their words. Statutes with public purposes – he points to the Sherman Act as an example – call for the use of more expansive techniques of legal development of the kind used in common-law domains.

18. This view of antitrust law has its own flaws from the standpoint of social choice theory. These will not be addressed here.

19. Standard examples here point to inventions like automobiles and their effect on tort law, etc.

20. Brian Marks, "A Model of Judicial Influence on Congressional Policy Making: Grove City vs Bell," Hoover Institution Working Paper in Political Science, p-88-7, 1988; Gely and Spiller, "A Rational Choice Theory of Supreme Court Statutory Decisions with Application to the *State Farm* and *Grove City*, Cases," *Journal of Law, Economics and Organizations*, 6 (1990): 263–300; John Ferejohn and Charles Shipan, "Congressional Influence on Bureaucracy," *Journal of Law, Economics and Organization*, special issue: 1–20.

21. Indeed, this conflict is at the root of both Terry Moe's emphasis on the importance of political uncertainty and McNollGast's focus on the attempts of an enacting congress to constrain future politicians. See Terry Moe, "Politics and the Theory of Organizations," *Journal of Law, Economics and Organization*, 7 (1991): 106–29, and McNollGast, "Structure and Process, Politics and Policy: Administrative Arrangements and the Political Control of Agencies," *Virginia Law Review*, 75 (1989): 431–82. See also Jeffrey Hill and James Brazier, "Constraining Administrative Agencies: A Critical Examination of the Structure and Process Hypothesis," *Journal of Law, Economics and Organization*, 7 (1991): 373–400.

22. Indeed, we might understand U.S. constitutional structures such as checks and balances and the separation of powers as devices that have the effect of enhancing the authority of statutes in exactly this way. Courts faithful to the Constitution's spirit might feel required to employ their interpretive resources to the same end.

23. John Ferejohn and Barry Weingast, "Limitation of Statutes: Strategic Statutory Interpretation," *Georgetown Law Journal*, 80 (1992): 565–82.

24. John Ferejohn and Barry Weingast, "A Positive Theory of Statutory Interpretation," *International Review of Law and Economics*, 12 (1992): 263–79.

25. William Eskridge, "Overriding Supreme Court Statutory Interpretation Decisions," *Yale Law Journal*, 101 (1991): 331–455.

26. "William Eskridge and John Ferejohn, "Politics, Interpretation and the Rule of Law," *NOMOS*, Forthcoming. The idea of an interpretive regime is closely related to Bruce Ackerman's notion of a constitutional regime, but our focus in this essay is primarily on statutes rather than constitutional issues. This is not to deny that interpretive regimes direct constitutional interpretation as well. However, the connection between a regime's orientation to statutes and its reading of constitutional provisions might be complex. It is possible to be a purposivist with respect to statutes and an intentionalist when reading the

John Ferejohn

constitution; indeed, I believe that this interpretive posture and its opposite may be found among actual interpretive regimes. See Bruce Ackerman, *We The People* (Cambridge, MA: Harvard University Press, 1991).

27. The substantive due process jurisprudence of Lochner-era courts amounts to a purposive construction of the constitution.
28. Legislative action was remedial and was undertaken to correct those rare instances where private interactions created helpless victims. These corrections were not aimed at displacing the system of private contracting and were to be narrowly bounded by specific legislative intent.
29. The best known such canon would be this: "statutes in derogation of the common law should be narrowly construed."
30. Because the deficiencies of private ordering were seen as widespread and systemic, legislative action was best seen as reforming broad areas of private interaction, and so should be interpreted in terms of their overall purposes.
31. A typical canon that would have been popular in that jurisprudence might be this: "remedial statutes are to be broadly construed."
32. This was accomplished by returning to a purposive or substantive reading of the constitution, this time finding privacy values behind it.
33. In the interpretive regime of the Warren and Burger courts, courts have generally made substantial use of nonstatutory materials in establishing legislative intent. Among these sources, a loose hierarchy of interpretive materials has evolved. The statute itself is considered to be the best evidence for legislative intent, followed by the legislative history materials (committee reports, floor debates, etc.), and then by subsequent events (court or agency interpretation and legislative action). As we descend the hierarchy, the materials become less controlling in the interpretation of a statute, as courts are forced to weigh the value of textual evidence not subjected to majority vote. See William Eskridge Jr. and Philip Frickey, "Statutory Interpretation as Practical Reasoning," *Stanford Law Review,* 42 (1990): 321–84.
34. The textualists' refusal to find privacy values in the Constitution might be seen as a restoration of an intentionalist view of the constitution.
35. New textualists would be intentional realists if they were to argue that only statutory evidence is admissable in discovering genuine legislative intent. However, a textualist could deny the reality of legislative intent altogether, seeing statutes as mere political settlements among competing groups. In that case, courts would be obliged to enforce the strict terms of a formally enacted statute but nothing more.
36. What is sometimes called the "plain meaning rule" – the idea that expressions of plain meaning of the statute are interpretive trumps that can override other techniques of construction – might be seen as the core constructive method.
37. In *Chevron v. NRDC,* the Court announced a policy of deferring to agency interpretations of statutes as long as those interpretations are consistent with the language of the statute.
38. In Aramco, the Court refused to defer to an agency interpretation (EEOC) that Title 7 of the 1964 Civil Rights act applied to U.S. employers of U.S. citizens in overseas operations. The refusal to defer to the agency interpretation was based on the fact that the statute did not explicitly cover the case (though rules of canonical construction that the Court uses on other occasions could be employed to argue that such coverage was implicit) and on the canon that statutes should be construed not to apply overseas.

39. Martin Shapiro, *Courts: A Comparative and Political Analysis,* (Chicago: University of Chicago Press, 1981), p. 135.
40. Many historians have argued that there is something about U.S. circumstances – the geographical isolation from Europe, the presence of a frontier, the abundance of natural resources, aspects of its history, etc. – that explain its unique institutional structure and political life. Perhaps the most influential such account is Louis Hartz's argument that the absence of a feudal heritage blocked the development of the sorts of class-oriented ideologies found in Europe: Louis Hartz, *The Liberal Tradition in America* (New York: Harcourt Brace, 1955).
41. Ackerman, *We The People,*
42. Pablo Spiller and Rafael Gely, "Congressional Control or Judicial Independence: The Determinants of U.S. Supreme Court Labor-Relations Decisions, 1949–1988," *RAND Journal of Economics,* 23 (1992): 463–92.

8

The rational choice theory of social institutions: cooperation, coordination, and communication

RANDALL L. CALVERT

INTRODUCTION

In both economics and political science, the study of institutions has achieved a new and increasing prominence over the past twenty years. This emphasis contrasts with economists' previous devotion to the neoclassical paradigm and, to some extent, with behavioralist and pluralist approaches to studying politics. In part this change is due to an interest in problems concerning particular institutional settings: the efficient structuring of the business firm, the nature and practice of economic regulation, the criticism or reform of democratic political institutions, and, more recently, the transition from command economies and totalitarian polities to more capitalistic and democratic forms. But, partly as a result, there has also been an increased appreciation of the need for positive economic and political *theory* that not only incorporates institutions and their effects, but also gives us tools to analyze institutional formation, maintenance, and change.

It is a measure of the importance of the idea of institutions in social science that the term often goes without an explicit definition in many studies to which it is central, even though writers who do define the term give it a great variety of meanings. This seems especially to have been true in political science, where an institution is variously a set of rules of the game that regulate lower-level political activities; a central and wide-

I am grateful for helpful comments from Arthur Denzau, Peter Hall, Doug North, Mancur Olson, Dave Weimer, and from workshop participants at the University of North Carolina Political Economy Working Group and at Harvard University's Center for International Affairs. Special thanks are due to Andy Rutten for his extensive comments on an earlier draft. As always, I claim responsibility for remaining errors and for suggestions not (yet) taken. Some of the research reported here was supported by the National Science Foundation through grants SES-8908226 and BNS-9700864, the latter through the Center for Advanced Study in the Behavioral Sciences, which generously supported the author as a fellow during 1990–91.

spread species of interest groups (Truman 1951); a highly formalized and elaborated type of organization (Polsby 1968); a method of preference aggregation (Riker 1980); and a set of norms, habits, rules of thumb, and other precepts for decision making and behavioral choices with which an organization or political group is endowed (March and Olsen 1989). Economists, for the most part, often use some form of the "rules of the game" analogy (e.g., North 1981: 201–2), although attempts at explicit definition are rare in the recent literature. Schotter (1981: 11), who takes the first self-conscious look at institutions by a game theorist, gives the following definition patterned after Lewis' (1969) somewhat narrower definition of a convention:

A regularity R in the behavior of members of a population P when they are agents in a recurring situation Γ is an *institution* if and only if it is true and is common knowledge in P that (1) everyone conforms to R; (2) everyone expects everyone else to conform to R; (3) either everyone prefers to conform to R on the condition that the others do, if Γ is a coordination problem, in which case uniform conformity to R is a coordination equilibrium; or (4) if anyone ever deviates from R it is known that some or all of the others will also deviate and the payoffs associated with the recurrent play of Γ using the deviating strategies are worse for all agents than the payoff associated with R.

Part 4 of Schotter's definition captures the idea of deterrent retaliation in a repeated game, in which Γ represents the stage game. Schotter is explicitly defining an institution to be some kind of equilibrium in some game, an approach that I will eventually follow to the letter.

Most of these definitions are either special cases or essential restatements of that of Durkheim (1895: lvi): "all the beliefs and modes of conduct instituted by the collectivity," that is, beliefs and conduct not depending solely on the judgment, will, or habits of individuals considered in isolation.[1] The "instituting" can be accomplished by any combination of purposeful design and spontaneous emergence. So defined, institutions include informal norms, complex formal organizations, and processes and rules designed for the channeling of political and economic activity – in short, any of the rules of the game by which individuals in society find themselves confronted when contemplating action. I know of no better general definition for addressing the present-day concerns of economists and political scientists, nor for use by the rational choice theorist, and I will adopt it as a general approach throughout this essay.

The recent institutional revival in economics and politics has often focused on the individual actor as the unit of analysis while trying to gain purchase on the analysis of aggregates, of organizations and institutions. This approach emphasizes an interesting and basic simultaneous determination. While the social rules of the game constrain the actions of individuals, the rules themselves consist of a pattern of individual actions and

217

expectations. The best tool social science has for portraying and analyzing this chicken-or-egg problem is rational choice theory, specifically the analysis of equilibrium in noncooperative game models. Accordingly, I adhere throughout this essay to the overall approach recommended by Schotter (1981) and treat an institution, for analytical purposes, as being a long-lived *equilibrium* pattern of rational behavior in some underlying *game* that society plays.[2]

The overall purpose of this essay then, is to assess the progress of and prospects for a rational choice theory of institutions that can be used to address the applied problems in which social scientists, especially economists and political scientists, are interested. Much of the recent literature on the theory of institutions in economics and political science has attempted to stretch previous theories and approaches to cover the need for such a theory. The remainder of this section examines several ways in which these attempts fall short, in that they fail to treat the chicken-or-egg problem of individual rational action and the "instituting" of malleable social constraints. A more successful theory must clarify three fundamental phenomena central to our thinking about institutions: the establishment and maintenance of endogenous incentives for *cooperation* among selfish individuals; the achievement of *coordination,* that is, of standards, organization, or conventions, in complex settings; and the way in which *communication,* which turns out to be central to the first two phenomena, can take on a life of its own in the definition and functioning of institutions. By viewing institutions as game-theoretic equilibrium phenomena, we can elaborate these processes while doing justice to the simultaneous determination problem of rational action and institutions. Later sections treat recent advances along these lines in understanding cooperation and coordination. They present several of my own attempts to address explicitly the problem of institutions, as well as explaining how certain recent, more general work in game theory has an important bearing on the problem. The concluding section briefly examines our first forays into the subject of communication as a game-theoretic phenomenon, an area of study that may have important implications for our understanding of phenomena, such as values, culture, and rhetoric, previously thought to be outside the realm of rational action. The whole theoretical framework carries a prescription for how empirical work on institutions ought to proceed, and this too is explicated in the conclusion.

Neoclassical economics, behavioral politics,
and institutions

Despite the impressive achievements of neoclassical economics, it has been clear for decades now that a full analysis of economic behavior and performance cannot proceed without a deeper understanding of economic objects purposely obscured in the neoclassical model. In political science, despite periods of intense concentration on political institutions, satisfactory explanations of institutional maintenance and change have proved difficult to achieve using tools borrowed from either sociology, psychology, or economics. In both fields, traditional work tended at bottom to assume the constraining ability of institutions, to examine behavior within fixed institutions, and to portray the change or maintenance of institutions as a phenomenon separate from behavior within institutions. Recent attempts in both fields to extend their most modern tools to construct theories of institutions have, I will argue, posed interesting problems but are incapable of addressing them fully.

Neoinstitutional economics. In real-life economic behavior, the presence of market institutions is critical for the functioning of the market. Neoclassical economics assumes all those institution-building problems to have been solved: Property rights are specified and enforced, a medium of exchange is maintained, potential customers and vendors can identify one another costlessly, traders can smoothly agree on prices in a setting of imperfect competition, and contracts are enforced. With this approach, neoclassical economists are able to concentrate on the matters of greatest interest, especially production and exchange. In addressing many real-world settings, however, it has become necessary to return to those institutional fundamentals, so often problematic to real economic agents, in order to understand how an economy works when the fundamental institutions are not given.

Within the past three decades (although precursors stretch back much further), an approach that now goes by the name of the "new institutionalism" or, in Eggertsson's terms, "neoinstitutional economics" (Eggertsson 1990), has taken those institutional arrangements more seriously. Relaxing neoclassical assumptions such as frictionless trade, commodity goods, and unitary, profit-maximizing firms, neoinstitutional economics brings an array of new concepts to bear upon our understanding of trade, production, and the institutional structure underlying market forces. Notable among these are new approaches to the ideas of transaction costs and property rights (Coase 1937, 1960).

An important strand of thought in neoinstitutional economics is that the design of institutions can determine the extent to which inherent transaction costs will stand in the way of achieving gains from trade. Transaction costs include, for example, the costs of organization, bargaining, and enforcement incurred when a group of actors attempts to purchase some property right valuable to all of them, such as in Coase's (1960) example of farmers paying a railroad not to run trains that emit

219

sparks that burn crops. An important implications of Coase (1960) and Demsetz (1972) is that, given a particular structure of transaction costs in some economic activity, there is in principle a best institutional arrangement to minimize the incidence of those costs. Other analysts have suggested that there are market-like forces that drive emerging institutions to the form necessary to achieve this second-best level of economic activity (Alchian 1950; Posner 1977), and some have proposed evolutionary mechanisms by which this emergence of the second-best might be accomplished (Rubin 1977; Nelson and Winter 1982).[3]

Yet another group of neoinstitutional economists, however, insists that economic arrangements often fall short even of this second-best status. North (1981, 1990) emphasizes that economic institutions are often determined for reasons unrelated to economic efficiency, and thereafter, having generated a constituency of support in government, in business, and even in the form of public "ideology," prove difficult to dislodge or to improve. This phenomenon of institutional development goes by the name of "path dependence." Levi (1988), a political scientist, examines in detail the incentives of governments in creating economic institutions, demonstrating for the case of France how those incentives can work against efficiency even for long periods of time. David's (1985) account of the QWERTY typewriter keyboard standard suggests that even if an institution is created for efficiency reasons, it may be impossible, if changing conditions later make the original institution dysfunctional, to alter it.

Such accounts of "third-best" institutions offer illuminating ideas about the emergence and maintenance of institutions, and their effects on economic activity. They lack a coherent theory to make them compatible with the theory of other aspects of economic behavior. To lay the path dependence phenomenon to transaction costs – by saying that institutions persist if the cost of changing them outweighs the gains – contributes little toward our ability to predict when the transaction costs of making the change might outweigh transaction cost saving resulting from the change. Moreover, none of these accounts has the purpose of answering the larger question of how the institutional rules of the game are enforced. Simply depending for enforcement on those who "control" the means of coercion would imply, on the surface, simply turning over all economic rights to the persons with the guns, obviating the economic plans of kings and businessmen alike. At present, the enforcement of property rights and other institutions is still a seldom addressed and poorly understood problem.

A neoinstitutional political science? Although there is no institution-free "classical" political science to modify, the field has gone through several approaches to the understanding of institutions that seem to be inadequate to present purposes.[4] These began with the early formalistic or legalistic institutional period, when much attention was indeed given to institutions, but often only to describe the formalized rules supposed to determine behavior in them. In reaction to this rather unsatisfactory approach, pluralists attempted to reorient the focus of political science and train it instead upon the actions of the interests comprising a society. From the pluralist viewpoint, an "institution" is just a formally and standardly organized social group (Truman 1951, pp. 26–7), and its members observe the rules of the group because people have a basic need for social acceptance and are socialized into groups (pp. 17–19). Likewise the behavioralist movement in political science, beginning in the late 1940s, about the same time as the blossoming of pluralist ideas, attempted to look at politics through the lens of individual behavior and individual psychology; its practitioners assumed to various extents that institutions are defined by the regular behavior patterns of individuals, and not vice versa. Behavioralism seems to view institutions not as constraints at all, but rather as the aggregated result of individual psychological propensities. This approach offers little hope of explaining changes in behavior that can result from formal changes in institutions, such as the alteration of legislative rules or the adoption of a constitution.

Some political scientists began a decade or two later to study individual behavior from a rational-actor viewpoint. Initially, they examined the workings of majority-rule and other processes of social choice without particular attention to any real institutions of real governments, in an attempt to pin down the basic forces underlying politics in those real institutions. Early rational choice analysts included a few stylized institutional features in their models,[5] but more concentrated work on alternative political institutions was inspired by the questions that neoinstitutional economists raised in their own field. Shepsle (1979) is the earliest direct suggestion that the problem of majority rule cycles, which had theretofore introduced instabilities into social models of voting institutions, might be mitigated by the constraints of procedural rules of the game.[6] Specifically, in a multidimensional game of majority-rule policy choice, if legislative committees could be created and each given a one-dimensional jurisdiction and full gatekeeping power, majority rule would be rendered stable. Shepsle and Weingast (1984), in an essay whose title itself paraphrases that of a classic Demsetz (1972) contribution to neo-institutional economics, go on to address much more broadly the way in which legislative structure could stabilize and determine legislative outcomes without being overwhelmed by majority-rule cycles and other social choice instabilities. Later work by the same authors generalizes to some extent beyond the case of one-dimensional committee jurisdictions (Shepsle and Weingast 1987).

Riker (1980) points out, however, that such legislative rules are themselves matters of choice by the legislature, so that we are still left with the problem of why majorities of legislators would allow themselves to be constrained by rules of their own devising. Riker demonstrates, in effect, the problem in assuming that legislators could commit themselves in advance to a particular set of institutional rules, given that, in any particular legislative situation, there are likely to be winning coalitions frustrated by those rules. This is precisely the problem of self-enforcement in institutions, to which I return later.

At present, most recent political science treatments of institutional constraints take essentially the Shepsle–Weingast approach. This includes the entire literature on spatial models of elections (e.g., Enelow and Hinich 1984), in which the institutions of electoral choice and the parameters of voter ideology often yield some measure of stability but are immune from endogenous change. It also includes much new literature on the influence of congressional committees and of bureaucratic agencies on policy formation (Weingast and Moran 1984; Gilligan and Krehbiel 1987, 1990). Although this literature has contributed much toward the analysis of political behavior under institutional constraints, it nowhere addresses the process by which such constraints are maintained. Disagreements over the relative influence of Congress versus the executive (Moe 1987; Calvert, McCubbins, and Weingast 1989) and of congressional committees versus chamber majorities (Krehbiel, Shepsle, and Weingast 1987) have at their root this ambiguity in the literature on the nature of governmental institutions (see the discussion in Calvert forthcoming).

Central problems for a theory of institutions

One important goal of a rational choice theory of institutions, as I understand it, is to flesh out these notions into a coherent theoretical whole compatible with the individual rationality viewpoint basic to the rest of economic reasoning – in other words, to provide an economics-compatible foundation for neoinstitutional economics. To get a clearer picture of what these central questions are, consider some of the conceptual problems that arise in understanding transaction costs, property rights, and rules of the game generally.

Transaction costs and institutional form. As Goldberg (1984) points out, the neoinstitutional literature seems to be of two minds concerning the precise nature of transaction costs. They sometimes appear as straightforward opportunity or resource costs. In this case, transaction

222

costs can be treated nicely using the tools of neoclassical economics: If a firm must erect fences or employ guards, say, to protect a property right, it bears a resource cost just like any other production cost. The firm must take this into account in choosing profit-maximizing methods and levels of production, including the organization of the firm, methods of contracting, and lobbying for changes in government regulation and enforcement.[7]

In other cases the transaction costs that neoinstitutional analysts refer to are not opportunity costs at all. Consider for example the problem of achieving collective action among farmers in Coase's (1960) example of the spark-producing trains. When farmers bear the liability for crop losses, to achieve the hypothetical gains from the trade they would all have to contribute appropriately to a fund for "bribing" the railroad to run fewer trains. It is difficult, however, to organize such collective action on the part of the farmers, and Coase refers to this as a transaction cost. But each farmer has an incentive to understate his willingness to pay for a reduction in train sparks. From the literature on incentive-compatible mechanisms under asymmetric information we know that there is no way to bring about an outcome to this problem corresponding to the perfect revelation of preferences without incurring some sort of efficiency shortfall. One is tempted to view this shortfall as a transaction cost. Notice, however, that it is *not* an opportunity cost: It does not represent an expenditure of resources that *could have been* put to some next-best use, because the asymmetric-information incentive problem precludes ever achieving a higher level of efficiency. The same is true for bargaining costs, at least where those refer to the difficulty of reaching agreement,[8] and to incentive difficulties resulting from principal–agent problems within the firm.[9] It is not possible to understand the effects of such costs simply by measuring resources devoted to their reduction (as in Wallis and North 1986) or by applying methods from the neoclassical theory of the firm. Rather, to gain a fuller understanding of the design and functioning of institutional forms it is necessary to model these incentive problems directly and to derive the properties of equilibrium behavior. The recent game theory literatures on collective action, bargaining, and principal–agent problems focus on this task:[10] the present survey examines issues more broadly related to the subject of theorizing about institutions.

The enforcement of institutional rules. One of the major achievements of neoinstitutional economics is its clarification of the importance of the property rights structure. However, an effective system of property rights must be consistently observed by the participants, and the question of how rights can be inculcated or enforced is not a particularly strong point

Randall L. Calvert

of neoinstitutional economics. This is a problem that arises in any discussion of rules of the game, such as political scientists' analyses of legislative procedural rules and constitutional rules. How can the rules be properly enforced within the purview of the system itself? This is the basic question that Durkheim and the classical sociologists leave unanswered: Is there any limit to the range of behaviors and beliefs that can be "instituted by the collectivity"?

Of course, one could "explain" obedience to such rules by positing that individuals have an internal drive toward obedience or cooperation per se.[11] Such an approach is undesirable for two reasons. First, it seems unlikely that a single, simple drive to "cooperate" or "obey" would explain the great variety of situations and definitions of cooperation or obedience that appear in social life. And second, such explanations are ad hoc and ignore the unquestionable fact that, in all societies, considerable ingenuity often goes into creating the circumstances to induce such cooperation (Ostrom 1990). Even more ingenuity goes into finding ways to beat such systems. The real question of obedience to the rules of the game is: In the *absence* of any inherent motivation for it, why do people cooperate sometimes?

Often we can explain the maintenance of cooperation or of rule obedience by appealing to some agency outside the institution that acts to provide the necessary incentives. For example, many features of our system of property rights are enforced by courts and police acting on laws against theft and so on. Such an explanation, however, assumes that the external agency will accurately carry out such enforcement – that the police will punish thieves and will not, for example, falsely prosecute people as thieves in order to extract extortion payments. Obviously, the enforcing agency is itself an institution whose coherence must be explained. Ultimately, any string of such explanations must come down to a *self-enforcing institution*. Social norms and political constitutions are perfect examples – there is no one outside to enforce them, and they must be seen as carrying sufficient means of enforcement with them. Indeed, most institutions involve some measure of self-enforcement. For example, a system of fiat money depends on the monetary authority to maintain a trustworthy currency, but it also depends on the mutual (and mutually supporting) expectation among economic agents that the money will continue to be accepted in trade by virtually all other economic actors. Likewise, consider the adherence of legislators to a system of rules of legislative procedure: An outside institution (the executive, the courts, the electorate, and the constitutional system in general) may require that the legislature maintain some system to delineate unambiguously when a law has been passed, but the details of that system are a matter of internal determination and internal enforcement in the legislature. Thus, even if we were to split off the legislature, for purposes of analysis, as a separate "institution," its rules would have to be self-enforcing in some respects. Recognizing that all the institutions involved in supporting the legislative system are inextricably interrelated, however, we must bear in mind that they are also all one big institution – and the one big institution must be entirely self-enforcing.

The game-theoretic approach to institutions. These two precepts of explaining the effectiveness of institutional constraint – that they must explain the countering of individual interest with incentives to cooperate, and that they must be ultimately self-enforcing – recommends one form of analysis over all others as an approach to building a theory of institutions, namely, equilibrium analysis in noncooperative games. Noncooperative game theory emphasizes the problem of individual choice and attempts to explain observed individual choices as the result of a balance, an equilibrium, of expectations about the actions of others and the incentives of the choosing individual. This approach draws a sharp line between the givens (available actions, preferences over outcomes, and how actions determine outcomes) and the results of game-theoretic analysis, namely, the taking of actions that are individually rational in combination. It assumes that any cooperative combination of actions must be supported as an equilibrium, thus placing the focus of institutional analysis exactly where it belongs: on the problem of constraining and channeling individual action.

It is clear from this discussion of central problems that any theory of institutions must offer a solid conceptual basis for explaining self-contained incentives for cooperation in an institution. This is the task to which I turn in the next section. In addition, the problem of applying rules of the game to new situations on an ongoing basis is a central one to all institutional settings. So is the question of how institutions can arise, and whether indeed they should be expected to carry with them any presumption of efficiency. In the third section I argue that such problems of emergence and maintenance boil down to the issue of coordination, about which a theory of institutions must also have a lot to say. Both cooperation and coordination are now being addressed fruitfully by the tools of noncooperative game theory. Finally, both empirically and theoretically, institutional solutions to problems of cooperation and coordination involve processes of rational communication. Such processes are also becoming productive subjects for game-theoretic modeling, but there is reason to believe that widespread reliance on these forms of communication in social institutions would give rise to a number of new phenomena, related to the sociological concepts of value, ideology, and culture, that game-theoretic models are perhaps just beginning to uncover at a theoretical level. In the final section, I summarize what we know about such processes thus far from a rational-actor standpoint. In addition, I draw, in the concluding section, some inferences about how the theory of institutions, as it is developing now, might guide empirical study in these fields.

COOPERATION

What usually interests us about the rules of the game embodied by institutions is their apparent *social function*. Generally speaking, that is, institutions lead people to work together in ways that those people wouldn't without the institutional constraint, usually so as to yield better outcomes for at least some participants. We do occasionally see examples of dysfunctional institutions,[12] and the theoretical approach suggested in this essay makes clear that this is possible in theory as well. Certainly the idea that institutions involve cooperation does not imply that institutions are always efficient – that all gains from cooperation will somehow be exploited. However, institutions usually connote some form of "cooperation" among at least some subset of the participants.

The nature of cooperation in institutions

By "cooperation" I mean precisely that an individual engages in some act whose immediate consequences for that individual, regardless of what others do *at that moment,* are negative, but which generates some positive benefits for some other individual (and usually for several others in a group). This definition is meant to subsume standard theoretical cases such as cooperation in a prisoner's dilemma, contribution to a public good, or high effort by the agent in a principal–agent setting. Usually cooperation is undertaken with the idea that other actors will be cooperating as well, for mutual benefit. In some institutions, a subset of individuals cooperates in order to coerce contributive effort from still others, yielding net long-run gains to the coercers and net losses to the coerced. Such an institution still involves cooperation in the sense that I intend.

Note well, however, that an institution-as-equilibrium, even one involving cooperation, does not necessarily embody efficiency; there may be some other cooperative arrangement that makes everyone better off.[13] Moreover, an institution does not necessarily embody any "individual rationality" condition, in the sense used in cooperative game theory, because some individuals may be worse off with the institution than without it.[14] Thus, cooperation can be used to characterize a great variety of institutions.

Still, institutions are not about cooperation alone. Cooperation does not adequately describe such actions as contribution in a threshold-type public good provision game (Palfrey and Rosenthal 1984) or accepting the lower "good" payoff in a battle-of-the-sexes-type coordination game. These types of actions maximize individual welfare even in the short-run or instantaneous sense; they are the subjects of the upcoming section on coordination.

For illustrative purposes, let us consider some important examples of economic institutions and the cooperative behavior they involve. The institution of fiat money can be maintained only if people generally are willing to cooperate by accepting inherently worthless scrip in return for valued goods and services. A system of property rights depends on the inclination of people to respect the rights of others in the use of goods and land, and to refrain from asserting rights not allocated to them. When any agent (insured person, factory worker, physician) acts in the interest of a principal (insurer, factory owner, patient), the act is one of cooperation. Finally, whenever one party to a contract carries out her side of the agreement, cooperative behavior has occurred. The reader will note that some of these forms of "cooperation" are, at least in the short run, one-sided, while others are inherently mutual. Also, some of these acts of cooperation are, in our society, enforced by the threat of official sanctions, while others depend on the presence of informal social sanctions or the incentives inherent in ongoing relationships of trade or reciprocity.

Many prominent political institutions involve cooperation as well. When politicians follow the rules of the game specified by a written constitution, they are cooperating. Common instances of such cooperative rule-following occur when an elected official voluntarily relinquishes office following an election loss, or when an executive official seeks the approval of superiors or of a legislature before issuing a desired order to subordinates. When an authority charged with the enforcement of a law expends effort or incurs danger in carrying out that charge, or refrains from exercising the powers of enforcement in circumstances not covered by the law in which the authority could thereby reap private gain, that authority is acting cooperatively. When a bureaucrat acts to promote organizational goals that differ from his personal preferences for policy, leisure, or career security, that official cooperates.

All sorts of informal social institutions amount to cooperative behavior. These include adhering to norms such as honesty, reciprocity in doing favors or bestowing gifts, or the preservation of some socially defined notion of honor. Also, any action by an individual to impose social sanctions, such as shunning of or withdrawal of trust from a person who has violated some norm, is an act of cooperation that preserves a feature of social structure often at some immediate expense to the enforcer. Often the expression of adherence to a value or ideal constitutes an act of cooperation in that it reinforces the expectation of social adherence to that value and of willingness to impose sanctions on its behalf.

Cooperative equilibrium and the rules of the game

The problem for a theory of institutions is twofold. First, the theory must explain how people will behave under a set of rules of the game. Second, it must explain why, under some circumstances, some sets of rules remain stable and succeed in directing people's behavior, and why in other circumstances rules undergo change. (I intend the latter problem to include that of establishing institutions). For the theory to do both these jobs consistently, the rules constraining behavior in the first instance must nevertheless be subject to change by the very people being constrained. In the case of rational actors, this can be a tricky problem: Why would rational actors allow themselves to be constrained by the rules from acting so as to increase their utility, when they could instead violate or change those rules?

One way to do this would be to represent institutions as binding rules, embodied in the available strategies and outcomes in our formal description of the game, and to give the players regular opportunities to reject those rules in favor of some alternative formulation. This two-step approach is essentially the one taken in the institutional analyses of constitutions by Buchanan and Tullock (1962) and that of legislative rules by Shepsle and Weingast (1984). Although we can learn a great deal from such models, they fall short of offering a proper theory of institutions, because their treatment of institutions is necessarily ad hoc. The analyst using this two-step approach must specify in advance what alternative institutional arrangements are available and the method by which institutions can be changed. Furthermore, in all such institutional models there is the implicit assumption that individuals can commit themselves to a set of binding rules for some period of time. Compare the case of, say, congressional budget procedures, which in several instances have been approved as rules by a majority and then, without further change, violated by other majorities through subterfuges such as the changing of economic projections.

A preferable approach, and the one I take throughout this essay, is twofold: to hold constant the formal description of the game, that is, of the players, payoffs, available actions, and the mechanism connecting actions and outcomes; and to let the institutional rules of the game be embodied in that formal game's equilibria. In this way, one can examine properties of the full range of available institutions, each of which must correspond to an equilibrium in the game. At the same time, one can maintain the requirement that adherence to the institutional "rules" be a matter of rational choice by the individual actors. This is the approach taken in Calvert (forthcoming). The underlying game should be viewed as the opportunity or problem that nature presents to the players, whose method of addressing the problem (both rules and behavior under the rules) is contained in the description of equilibrium.[15] The following model illustrates more precisely the way in which the institutional rules of the game can be represented by features of equilibrium.

Institutions as equilibria in an underlying game.   Calvert (forthcoming) addresses the general problem of cooperation through institutions in the simplest way possible, by taking the underlying game to be a repeated prisoner's dilemma (PD) played by randomly matched pairs of players in a large group. In that setting, as in most problems posed by nature in real life, there are equilibria embodying a lack of cooperation, that is, a lack of institutional structure, as well as equilibria corresponding to various self-supporting systems of cooperative behavior. To capture the opportunities that the players have for maintaining institutions of the latter type, players in the game have opportunities to communicate at various stages during play. To capture the difficulties of monitoring and agreeing, it is assumed that communication is costly and that players have direct knowledge only about the outcomes of their own interactions, never about the interactions of other pairs of players.

Specifically, let the set of players be indexed by $\{1, 2, \ldots, n\}$. Represent the payoffs for each PD interaction as follows:

	C	D
C	1, 1	a, −b
D	−b, a	0, 0

where $b > 0$, $a > 1$, and $a - b < 2$. In each period $t = 1, 2, \ldots$, players are first paired off by a random mechanism. Players then have an opportunity to engage in costly communication, described in detail later. After this communication round, the players in each pair play one iteration of the PD. Following that, there is a second round of communication, and then the whole process is repeated in the next period, beginning with the random matching. Players discount their payoffs in future periods by some discount factor $d < 1$ per repetition.

As in any noncooperative game, communication is represented by a rigidly defined process that may, however, include arbitrary complexities

Randall L. Calvert

based on the purpose to which it is to be put by the analyst. Here, in each round of communication each player has the option of sending one message from a message set M, or of sending no message, to each of the other players. For each other player to whom a message is sent, the sender bears a cost $c > 0$ in utility. The receiver of a message has the opportunity to deliver a costless reply, also drawn from M, to the sender. In a model such as this one, the method of analysis is to make M contain at least as many messages as needed to support the equilibrium being examined; by implication, any message other than the expected ones in that equilibrium will have no effect on any player's actions. For some equilibria, a given communication round may not be used at all — that is, no message sent will have any effect on present or future behavior, so the sender may as well not send it and save the cost.

Representing formal and informal institutions as equilibria. Within this simple structure it is possible to represent several simple institutions (and noninstitutional behavioral arrangements) that may ensue in this cooperation problem. First, of course, is the equilibrium[16] in which no player ever plays C in the PD or communicates in the communication rounds. This is an equilibrium regardless of the values of the parameters in the model. A second equilibrium also makes no use of costly communication, but rather has each player treating each of his or her series of interactions with each possible partner as a separate, two-player, repeated game, in which some two-player repeated PD equilibrium strategies, such as Tit for Tat, are used. The effective discount factor for each of these two-player series depends on both d and N, and the equilibrium exists provided that d is sufficiently large and N sufficiently small. This is not an institution in any usual sense of that term, since there is no involvement of the group in whether people cooperate or not: Each act of coordination benefits only the partner of the cooperating player, and defections are punished only by the wronged partner.

A real "norm" of reciprocity, for example, which might indeed qualify as an institution, would normally be expected at least to involve the whole group in the punishment of any defector. The Calvert (forthcoming) model goes on to examine two such institutions, one decentralized in the manner of an informal norm, and the other centralized in the manner of a formal organization. Interestingly, there are circumstances in which the earlier simple two-player reciprocity arrangement is impossible, but in which one of these more complex, true institutions could persist and support cooperation. Each institution is an equilibrium in the repeated game, each based on the Tit-for-Tat strategy but involving all players in the punishment of any offending player. In each version, the information necessary to implement such punishment is disseminated by means of

230

costly communication; in the decentralized institution, every player communicates regularly with every other player, while in the centralized institution one player is designated as a central director, and other players communicate exclusively with this director.

The decentralized institution works as follows. In each period, following the play of the PD, each player then sends messages to all $n - 2$ players other than her current partner at a cost of $(n - 2)c$, telling who her current partner is and whether that partner cooperated or defected. Players reported to have defected inappropriately, and players who fail to report their partners' actions, are subject to punishment by all succeeding partners, who play D against the offending player until she makes "restitution" by cooperating once unilaterally; otherwise all players cooperate. If a player does depart from the equilibrium path by not reporting or by defecting in period t, that player immediately makes restitution by cooperating in period $t + 1$ and then resumes communicating and cooperating as originally prescribed. Notice that it is rational for each player to carry out the assigned punishments, because a punishing player gets the high payoff of a when the offending player makes restitution. Finally, as demonstrated in Calvert (forthcoming), no player finds it rational to lie about a partner's action provided that either (1) all communication is strictly private, so that one can never make one's partner aware that one has lied, or (2) an additional punishment scheme is superimposed in which a player lied about will retaliate by lying about the same partner at the next opportunity. This combination of strategies is an equilibrium provided d is sufficiently large, N sufficiently small, and c sufficiently small. However, the bounds on d and N are not as severe as in the pairwise Tit-for-Tat equilibrium described earlier.

This decentralized institution resembles a true reciprocity arrangement, although it could appear in the real world either as an informal but implicitly agreed-upon "norm" or as a formal written description of rules specifying that players are to play C or D under certain circumstances and communicate certain messages in the manner described. The institution could be brought into being through additional communication among players concerning the institutional form, either before or during play of the repeated game, in which someone proposes the decentralized arrangement. If there had been no previous means for the players to extract as much of the available gains (namely, $1 - (n - 2)c$ out of a theoretically available maximum of 1 per period), then once that suggestion is made, its status as an equilibrium gives everyone the incentive to adhere to it.

If the group of players is large, an alternative institutional form can generate even higher net gains from cooperation than the reciprocity institution, providing an average payoff of $(1 - 2c)(n - 2)/n$ per player each period. This is done by means of centralized communication, illustrating how an institution *cum* equilibrium can incorporate some real organizational structure in contrast with the decentralized institution in which every player played an identical role. Arbitrarily designate a player, say player 1, to be the "director." If a player is paired with player 1 in any period, both always play D (a way of saying that the director does not participate in the underlying game). In each period, following the pairings, each of the remaining $n - 2$ players reports the identity of his partner to the director, at cost c; the director replies (for free) whether that partner is in good standing. The PD is then played by all; players not paired with the director play D if in good standing and the partner is in bad standing, and C otherwise. Then in the second communication round, each player not paired with the director pays c to report to the director the action of his partner in the PD of this period. Again, any player who departs from the path of equilibrium play and enters bad standing immediately makes restitution. All players begin the game in good standing and enter bad standing upon either (1) failing to report as required, or (2) being reported to have failed to play C as required. Upon making restitution, a player regains good standing. Lying about one's partner is deterred as in the decentralized institution; dishonesty by the director (such as extortion or accepting bribes) can be deterred by the addition of a system of fees paid to the director, together with a refusal to play C or to pay the fee if the director appears to have committed extortion or bribery. These strategies are in equilibrium provided that d is sufficiently large and c sufficiently small; this result does not require small n, although of course it does require $n > 3$ so that there is a pair of players left over to cooperate once the director is "removed" from play.

This centralized institution is the beginning of a formal organization: One player is designated to play the role of an official and, at the word of the official, players carry out punishments against other players. All such punishments are rational to carry out as directed but never at other times, and the honesty and accuracy of the official in applying the punishments is assured. Emergence of the institution is possible in the same way as for the decentralized institution; the system of fees can be calibrated to ensure that players are indifferent about serving as director or remaining a regular player.

Lessons from this approach. This analysis demonstrates several things. (1) It is feasible to depict the institutional rules of the game as being endogenous without making ad hoc assumptions about the forms of institution available. (2) A wide variety of realistic institutions, including formal organizations, can be depicted as equilibria in underlying games. (3) If this is done, the resulting model is compatible with any theory about the process of emergence of institutions in which these equilibria are stable outcomes, such as preplay negotiation or adaptive learning. (4) Such a model gives conditions on the parameters (discount factors, group size, payoff values, etc.) under which the institution can exist; if the conditions for equilibrium are not met, then the institution is impossible given the underlying game assumed. (5) Further, if parameters are subjected to some exogenous change, the model generates a prediction of the change that the institution will undergo in response. Where precise equilibrium behavior (e.g., mixed strategy probabilities) depends on the parameters in question, marginal changes in those parameters are reflected in marginal changes in equilibrium behavior, unless that "type" of equilibrium ceases to exist. In the latter case, the model predicts a discontinuous change in behavior, namely, the destruction of the institution and its replacement by some other, which, depending on the nature of the game, may be impossible to predict beyond saying that it will be among the set of equilibria of the new game.

Further research into this approach to analyzing institutions should pursue the construction of institutions in more substantial "underlying games." Although the PD is an archetype, and although it will doubtless prove infeasible to examine very complicated underlying games, other stylized processes may prove informative in the explanation of other types of institutions. For example, in studying rules of legislative procedure as an institution, we might assume that the legislature ultimately generates alternatives and selects them by a basic majority rule process, as in Baron and Ferejohn (1989). It should be possible to express procedural rules, committee or party structure, and leadership arrangements as features of equilibria in this underlying majority choice game.

Other aspects of cooperation in institutions. Even at the level of abstract cooperation problems, there are special features seemingly important in the functioning of real-life institutions that are not captured at all by the random-matching, two player PD model. One is that cooperation often involves more than two players in a single interaction, as portrayed in the standard collective action problem. The enforcement of cooperation in such problems can be far more complicated than in the case of two-player interactions. Another complication is that real-life cooperation problems often involve variations from one "iteration" to the next, complicating any attempt to maintain a prescribed pattern of cooperation. In the remainder of this section, I summarize the models and results of some first-cut analyses of these problems in order to demonstrate the additional potential of a rational choice theory of institutions based on game-theoretic equilibrium.

233

Problems in which prescribed cooperation must vary with the situation

The model. Let us begin by sticking temporarily with the two-player PD problem, dispense with the random-matching business, and consider what happens when the players are in possession of private information that affects the social desirability of cooperation and that varies from one period to the next. In order to let this private information be of a particularly simple form, we change the labeling of the PD game in the following manner. Each player receives a benefit of b times the number of players who choose C (0, 1, or 2), where $b > 0$; and each player i bears a cost c_i for choosing C and no cost for choosing D. If both players choose D, we again let the overall payoff be 0. This yields the following game, which we label G:

	C	D
C	$2b - c_2$ $2b - c_1$	b $b - c_1$
D	$b - c_2$ b	0 0

Assume that each c_i can take on the values c' and c''. The first of these satisfies $b < c' < 2b$, so that setting $c_1 = c_2 = c'$ makes G a prisoner's dilemma game. However, $c'' > 2b$, so that if a player has $c_i = c''$ then that player actually prefers mutual defection over mutual cooperation. The value of c_i is private information to player i, selected according to the common-knowledge probability $\Pr\{c_i = c''\} = p$ for $i = 1, 2$. Finally, suppose that G is to be played repeatedly, with the players discounting future payoffs using a factor $d < 1$, and that each c_i is selected anew at the beginning of each iteration.

It is easy to show that classical, or first-best, efficiency (Holmstrom and Myerson 1983) requires the players to cooperate whenever they have the low value of c_i and to defect when they draw the high value. Since the value of c_i is private information, however, it is impossible to enforce such a pattern of cooperation in equilibrium. Thus thwarted, the candidates could ignore the varying payoffs and just play Tit for Tat or a more severe punishment scheme, provided that the high cost value c'' is not so high that it cancels out the future gains from cooperation. Such an equilibrium would fall considerably short of efficiency, since each player would occasionally have to bear the high cost, in effect throwing away some of the gains from turns in which that layer engages in low-cost cooperation.

The rational choice theory of social institutions

Using communication to get more cooperation. Calvert (1993) examines a method of using communication along with the play of G to achieve a higher proportion of the available gains from cooperation in this problem. A communication round is inserted in each period prior to the play of G. Again, communication is portrayed as a specific process of players sending messages to other players from a set of possible messages. In the present model, there is no cost to communicating, and it is assumed that communication can involve a third person, called a "mediator," whose payoff is independent of the outcome. For such communication processes, the revelation principle (Myerson 1985) proves that any outcome achievable by the players in equilibrium can be achieved as the outcome from a particular, simple form of communication process: an "incentive-compatible direct mechanism." In a direct mechanism, the complete communication process is as follows: (1) players simultaneously and privately, but not necessarily truthfully, report their private information to the mediator; (2) the mediator applies to those reports a mediation rule, known to the players, that yields a suggestion of how each of the players should act in G; and (3) the mediator privately communicates the relevant suggestion to each player. The direct mechanism is incentive-compatible if, for a given mediation rule, there is an equilibrium to the whole single-period process of communicating and playing G in which the players always report the truth and always follow the mediator's suggestions. In general, in order to provide the players with the incentive to tell the truth, it is necessary for the prescribed choices in G to fall short of classical efficiency: by making it sufficiently likely that *neither* player will choose C when *either* player reports the higher cost, the rule makes it unattractive for a low-cost player falsely to report high cost. Within the incentive compatibility constraint, however, there is a set of mediation rules that are Pareto efficient from the standpoint of overall payoffs to the players. Such a rule is said to be "incentive-efficient" (Holmstrom and Myerson 1983). Obedience to the suggestion is ensured if the suggested combination of moves is always an equilibrium in G, or (as in the present model) if the distribution of suggestions is such that each player finds it rational to obey the suggestion made to her, given the distribution of suggestions that could have been made to the other player. In the case of G, this will again require some departure from the classically efficient choices, so that low-cost players are sometimes told to choose D.

Calvert (1993) addresses the problem of finding a good mediation rule when the whole process of communication and play is repeated with discounting. In the repeated game, there is an additional source of incentives to ensure honest reporting and obedience: The mediation rule can punish failures to obey or, if discovered, failures to report honestly, by inducing cooperation failures in future periods. By reducing the use of cooperation failures in the current round to enforce obedience, there is a gain in average payoff in the play of G. An efficiency gain results since the future cooperation failures are never invoked in equilibrium play of the repeated game – as with Tit for Tat in the traditional repeated PD, the threat of future "retaliation" is sufficient to deter a player for whom C is suggested from ever choosing D. The resulting mediation rule provides the players with higher payoffs than they would get from application of a one-period incentive-efficient rule, and with higher payoffs from the repeated game than they could achieve using Tit for Tat without communication.

The analysis in Calvert (1993) cannot identify incentive-efficient mediation rules because, apparently, present tools are insufficient to analyze the use of future periods to deter dishonesty as well as disobedience. Conceivably, some sort of "review strategy" by the mediator could be used to detect likely patterns of dishonest reporting and trigger "retaliation," in the form of induced mutual play of D, by the mediator in a future period. This approach is used in the literature on repeated games without discounting and with hidden action (imperfect monitoring), but the same tools do not carry over to the discounting, hidden-information setting used here. Calvert (1993) offers some reasons to believe that communication is actually necessary in order to achieve incentive efficiency in the repeated-G problem – that the players cannot achieve as high a payoff from the direct use of review strategies without communication. However, the result remains to be proved even for this specific case.

Lessons from this approach. The analysis of efficiency gains through communication in the repeated version of G demonstrates several interesting features of cooperative institutions that were not apparent in the complete-information repeated PD. Most importantly it demonstrates how critical it is for participants in a cooperative activity to have agreement on exactly what is expected from each player in all circumstances. In the game examined here, disagreement about whether a player should be required to choose C in a given period could lead to a player being punished for what he thought was an acceptable action; such inappropriate-seeming punishment, in turn, can lead to retaliation by the punished player, and the result is that both players end up unnecessarily forgoing gains they could have had if they had been able to cooperate during the periods of mutual recrimination. This complication does not arise in the conventional repeated PD, since there it is obvious that, if cooperation is achievable at all, full cooperation can be achieved, so that every player is expected to choose C in every period. Here, variation in the expected choices is desirable, the more so the higher is c''. The problem of arriving at essentially (or, in real life, at least substantially) identical expectations must be solved before stable mutual cooperation can be established; to say that the players' expectations are aligned is almost identical to saying that an institution has been established. (The remaining problem is that incentives must be present to make it in each player's interest to meet those expectations.) The upcoming section on coordination returns to the issue of establishing similar expectations.

A second feature of institutions generally that is demonstrated by the two-player PD with varying costs is the importance of communication in the course of play – in a different form and for a different reason than in the case of the random-matching PD model, which used communication solely for purposes of reporting and monitoring. Here, at least when c'' is large, the rules of the institution must allow for some defection; relative efficiency may require that at least some of those defections go unpunished. Since the circumstances for such leniency are based on players' private knowledge, some way must be found to let the players, explicitly or implicitly, "plead hardship" and avoid being required to obey the usual rules designed to apply when cost is low. The institution, in short, gets input from players in the form of these claims, and bases its "rules" on that input. Players, as a result, have opportunities to try to manipulate the institution's rules. The design of an incentive-compatible direct mechanism to achieve such cooperation makes clear the costs of that manipulative opportunity, by focusing directly on the need for cooperating players to guard against or take into account their partners' and their own temptation to manipulate. Any such mechanism is designed, by definition, to cancel out such manipulation, at some cost in terms of the achievable payoff level.

Cooperation in collective action problems with many players

In his examination of cooperation in the repeated PD, Axelrod (1984) discusses the possibility of explaining such achievements of social order using arguments derived from his analysis of Tit for Tat in the two-player game. Similarly Taylor (1976) supports the possibility of social order in anarchic communities enforced by the threat of retaliation by other players against any unilateral defection in a many-player PD setting. A number of important new complications arise when we move from the cooperation problem among pairs of players to that involving many players simultaneously – a class of problems generally termed "public good" or "collective action" problems, of which the two-player PD is just the simplest special case. Punishment within the group by withholding cooperation is harmful not only to the defector, but to the whole group. Off the equilibrium path, efficiency[17] then would require the use of the minimal amount of punishment necessary to deter defection, which creates a second problem of choosing which players get to do the punishing and thus avoid contribution costs (Hardin 1982). Or, if the punishment for defecting is to be assessed outside the collective action problem itself, say, through a system of enforced fines or of defection in other interactions, the carrying out of punishment is itself normally a collective action problem (Laver 1983, pp. 55–9). Additionally, the resources for such punishments cannot be put in the hands of a centralized organizer, because that organizer then has an incentive to misuse the resources to extract concessions from players who have not violated rules (Frohlich, Oppenheimer, and Young 1971). Difficulties in monitoring and policing the application of punishment may thus render the punishment a less credible deterrent in the original game. For reasons such as these, theoretical lessons learned about two-person cooperation problems do not necessarily carry over to the case of many-player problems.

One concrete example of these difficulties is the problem of using a trade embargo to enforce judgments of noncooperation in international agreements or norms. Suppose that a public good, the absence of military threats in a region of the world, is provided by the act of refraining from threatening one's neighbors or by eschewing a large offensive capability. A failure by any nation to observe such restraint makes it necessary for many nations to maintain stronger defensive forces, rapid-deployment troops, and the like. But as long as others are militarily weak, the temptation to engage in a little militarization and threat may prove irresistible. This temptation can be countered by a willingness on the parts of other nations to punish an offender: (1) by building up military capabilities themselves so that the offender, too, faces a threat; (2) by engaging in a high-cost military expedition to take out the offending government; or (3) by individually punishing the offender through refusal to deal with it diplomatically or economically – an embargo. Alternative 1 hurts everybody even more, as the presence of widespread military power makes all nations even more insecure; because each nation would like to be one of the more secure ones, any attempt to impose limited punishment while maintaining some of the public good is prone to break down completely. Alternative 2 presents another public good problem, as each nation will prefer that others carry out the expensive punishment task without them. Alternative 3 is difficult to maintain, because each nation is asked to give up gains from trade with the offending nation; and adherence to the embargo may be difficult or impossible to monitor and enforce due to its decentralization and to the even more limited willingness of nations to enforce the embargo by means of second-order embargoes against any cheater.

By no means, then, is the theory of collective action among larger groups of selfishly rational players a settled matter. There is a need for new theory to examine the difficulty of arriving at a system for enforcing such cooperation, of limiting the options of the enforcer, and of ensuring the proper level of retaliation.

Enforcing public good contribution through a separate, two-player prisoner's dilemma.   One attempt to examine the embargo problem is presented in Calvert (1991). This model differs from other examinations of the accountability problem (Frohlich et al. 1971) or the many-player collective action problem (Hardin 1982) by focusing on the possibility that different "types" of players, having different degrees of trustworthiness in two-player interactions, might be forced to reveal their types by their willingness to contribute to a public good. The simplest model of the situation is as follows. Suppose that a group of players $\{1, 2, \ldots, n\}$ (n being even) is to play one public good contributions game (PG), following which they are to be randomly paired up once in order to engage in a two-player repeated PD. PG, of course, represents the provision of a large-group public good such as military restraint among nations, while the two-player repeated PD represents trade between two nations.

In PG, each player has the choice of contributing or not; every player bears a net loss of z for contributing to the public good and receives an additional positive payoff $u(k)$ if k others, $k \leq n - 1$, contribute. (Naturally, u is increasing in k; let $u(0) = 0$.) Thus, if k players contribute and $n - k - 1$ do not, the remaining player receives $u(k) - z$ for contributing and $u(k)$ for not contributing; since this is true for all values of k, not to contribute is a dominant strategy for every player. However, the payoff when every player does this is 0, whereas the payoff to every player if all contribute is $u(n - 1) - z$.

The structure of the PD is the same as in the previous models: In each period, each player receives b times the number of players choosing C (0, 1, or 2) and pays an additional cost of c_i for choosing C. Again, c_i is private information and can take on the value c' or c'', where $0 < b < c' < 2b < c''$. As before, the PD will be repeated with discount factor d. This time, however, we assume that all values of c_i are fixed before the play of PG, and that it is common knowledge that m of the players have drawn the low-cost value.[18] Notice, then, that c'-types can gain from mutual cooperation, but c''-types will prefer mutual defection to mutual cooperation. Finally, assume that $u(m - 1) > z$ so that, in the end, a public good really will be provided in PG.

Now suppose that players use the following strategies. In PD, c''-types always choose D, while a c'-type will play Tit for Tat if her opponent contributed in PG, but always choose D otherwise. In PG, only c'-types contribute. For this strategy combination to be an equilibrium requires first that $z > bm/(n - 1)$, so that high-cost types will not contribute just to take advantage of the first-move PD unilateral cooperation in case they are paired with a low-cost type, and second that $z < b(m - 1)/[(n - 1)(1 - d)]$, so that the PG contribution will be worthwhile for the low-cost type, in order to gain the cooperative payoff from the PD in case of being paired with another low-cost type. As long as $d > 1/m$, there are values of z that satisfy both conditions.

Lessons from the analysis. This model says something very simple about the embargo problem: If the public good is valuable enough and if there are enough PG participants who stand to gain from cooperation in the PD, then the full contribution of those "trustworthy" participants in the PG can be induced once a connection between willingness to contribute and trustworthiness in two-agent interactions has been established in the players' mutual expectations. Only in this way could unmonitored punishment at the two-player level, such as the embargo, be used to enforce general collective action.

There are many ways, in principle, to enforce *n*-player collection action – too many ways, in the sense that it may be hard for one specific system to emerge. Where explicit design of an institution is possible, the problem is not always insuperable, although the creation of a system of rules both agreeable to the participants and successful in supporting the desired behavior as an equilibrium may be partly a matter of luck. There are many systems of large-scale cooperation in the real world, however, that are apparently never matters of explicit negotiation or planning. When large, complex, explicitly designed institutions, such as written constitutions, do function more or less as intended, they do so only because the written rules are supported by a system of norms as well. In all such cases, people have to blunder into institutions. And when there are too many incompatible ways to make institutions work, it is often hard to imagine how such blundering succeeds.

The enforcement of public good contributions with PD cooperation or defection, as portrayed here, is an attempt to show how a relatively simple form of enforcement could work. In this model, the players likely to prove bad partners in one-on-one interactions are induced to voluntarily separate themselves, through the play of the PG, from those who would be good partners. A modest application of communication or rhetoric ought to be sufficient to induce people to expect, and thus to participate in, such a separation process. If some collective action could be initially supported through processes like this one, it is easier to believe that more complicated collective action regimes might form through some combinations of trial and error, negotiation, imposition by the strong upon the weak, and adaptive learning.

240

The rational choice theory of social institutions

The problem of arriving at agreement. Still, arriving at such agreements is a central problem in understanding the formation of institutions. It is the subject of the second fundamental branch of the theory of institutions, namely, the solution of problems of coordination. The next section examines some of the ways coordination problems appear in social interaction in general, and in the process of creating or maintaining institutions in particular, and examines some models of how coordination problems might be solved in a game-theoretic setting. In general, these models attempt to represent how, in the course of playing a game, players can eventually arrive at one out of a multiplicity of equilibria. This approach contrasts with the traditional account in which equilibrium is "explained" simply as the result of an instantaneous, preplay process of independent reasoning by the players; such accounts founder on the problem of multiple equilibria.

COORDINATION

Besides providing and embodying the necessary incentives for cooperation, institutions perform another general function: They coordinate individual action. The problem of coordination is as basic to social, economic, and political interaction as that of cooperation. A coordination problem, roughly speaking, is one in which several individuals share a desire to achieve one of several outcomes (behavior combinations) universally regarded as good ones, but have difficulty doing so (1) because they must choose among several such outcomes, and communication is somehow imperfect; and (2) in some cases also because, due to differing preferences, they disagree about which of these good outcomes is best. The "pure coordination" game is the simplest example embodying only the first characteristic; in it, all players agree completely in their preferences over the outcomes of a game, but unless they can coordinate their choices they stand only a moderate chance of satisfying that preference. The 2×2 pure coordination game can be represented as follows:

	C	D
C	1 / 1	0 / 0
D	0 / 0	1 / 1

The simplest game involving both characteristics of the coordination problem is the "battle of the sexes" game (Luce and Raiffa 1957, pp. 90–

1), in which the players agree that some of the outcomes are better than the others, but disagree over which of the good outcomes is best:

	C	D
C	1 / 2	0 / 0
D	0 / 0	2 / 1

Simple and derived problems of coordination

Setting standards for industrial production is perhaps the most basic example of a coordination problem. In some cases, no participant cares what the standard is, as long as there is some standard. More often, various participants have some preexisting investment in a given potential standard and would prefer to see that one adopted; but if a different standard is adopted they will adhere to it and be better off than if no standard had been adopted and they had maintained their original production approach.[19] Another common type of coordination problem occurs whenever people in a group organize and specialize in order to accomplish some group task valuable to all, such as military defense. Even if we assume that the cooperation problem of getting people to participate at all in defense has been solved, and even if every individual is indifferent about what specialized task he is assigned, there are gains from assigning different duties to different people so that all tasks are accomplished on time. Without some discussion, direction, or previously established practice, such coordination is unlikely to occur spontaneously in a large group. An important function of some institutions is to foster such coordination.

Coordination problems derived from other institutional problems.
Coordination problems are even more important, however, because they often arise in the course of efforts to solve other problems of social action or social order.[20] Consider an iterated collective action problem of the sort discussed previously in the section on cooperation. If such a game has any complexity at all, as in the example of the PD with hidden information or in the many-player PD, there are multiple ways of "solving" the problem of motivating cooperation. The difficulty lies in having all participants choose *the same one* of these solutions. If players have different expectations about when and by whom cooperation is expected, and about when, how, and by whom punishment or reward is to be

carried out, they are likely to end up punishing one another for actions intended to be appropriately cooperative. A system of incentives would break down under such circumstances, and cooperation would fail.

To achieve cooperation in a moderately complicated repeated game, then, it is necessary to make sure that all players arrive at the same expectations about which of many available equilibria they will all adhere to. Nearly any interesting problem with multiple equilibria is a coordination problem.[21] Consequently, any repeated game presents an initial coordination problem, namely, the identification of appropriate cooperative actions and appropriate rewards and punishments. The institution specifying rules for cooperation, reward, and punishment is a solution to that coordination problem. And like the solutions to a coordination game, such an institution can be specified and agreed upon in some preplay communication round, or it can emerge through trial and error in successive play of the original game. The problem of designing an institution, or evolving an institution, to accomplish cooperation is precisely the problem of agreeing upon one solution to a coordination game.

Such derived problems of coordination do not appear only once, at the outset, in a repeated cooperation game. If the cooperation game is repeated with variation, as in the case of the PD with hidden information in the preceding section, then in principle *each iteration* brings up a coordination problem: How is "appropriate" cooperation to be defined in the current iteration? If it is not feasible to describe in advance all possible contingencies that a cooperative institution might face, a difficulty that is endemic in the writing of any contract or set of rules, then new problems of specification must constantly be solved within any ongoing cooperative institution. In real life, whenever we disagree over the application of a rule to a specific situation, or argue about what precedent is applicable in a specific case, then (assuming we have a common interest in the use of orderly procedures to determine appropriate behavior) we are addressing a problem of coordination.

Need for a theory of coordination. To sum up, a well-developed theory of coordination games is necessary not just to understand institutions that function primarily to organize effort or to set standards, but more importantly to help us understand the emergence or design of institutions, and the conduct and maintenance of nearly any institution to foster cooperative behavior, broadly defined. Conversely, any theory that satisfactorily addressed these questions about institutions would constitute a theory of coordination games. To set standards or organize effort is to solve a coordination problem. To design an institution through explicit bargaining or planning is to solve a coordination problem. The emergence of an institution over time is a process analogous to the development of a pattern of coordination among players in a repeated coordination game, when no focal point or convention initially exists. The maintenance of an institution requires the repeated, successful play of coordination games in which the solution to previous games is at best an imperfect guide to the solution of a new game.

Schelling (1960), the first game theorist to address coordination, introduced the notion of the "focal point," a coordination outcome that, prior to the play of the game, has obvious mutual significance to the players due to their common experience or common observation of the way the game is presented. Recognizing or creating focal points is one important way in which the players can successfully coordinate. In addition, Schelling examined the importance of communication and commitment strategies in "mixed-motive" coordination games such as the battle of the sexes game. However, Schelling and other analysts regarded these aspects of the solution of games as being somewhat beyond the purview of game theory itself. For many years his extra-game-theoretic, intuitive approach to coordination games was the only available theoretical treatment of the problem, but the theory has recently begun to move to the specification of more rigorous models. Since coordination is so closely relevant to the problem of institution formation, the main job of the present section is to examine in detail the directions that this research has taken thus far.

The establishment of conventions

Schelling's theory of focal points depends on the players having common experiences. Based on this common experience each player can examine the form in which a game is presented and make educated guesses about how the other player will react to that presentation. For example, consider a game that involves choosing a location on a map at which to meet the other player. If it is common knowledge that the two players have identical maps before them and have common experience with the features of maps, and if there is a unique, easily recognizable prominent point on the map — say, a crossroad — then the players are likely to coordinate successfully on that point. This simple game is analogous to the situation of people interacting in a problem of social coordination, such as the choice of proper actions in a repeated game, when some convention[22] has already been established (Lewis 1969; Hardin 1982). A central question necessary to the understanding of institutional formation is: How are conventions established in the first place? For institutions are often conventions, embodying either the solution to a direct problem of coordination or the solution to the problem of choosing among the many equilibria in a problem of cooperation.

The rational choice theory of social institutions

Equilibrium selection in games.   From the pure game theorist's point of view, the problem of coordination is a special case of the problem of *equilibrium selection,* that is, the criteria or process by which the analyst or players can arrive at one equilibrium as a prediction or outcome, in a game that has several equilibria. The game theory literature develops two major approaches to the problem of equilibrium selection: (1) equilibrium refinements, in which additional criteria, concerning behavior following mistaken violations of equilibrium or concerning rational learning, are applied to narrow the set of Nash equilibria thought to be relevant for predictive purposes; and (2) what we may generally call "learning in games," in which players are portrayed as adjusting their stage-game strategies across iterations, in response to the observed previous actions of other players. The first approach, although useful in certain special cases of games of incomplete information (see e.g., Kreps and Wilson 1982), has proven unsuccessful in solving the general problem since one can design versions of the folk theorem to show that in a repeated game with sufficiently light discounting, there are multiple equilibria meeting any of these refinement criteria.

The learning-in-games approach, however, has considerable relevance for the problem of coordination and thus for the emergence of institutions. In particular, this approach addresses the phenomenon of institutional emergence without purposive design. Models of learning in games employ some process of natural selection or adaptive learning to portray the process by which individual players react to the previously observed actions of other players, and study the dynamics and steady states of such systems. Suppose that a large pool of players is to play a game repeatedly, either as one large group or in smaller groups through a random-matching process. This literature assumes always that there are no history-dependent strategies across these repetitions, although each individual game in the model may represent an entire repeated game that does involve internally history-dependent strategies. Imagine any starting point at which players use an arbitrary distribution of strategies. After one play of the game by everyone, some adaptive learning takes place: for example, each player compares her payoff to the average payoff attained by all other players; the lower the ratio of own payoff to average payoff, the more likely that player is to change to a different strategy for the next period. When a player does change, she changes to one of the strategies used by one of the other players, favoring those used by the players receiving higher payoffs. The result of such an analysis is a phase diagram describing the evolution of the strategy distribution in such a system and exhibiting the stable points of the system. If the distribution enters the neighborhood of one of those stable points, it will approach the point and

245

stay there. Elementary versions of such evolutionary models can be found in Maynard Smith (1982) and Axelrod (1984). Examinations of how such stable points compare to Nash equilibria under various learning dynamics are pursued by Jordan (1991), Milgrom and Roberts (1991), and Samuelson (1991), among others; the overall lesson is that, except for certain special situations, the stable states of these evolutionary systems tend to correspond with the Nash equilibria of the game. Importantly, there is no guarantee that the equilibria emerging from such a process will have good welfare properties, such as efficiency.

In none of these learning-in-games models do the players engage in fully strategic behavior; that is, each player ignores the fact that others will also be looking at past behavior and adjusting their strategies accordingly. Certainly, the players ignore the fact that their individual adjustments have implications for the quality of the equilibrium in which they will eventually settle. While such models are appealing representations of some forms of institutional emergence, then, they do not capture the important category of situations in which participants in an ongoing interaction actually worry about the establishment of precedent, or about the implications of their actions for future rules of thumb that others will follow.

The Crawford–Haller model: learning to coordinate. By introducing an innovative new theoretical device, Crawford and Haller (1990) offer a rigorous approach to the emergence of convention in games of pure coordination (in which all players have identical payoff functions). Their approach is related to the learning-in-games approach, but it portrays the players as being fully strategic, aware that their actions in search of a coordination equilibrium will combine with the efforts of other players to determine the eventual outcome. Suppose that two players are to play a large number of identical repetitions of a pure coordination game; for illustrative purposes consider the 2 × 2 game of pure coordination illustrated previously. The absence of a predefined convention or focal point depends on a rigorous insistence by the analyst that, at the outset, the players share no information about the way the game is labeled or presented. So, for example, while Player A sees herself as the row chooser and the payoff matrix as having 1 in the upper-left and lower-right outcomes, Player B may be viewing the game with himself as the row chooser and the payoffs in the opposite corners, with strategies relabeled appropriately. They are playing the same game, and the payoffs will correspond, but they have different ideas about how to describe the game. Thus, it is meaningless for Player A to say to herself, "I will guess that my opponent will aim for the upper-left outcome, since we both speak English and English is read from the upper left," because Player B may not see the same picture or may speak Hebrew. Importantly, Crawford and Haller assume both players to be fully aware of this difficulty. In locating a focal point, then, the players have nothing initially to go on; in the absence of any criterion, the only reasonable prediction either of them can make about the other's play in the first round is the mixed strategy that chooses each strategy with probability $1/2$. Since this is an equilibrium in the one-shot game, those expectations are consistent.

A second theoretical device necessary to implement the idea of no focal point depends on the notion of *symmetric* and *attainable* strategies. Two of a player's strategies are *symmetric* if they yield the same array of possible payoffs, perhaps given some rearrangement of the rows or columns corresponding to the other player's symmetric strategies. Likewise two *players* are symmetric if they are in identical strategic positions in the game. A strategy profile is *attainable* if symmetric players always employ identical mixed strategies, and if each player assigns the same mixed strategy probability weights to any two symmetric strategies. In the absence of any common-knowledge distinctions among such players and strategies, Crawford and Haller argue that no player has any reason to predict any distinctions between the strategies of symmetric players (themselves included) or among the weights placed on symmetric strategies. Thus, in isolated play of a coordination game, or on the first play of a repeated coordination game, only the attainable strategies are relevant.

As they play the repeated game, however, the players develop some common-knowledge[23] distinctions among strategies and players that were originally symmetric, and new profiles become attainable. In the 2×2 example, once the players first hit (randomly) on a coordinated outcome, they can distinguish, for each player, the action taken on that repetition from the action not taken. They then have available the following continuation strategy, which Crawford and Haller argue is inherently focal: continue to take that same action, successfully coordinating on every subsequent turn. Even in the rather complicated-looking examples that Crawford and Haller examine, the expected waiting time until perfect coordination is achieved may be surprisingly short. In the 2×2 pure coordination game, the average number of periods spent before coordination occurs is just 1.

When precedent is an imperfect guide.   One feature of the Crawford-Haller approach limits its applicability to the kind of coordination problems generated in the emergence or maintenance of institutions. Those complex coordination problems would often involve shifting situations, in which lessons learned in previous iterations may be of only partial relevance. Crawford and Haller assume instead that the "labeling" each player places on the game stays constant across all repetitions, a regularity that drives the relatively rapid achievement of coordination in their examples. Also, the assumption that the players will choose to repeat the "same" strategies that yielded their first successful coordination, an assumption that is somewhat arbitrary to begin with, is even less appealing when the meaning of actions and strategies may change across iterations.

Calvert (1991) examines an extended version of the Crawford–Haller model, for the 2×2 case only, that takes the variation of players' perceptions across iterations explicitly into account. That is, it addresses the problem of what happens when even a newly established convention is not a perfect guide to future behavior, as would be the case when trying to agree upon the proper requirements of cooperation in a repeated game whose iterations are not identical in terms of payoffs, participants, and the like. The model does so by explicitly depicting the "labeling" of the game that each player is using. Suppose again that each player sees himself as the row chooser, and now suppose further that the rows are presented in reverse order in some iterations of the game. However, neither player is directly aware of differences in his own labeling; from each player's point of view, it is the other player who occasionally behaves as though seeing a different labeling, and as though choosing the same *label* as before – for example, always choosing the "top" row.

As in the Crawford–Haller model, the players begin by playing the lone attainable equilibrium, choosing each action with probability $1/2$. Suppose their first success occurs on a turn in which Player A chose the top row. Arbitrarily label Player B's type on this iteration as t (a player's "type" on a given iteration denotes the way that player labels the game on that play). Now with some probability p, on any subsequent iteration Player B will (appear to) be of the opposite type, t', which sees the game with the opposite labeling of B's actions and, from Player A's point of view, does just the opposite of what type t would be expected to do. (Simultaneously, Player B sees himself as the row player in the identity-matrix game and sees Player A as taking on two different types.) Thus, if the players conduct themselves exactly as in the Crawford–Haller model, playing the "same" strategy forever once they initially coordinate, they will successfully coordinate on a proportion $1 - p$ of all subsequent iterations.

Of course, A has no way of knowing what the true type of B was on the iteration where they first coordinated. Suppose A knows only that one of B's types occurs with probability p and the other occurs with probability $1 - p$. The best policy would be, if possible, to coordinate with the more common b-type, and just endure the resulting loss when B happens to be the other type. The optimal long-run average payoff would then be $\max\{p, 1 - p\}$. If the first coordination happens to occur when B is his most common type, then this payoff is rapidly achieved. However, if the players are not so fortunate, they will receive a lower payoff, min$\{p, 1 - p\}$. By noting the numbers of successes and failures thereafter, they may realize their "mistake" and start over again, continuing to do so until the higher payoff is achieved. The Calvert (1991) model goes on to address how public information correlated with the players' true types could be used to improve payoffs further, by allowing them to establish different conventions for different circumstances.

Lessons from the analysis. Both the learning-in-games approach and the Crawford–Haller model of establishing convention apply most directly to the emergence of institutions when a pattern of cooperation and enforcement is to be chosen once at the beginning of a repeated cooperation problem. Although both shed light on how we can bring the ideas of focal points and equilibrium selection properly within the purview of game theory, there is much more to be done before these results will apply directly to questions of institutional formation. If the convention in question concerns equilibrium choice in a repeated game, a direct application of their model would portray the players as, in effect, playing the whole repeated game for each "iteration" of the Crawford–Haller game. Then, the players would look back to see if they had been agreed on the equilibrium cooperation and enforcement scheme and, if so, follow it the "next time" the repeated game was encountered – not exactly the way one would want to model this problem. Instead, it would be more in keeping with the way one normally thinks about the process to portray the players as beginning the repeated cooperation game unsure what their partner's expectations are going to be, and as progressing toward similar expectations as the patterns of cooperation emerge from play. A fundamental problem for players taking this iteration-by-iteration approach is that an opponent's strategy in the repeated game cannot be inferred precisely from the observation of any finite sequence of moves. Thus, the coordination problem faced by participants in a "new" cooperation problem embodies difficulties not reflected in the solution of the simple repetition of one-shot pure coordination games. Still, the approach introduced by Crawford and Haller might point the way toward additional theoretical innovations that will give us a handle on the process of institutional emergence.

A fundamental result of all these models concerning the emergence of coordination outcomes and thus of institutions is that there is absolutely no general built-in drive toward efficiency of the resulting institutions. Crawford and Haller give an example in which, even though precedent is a perfect guide to future behavior, the players should fail to achieve an ex post efficient outcome. Consider a symmetric, two-player pure coordination game having a large number of strategies, with nonzero payoffs appearing on the main diagonal only. Suppose that most of the nonzero payoffs are 3, but that a very few of them are 2. Here, achieving the lower-payoff, coordinated outcome presents less of a challenge than achieving a higher-payoff one, because there are fewer such outcomes to coordinate among. For appropriate parameter values, then, the Crawford–Haller model would predict that the players would aim for, relatively quickly achieve, and stick with a pattern of play ultimately yielding a payoff of only 2 on each turn. An observer, seeing the result of the players' efforts, might say that the players have irrationally failed to take actions that would make them all better off. Only given the proper model of how the "inefficient" outcome was arrived at does it become clear that the players acted to maximize ex ante expected payoff – and that it would still be irrational for them to respond to the outside critic by trying to improve their payoff after the fact.

Considerations very similar to these often provide compelling explanations of the maintenance of inefficient equilibria in the real world. David (1985) presents his history of the QWERTY keyboard standard as just such a situation. Similarly, citizens may willingly maintain an unsatisfactory constitution if the attempt to switch to some superior one would subject them to a lengthy period of costly disorder due to the difficulty of coordinating expectations on a particular new set of political rules of the game.

Cheap talk and coordination

The Crawford–Haller model takes a radical approach in assuming that there is no preexisting information of any kind that would help the players coordinate, and further that there is no ability to communicate meaningfully about the problem except implicitly through the actual play of the game. In most situations of institutional formation and maintenance, and certainly in direct coordination problems, this is by no means the case, and surely communication plays an important role in coordination. Although is it important for the theorist of institutions to understand the situation in which there is no preexisting convention, it is also important to gain some purchase on the way communication can be used in such problems.

In a situation like the pure coordination games examined by Crawford and Haller, a little communication would go a long way toward solving the problem: All it takes is one person to announce an outcome to all the players, and a focal point is successfully created. Of course, if there are numerous such "announcements" floating around, a coordination problem remains, but one would have to conclude that pure coordination games in the real world are relatively easily solved. The same cannot be said for situations in which there is some degree of underlying disagreement about which of the "coordinated" outcomes is most desirable. In the case of standard-setting in which different manufacturers have preexisting stakes in different possible standards, or in a problem of task organization in which some tasks are more odious than others, communication inevitably involves a measure of negotiation, bluster, and threat about who gets the most benefit from any ultimate coordination agreement. Obviously, the design of an institution or the determination of precedent involves serious interest conflict of this sort. In such cases communication need not lead directly to smooth acquisition of a convention, and the theoretical problem of how communication might contribute to coordination is a substantial one.

The Farrell model. Farrell (1987) uses a simple model of rather disagreeable communication to show how even the most unpromising of methods can improve expected payoffs in a mixed-motive coordination problem. Suppose that two players are to engage in one play of the battle of the sexes game with payoff values of 2, 1, and 0. With no communication, about the best they can hope for is the symmetric, mixed-strategy equilibrium, which yields successful coordination with probability $4/9$, and an expected payoff of $2/3$ to each player. In contrast, each player would receive a payoff of 1 by just accepting the other player's favorite outcome with certainty, and an expected payoff of $3/2$ in the best symmetric correlated equilibrium strategy.[24] Farrell augments the play of this game by allowing the players a round of "cheap talk" communication before play. That is, before playing the game, the players can send one of two messages to one another, where the messages have no cost and are in no way binding as promises or threats. In the augmented-game equilibrium that Farrell examines, there are two messages whose effective meanings are "I will play the strategy corresponding to *my* favorite outcome" and "I will play the strategy corresponding to *your* favorite outcome." The equilibrium is as follows: the players send the "my way" message with a high probability but not with certainty; and if by chance one player says "my way" and the other "your way," they choose the corresponding strategies in playing the actual battle of the sexes. If they both send the same message, however, they go ahead and use the symmetric, mixed-strategy equilibrium just as if there had been no communication in the first place. Thus, in effect the players get two chances to coordinate rather than one; this improves their chances and their ex ante expected payoffs, even though the equilibrium probability with which a player sends the "your way" message is lower than the probability of actually playing that way in the symmetric equilibrium in the original battle of the sexes. Adding more rounds of such communication, Farrell examines an equilibrium in which, if ever the players send compatible messages, they ignore all further messages and play according to their "agreement." This gives them even more "chances" to coordinate, and raises expected payoffs even though the more rounds of communication there are, the smaller the early-round probability of sending the "your way" message. The probability of coordination, and the expected payoff, gets ever larger as more communication rounds are added, although in the limit it does not approach the correlated equilibrium level.

Optimal coordination with cheap talk. Even this kind of "yes I will, no you won't" negotiation actually improves the players' ability to coordinate. As Banks and Calvert (1990) point out, the players can do even better if their communication is less pejoratively labeled – they can in fact achieve the correlated equilibrium by engaging in a one-round, unmediated, mixed-strategy communication process that, without actually requiring that the players be in physical contact, amounts to the joint flipping of a fair coin. Although it is far from obvious that all mixed-motive coordination games can be thus perfectly solved by proper communication, it is clear that communication is critical to the ability to settle on a coordinated outcome when interests conflict.

Bargaining problems. In some respects, the battle of the sexes game resembles a simple bargaining problem. Indeed, as Schelling (1960) suggested, every bargaining problem presents a coordination problem, since there is some chance that bargainers will fail to reach an agreement due to their holding out for a better deal, despite the existence of some potential agreement that would have been better than failure for both players. This does not happen in complete-information models of bargaining, however, because players in those games are, in effect, fully informed about the extent of their opponents' willingness to give in (see, e.g., Rubinstein 1982). When bargaining models include asymmetric information, however, coordination failure appears as the occasional failure, in equilibrium, of the players to reach an agreement as early as possible (thus incurring discounting or the possibility of an exogenous breakdown) (Rubinstein 1985). Here, then, communication consists of the bargainers' offers and counteroffers, and successful coordination consists of the reaching of agreement before any "shrinkage" of the available gains occurs.

Lessons from the analysis. Bargaining over the details of institutional design, inasmuch as it reduces to the classic problem of bargaining to divide a fixed "pie" of available gains, should look essentially the same as any other bargaining process from a theoretical standpoint, whether the process is modeled as a cheap-talk game or as an offer-counteroffer negotiation. The communication in such processes enables the players to achieve a mutually advantageous outcome in the form of an institutional arrangement; the uncertainties of the process may limit the extent of those mutual gains, however.

Again, though, one must bear in mind that the "communication" that determines institutional choice in the real world is not always of the preplay variety common to bargaining and cheap-talk models. If the actual bargaining over institutions takes place in the process of play of the underlying game, rather than in some preplay communication round, new complications may arise. In the end, the same cautions apply to bargaining models and cheap-talk coordination games as in the pure coordination process of the Crawford–Haller model: The theory of institutions, although conceptually advanced by these models of communication and coordination, awaits further theoretical innovations before it can address realistic processes of institutional formation from this approach.

Institutional choice behind a partial "veil of ignorance"

In some real-world processes of institutional design, the conflicts inherent in the cheap-talk and bargaining models are alleviated somewhat by the fact that at the time they choose institutional rules, participants do not know the specific issues they will be dealing with or interests they will be pursuing under those rules. A model due to Banks and Calvert (1992) examines some of the considerations inherent in the choice of institutional rules under a partial "veil of ignorance" about each individual's eventual stakes when acting under those rules. This model centers on a battle of the sexes game with asymmetric information about payoffs. Two players are to play one iteration of the following basic game:

		x		y
		0		1
x	0		t_1	
		t_2		0
y	1		0	

where $t_i \in \{a, b\}$, $b > a > 1$, and the t_i are private information, determined according to Prob$\{t_i = b\} = p$, where the value of p is common knowledge. This basic game could represent either a primary coordination problem, such as the setting of standards, or a stylized version of the coordination problem derived from some underlying problem of equilibrium selection, such as in a repeated cooperation problem. If the game represents a derived coordination problem, then the institutional design problem would be simply to solve this coordination game, and thus agree upon an equilibrium for the underlying game. If the basic game represents a primary coordination problem that may be repeated, then an institution would be some sort of system in an augmented version of the game, allowing for the smooth and profitable solution of the primary coordination problem each time it arises. The Banks–Calvert analysis concerns the latter case.

Accordingly, let us augment the basic game by adding an opportunity for communication. Prior to playing the basic game, the players can communicate by sending messages to one another according, once again, to some precise process specified by an extensive game form. I also assume that a third "player," in the form of a disinterested mediator, takes part in this communication phase; however, the mediator's communication adheres strictly to a set of rules or specifications that are common knowledge to the two regular players.

In the Banks–Calvert analysis, the stage of choosing an institution is left outside the augmented game. Rather, the strategy there for examining institutional choice is to derive the expected utility of each player ex ante, that is, before they know their own true t_i values, for each possible institutional arrangement. In this setting in which the players are in completely symmetrical positions, then, such normative properties of institutional alternatives ought to inform the players' choice of an institution. But what exactly is the nature of the institution that players in this game are to choose before the augmented game itself is played? The relevant institution here consists of (1) the rule to be used by the mediator when she participates in the communication phase and (2) the equilibrium to be followed by the players given that rule. This approach fits into our overall scheme of institutions as equilibria, strictly speaking, since the mediator receives no payoff and is thus indifferent about using one rule or another. To be slightly more realistic, we could instead portray the mediator as receiving some sort of commission or reward based directly on the total payoff that the other two players receive. However, there is no room in the present model for a mediator whose interests conflict with the ex ante preferences of the other players.

Naturally, the set of equilibria of the augmented game depends on the particular specification of the communication process. However, Banks and Calvert use the revelation principle (Myerson 1985) to abstract away from the particular communication process and discover the set of possible distributions over outcomes that are available to the players in some equilibrium of some allowable communication process. In carrying out this analysis, it is possible to discover general properties that must be true of any efficient, symmetric process for communicating and choosing actions in the basic game.[25] Assuming that such processes would indeed be the attractive ones for players deciding upon institutions under a veil of ignorance, then, we learn about the properties that would characterize any agreeable institutional choice by the players.

Properties of the optimal mechanism.   The optimal mechanism has several interesting properties from the standpoint of understanding the role of institutions. First of all, even without communication in each period, the players in this game achieve higher ex ante expected payoffs than they would if the game were played with complete information about payoffs.[26] Second, however, the addition of communication definitely provides a further improvement in payoff. Third, the payoff from any such mechanism is bounded away from the classically efficient level, which the players could achieve only if they could credibly bind themselves to report their true payoffs. Fourth, the optimal mechanism requires, in general, the use of an impartial mediator of the type portrayed (but not actually required) in the Calvert (1993) model discussed earlier. The only exception is when parameter values are such that the optimal mechanism is for the players to simply flip a coin together to decide between the coordinated outcomes — that is, to play a correlated equilibrium that does not attempt to take their private information into account at all. Fifth, in order to elicit information from the players in the most profitable way for them, the mediator's rule must sometimes lead the players into coordination failures. As a result, the privacy of the mediator's communications is important to the optimal mechanism, again in contrast to the mechanism examined in Calvert (1993). If the mediator's suggestions were public, the players would not obey a suggestion that they play uncoordinated strategies.

Lessons from the analysis.   The basic game in the Banks–Calvert model is an example of an important class of problems in politics and institutional design. First, of course, it is a game with mixed motives, and hence with distributional consequences that coexist with the mutual desire for coordination. Second, the possibility that players' stakes in their preferred outcomes (the t_i) may differ means that there is some ex ante uncertainty in each player's mind about what his preferences will be when the agreed-upon institution is actually put into effect. The decision on institutional structure is made at this ex-ante stage, so that each player has some stake in designing effective rules, and is not merely feathering his own nest; the initial symmetry of the game makes it plausible that any agreement would result in an institutional structure that would treat the two players identically, and so the analysis concentrates on efficient, symmetrical institutions.[27] Third, the presence of asymmetric information about the stakes, even once the players learn their own true payoff values, reflects an important feature of bargaining in many real-life economic and political situations. The individual actor often appreciates his own costs and outside opportunities better than any other actor does.

The Banks–Calvert results indicate that in a decision problem characterized by mixed-motive coordination and asymmetric information, communication is central to any institution that would allow the participants to realize the available gains from coordination. Moreover, *private* communication is critical, as is the role of the trusted intermediary who can make suggestions and carry credible information. Because of the need to elicit credible information from the players, even the best possible institution must sometimes yield outcomes that are ex post inefficient. And due to the information asymmetry in such a problem, the best available institution will fall short, even in terms of ex ante efficiency, of the payoffs that would appear available in the absence of incentive problems. Again, the institutional critic operating without benefit of the theory would find fault with what the theory shows to be the optimal institution; these faults are in fact insuperable obstacles in a world of mixed motives and asymmetric information.

CONCLUSION

It remains to examine three important issues emerging from the analyses surveyed. First, the role of rational communication in many of these models of cooperation and coordination indicates that similar models may offer interesting possibilities for the study of communicative phenomena such as rhetoric, ritual, and symbolic speech, often regarded as elements of culture not amenable to rational choice analysis. Second, the rational choice theory of institutions focusing on these processes of cooperation, coordination, and communication offers a useful agenda for the empirical study of institutions, and I will examine the steps that one should take in any empirical analysis based on the theory. Finally, I contrast the theory sketched in this essay with some current critiques of the rational choice approach, and argue that the theory is capable of much more than it has already accomplished and much more than its critics expect.

The role of communication in institutions

In several of the models of coordination and of cooperation, the ability for the players to transmit messages to one another, even if those messages are purely cheap talk, produces an array of opportunities and complexities in the interaction of rational agents. Even in the simple, stylized games of coordination and cooperation amenable to theoretical analysis, the opportunity for cheap talk alone produces important new results and the possibility of significant improvements in outcomes, as illustrated in Farrell (1987). Whenever people operating within an institution need to establish precedent, assign specialized roles, define appropriate levels of cooperation, or take individual private information into account, they can do it most effectively by communicating, by stating suggestions, intentions, or information. As illustrated in the Calvert (forthcoming) model of Tit-for-Tat cooperation using centralized communication, an institution may function by defining not only special times and messages for communication, but also by specifying that certain suggestions from certain players are always to be followed. As long as those suggestions are backed up by some player's rational willingness to apply sanctions when appropriate, that suggestion is an order, and that player is authoritative. In this way institutions define and use communication as integral parts of their systems of incentive and coordination, and the theory of communication in games is critical to any rational choice theory of institutions.

It is worth considering the subject of communication separately from those of cooperation and communication as well, however, because of the complex ramifications that the widespread use of communication in those types of problems may have. Signals about intended or promised actions in one game might yield inferences about a player's preferences, the state of a player's knowledge and expectations, and so on that in turn tells others something about that player's likely behavior in other, related interactions. Thus, a promise of cooperation now, in some cheap-talk equilibrium, may not only presage the keeping of that promise but also foretell cooperativeness in other settings later.

The implications, however, go much deeper than this. The expression of a value, that is, of a principle justifying some norm or other prescribed behavior, in communication preceding the play of a complex problem of repeated cooperation ("I believe that all players ought to expect others to cooperate when in situations resembling X") may not only signal an intention to adhere to the value (to hold the expectation and to intend such cooperation), but also serve as a convention-creating, focal statement in the sense of Schelling (1960) that helps actually implement such expectations and behavior by all players in equilibrium play – that is, helps create the value as a matter of mutual expectation among the participants. The mere stating of such expressions may itself come to be expected of players who want to continue cooperative arrangements with others, giving rise to ritual and symbolic expressions of value unconnected with specific instances of cooperation. Moreover, rhetoric acquires

257

an important role in a setting like this, as various players attempt to connect potential interpretations or precedents for the current situation with particular rules already established, using statements of *values* that have previously been applied successfully in attempts of this sort. This whole approach is suggested obliquely in Hardin (1982) in his discussion of how conventions arise. Johnson (1991b, 1993) gives an interpretation of the "communicative action," as opposed to "strategic action," of critical theorist and sociologist Jurgen Habermas (1984) that works in more or less this way. Elsewhere, Johnson (1991a) describes and motivates (although he does not formalize it mathematically) a theory of cultural change through the strategic manipulation of cultural symbols. The overall approach of Johnson's theory is closely compatible with the ramifications of widespread rational communication sketched here. In short, widespread communication in a setting of multiple, complex games among overlapping sets of players could give rise to rich expressions of norms, values, and even a somewhat stylized model of culture.

Current models of the achievement of coordination without benefit of preexisting conventions (Crawford and Haller 1990) offer hints at how a variety of signals having no inherent meaning can, when used in conjunction with individuals' actions in coordination and other problems, acquire meanings in the form of common-knowledge expectations about actions that the signals invoke. In a theoretical world of "learning to cooperate" and of learning to coordinate under asymmetric information and varying situations and experiences, such signals could come to have an even richer variety of meanings. The development of language, which is after all just one social institution, might be portrayed in terms developed from these coordination models. Perhaps the resulting theory can be connected with philosophical theories of language that see the meaning of utterances as inhering in their correlation with acts.

An empirical research program

The idea of institutions as game-theoretic equilibria can be fruitfully applied to analyze the stability and effects of institutions in various areas of social life. Such an analysis would begin with a description of an apparent institution and the associated patterns of behavior. To check this description for consistency, the analyst should construct a model of the institution along the lines of the models surveyed here. First, such a model requires a portrayal of the game that underlies a given institution: the production of value, the opportunity for gains from trade, cooperation, coordination, or whatever. Along with this basic interaction, most institutions depend upon information transfer, and so sufficient opportunities for communication must be built into the game. The resulting game can then be solved for its equilibria. Given the limitations on our analytical capabilities, this model will necessarily be a very simplified and stylized version of the observed situation; the goal, however, is to include whatever features are necessary in order to derive the most interesting features of the institution.

The institutions and behavior observed in real life should correspond roughly to one of the equilibria to the game so constructed. The utility of this analytical process begins at this point: If there is no such equilibrium, this may be an indication that there is some fault either with the description of the underlying problem or with the description of the real-world institutions. In that case, one returns to the real-life institution to try to determine, perhaps using the game-theoretic reasoning derived thus far, what might have been omitted or misspecified in the original description. The model should help the observer know what to look for.

Once a suitable fit is found between the model and the observed process, it is possible to examine the model to derive explanations and predictions about the institution. The game-theoretic analysis offers comparative-statics statements about how the model's equilibrium behavior varies with variations in the game's parameters (payoffs, number of players, discount factors, etc.). These constitute predictions about how marginal changes in the real-world environment will influence real-world behavior. It may be possible to identify parameter changes under which the observed institutional features would cease to be in equilibrium (as happens in repeated-cooperation institutions if the discount factor drops below a certain value). Further, interrogation of the model yields results concerning Pareto improvements that might be available under alternative equilibria, or strategic opportunities for coalitions. Empirical analysis of such a model would consist of tests of those comparative statics results, along with the detection of infrequent behavioral patterns predicted by the model but not previously noticed in the real-world case at hand. When such predicted patterns fail to hold, the analyst goes back to the model and to the description to determine what changes might render the description consistent again.

Such a program of study does not aim to "test" the basic notion that an institution is an equilibrium among rational actors. Rather, it takes this basic notion as a given method and tests the models that the analyst derives using the method. It has the great virtue of imposing a discipline on the description of institutions and institutional processes, forcing them to be consistent with the simultaneous rationality of all the actors given their information and basic goals. Whether this method is valid overall will depend on an assessment of its usefulness as a guide for theoretical and empirical analysis, by comparison with other methods. At present, I do not think that any alternative method offers such a coherent overall approach to the study of institutions. I conclude by examining some of those alternatives and the critiques of the rational actor approach that they embody.

Alternative approaches

Some recent criticism of rational choice theory has advocated nonrational, or radically non-self-interest, approaches to understanding institutions, especially in the case of informal institutions manifested as social norms. Levine (1981), Maass (1983), and Quirk (1990), for example, attribute the development of regulatory institutions to a built-in preference of legislators and regulatory officials to make good public policy, rather than to the incentives created by electoral and governmental political structures. More generally, Elster (1989) insists that adherence to social norms is a result of generalized other-regarding preferences, or "altruism," rather than to any promise of reward or threat of sanctions in the form of social pressures. These approaches suffer for a couple of reasons by comparison with the rational choice approaches discussed in this essay. First is the issue of parsimony: if rational choice and self-interested preferences can explain seemingly altruistic behavior, why adduce altruistic basic motivations? Altruistic motivations are less appealing as a starting point anyway, since, second, they are invariably inferred post hoc from the observation of behavior – it is difficult to state a single, abstract altruistic motivation that would be evoked by each of the multitude of social situations in which people behave in a seemingly altruistic manner. Third, altruistic motivations do not always determine behavior, since behavior is often selfish; a similar act of cooperation may be commonplace in one culture, and rare in another. An altruism-based theory must explain this variety as well. On the whole, a lot of work must be done by an altruistic-motivations theory to explain selfless-seeming behavior – and such a theory must still have a selfish component![28] Why not let the selfish motivations do all the work, abetted perhaps by incomplete information and bounded rationality? Despite the lively literature that has developed in criticism of rationality models in general and of self-interest approaches in particular,[29] the self-interest model still seems by far the most promising direction for a theory of institutions. Indeed, as the new theoretical advances cited in this essay should indicate, we are only beginning to realize the potential of game-theoretic techniques for this purpose.

NOTES

1. North (1990: 3) ultimately employs an almost identical definition: "the rules of the game in a society, or, more formally, . . . the humanly devised constraints that shape human interaction."
2. At least, this is the approach Schotter advocates in his chap. 2 (1981); but contrast his conceptual description in chap. 1, in which he emphasizes a dynamic and nonequilibrium conceptualization. His actual analysis draws on assumptions of myopic, dynamic adjustment based on stage-game preferences.
3. The idea of efficient or otherwise "good" institutions resulting from an evolutionary process is central to Hayek (1967, 1973) and has been employed by numerous others. However, Knight (1992, chap. 4) criticizes this approach, arguing that most of its practitioners fail to specify adequately the details of the selection mechanism that would yield the hypothesized good results.
4. Fuller accounts of the development of institutional and noninstitutional political science include Somit and Tannenhaus (1967), Eulau (1963), and Olson (1965, chap. 6).
5. Consider the importance of the governing agencies, constitutional-choice, and supermajority institutions basic to Downs (1957) and Buchanan and Tullock (1962). Indeed, the latter were explicitly interested in how various choices of supermajority criteria could effect the size of externalities imposed by, and thus the overall benefits from, government action.
6. Kramer (1972) had made the same modeling step, that of one-dimension-at-a-time movement in the policy space, although he did not emphasize the application to institutional channeling of majority voting. See especially Kramer's discussion at pp. 166–7.
7. These are the kinds of transaction costs that Wallis and North (1986) attempt to measure, by measuring the resources devoted to financial services, legal representation, transportation, etc.
8. Buchanan and Tullock (1962) treat "the cost of higgling and bargaining" as a transaction cost in their analysis of the proper size of a constitutional majority. The cost of traveling to reach a partner for bargaining would be a straightforward opportunity cost, but the possibility that "higgling" will delay or even prevent the reaching of an agreement is inherent in the incentives of any bargaining problem under incomplete information, and is thus not an opportunity cost. The original treatment of bargaining under asymmetric information is Rubinstein (1985).
9. See, e.g., Coase (1937), Alchian and Demsetz (1972), and Jensen and Meckling (1976). Again, such "costs" represent incentive and information problems that often cannot be overcome by the straightforward application of more resources.
10. For an overview of what such approaches tell us about incentives in organizations such as the firm, see Miller (1992) and Milgrom and Roberts (1992).
11. This is the approach taken straightforwardly in, for example, Keohane (1986), Koford and Miller (1991), and Margolis (1982). Some authors, such as Frank (1988) and Boyd and Richerson (1985), take a more sophisticated approach, proposing that specific learning and selection mechanisms might bring about the evolution or inculcation of obedient or altruistic motives. However, these approaches also involve methods that are at root game-

theoretic, in that they attempt to show how initially selfish motives are supplemented by rational equilibrium processes. Nevertheless, they too end up claiming an extremely broad propensity to cooperate, offering little to help us understand why altruistic motives are effective in some specific circumstances and not in others.

12. Not to be confused with descriptions of institutions that merely fall far short of efficiency. A dysfunctional institution or rule would be one that all or most affected individuals would be better off without. For example, current descriptions of Russian attitudes toward successful entrepreneurship (that those who prosper relative to others through innovation or arbitrage should be punished – a set of norms and values and thus an institution) portray that value system as being dysfunctional. Such values constitute a kind of equilibrium trap that makes most Russians worse off but from which each individual Russian is powerless to escape unilaterally. On the other hand, Turnbull's (1972) description of the social order of the Ik, and Banfield's (1962) account of "amoral familism" in southern Italy, portray institutional systems that fail to realize many of the gains that would presumably be available through alternative patterns of social order. These are inefficient, but not necessarily dysfunctional, institutions. The section on coordination, later, gives the theoretical underpinnings of the persistence of both inefficient and dysfunctional institutions.

13. Indeed, my notion of institutional cooperation does not even rule out the existence of dysfunctional institutions.

14. It is critical to distinguish between the assumption that individuals are rational in their actions and the stronger assumption that individuals will not participate in an institution whose existence makes them worse off. Viewing institutions as equilibria merely requires each individual to behave rationally *given what all others are doing;* this is weaker than an "individual rationality" condition for the *existence* of an institution, such as a normative or contract theorist might assume (see e.g., Buchanan and Tullock's, 1962, pp. 85–96, unanimity condition for an ideal world in the absence of bargaining costs and Gauthier, 1990, pp. 200–1, on the normative requirement that social choice mechanisms be an improvement over the state of nature for every individual). Compare, for example, the definition given by Luce and Raiffa (1957) of noncooperative-game equilibrium (pp. 60–5, 104–5) with their individual rationality condition for cooperative games (p. 193). Viewing institutions as equilibria carries no normative or welfare implications whatsoever.

15. Alternatively, the underlying game may be taken both from nature and from some exogenous institutional structure assumed to be fixed; the model then serves to analyze the feasibility and effects of additional institutional details.

16. Throughout this analysis, the equilibrium concept employed is subgame-perfect Nash equilibrium. Thus in particular, any threat to defect or promise to cooperate off the path of equilibrium play is rational to carry out.

17. "Efficiency" off the equilibrium path becomes a relevant consideration if we introduce into the game the possibility of mistakes or "trembles" in the choice of strategies, or if we contemplate extending the analysis to allow considerations similar to those in Calvert (1993), involving the possibility that occasional, adverse, private-information payoff values might force otherwise cooperative individuals to defect.

18. The model as given in Calvert (1991) is made marginally more interesting by

letting the players draw new cost values in every iteration of PD, but according to different probabilities of the low-cost draw, determined prior to PG. The probability of drawing a low cost is either q_h or q_l, with $q_h > q_l$, and the probability of drawing q_l is known by all to be p, so that the expected number of more-often-low-cost types is pN. Then q_l must be assumed sufficiently low that q_l types can maintain cooperation using a mechanism such as that described in the previous PD game with asymmetric information, while q_h is too high for that to be possible. The result is interesting because q_h types then have an incentive to masquerade as q_l types even in the PD. However, the formulation presented here is much simpler and gets the general point across.

19. Of course, if there are participants who are better off with their accustomed practice and no standard than they are with the less-preferred standard, then the problem is no longer simply one of coordination.

20. Hardin (1982, chaps. 10–14) was apparently the first to consider this problem in the context of institutional emergence.

21. This is not universally true since, with more than two players, it is possible to write down a normal-form game with multiple equilibria in which some disagreements about equilibrium would yield Pareto improvements. However, in the case of repeated cooperation problems, in which the multiplicity of equilibria involves various cooperation requirements and retaliation schemes, this happy accident is unlikely to occur. Rather, punishments for well-intentioned behavior will lead to failures to achieve available gains from cooperation.

22. A convention is a pattern of behavior that almost all participants expect almost everybody to engage in, and having the properties that: given this expectation, most individuals would maximize utility by engaging in that same behavior pattern as well; but there is some alternative behavior pattern such that, if almost everyone else engaged in the alternative instead, then each individual would be best off engaging in the alternative as well.

23. That is, the distinctions are known to both players; both players know that both players know the distinctions; both players know this; and so on, ad infinitum.

24. That is, an equilibrium in a version of the game in which a mediator privately suggests an action to each player according to some probability rule known to both players, after which the players take action but need not follow the suggestion. In a correlated equilibrium, it is rational for each player to follow the mediator's suggestion, assuming that the other will do so.

25. Banks and Calvert (1990) smooth out some important details by proving that there can be no asymmetric mediation rule that would yield efficiency gains over the efficient symmetric rule, and that the set of symmetric rules under the revelation principle corresponds exactly (in payoff yields) to the set of symmetric equilibria in all possible general communication processes.

26. This happens, ultimately, because the existence of the two different player "types" defined by $t_i = a$ and $t_i = b$ gives the players an extra means for distinguishing themselves (even though the types are private), and thus makes it easier to reach a coordinated outcome, which by definition requires the initially symmetric players to take different actions. See Banks and Calvert (1990: pp. 11–12).

27. Asymmetrical situations could in principle be examined by assigning the players different probabilities or payoff values.

28. Margolis (1982) offers a theory of combined selfish and altruistic action that claims to accomplish the whole job; but it is, in the form given at least, a nonrational model. That is, there is no well-defined preference that individuals can be said to maximize. Rather, the model makes an arbitrary assumption about how the individual trades off selfish against altruistic actions, and employs an unexplained criterion, unrelated to preferences, that controls the trade-off.
29. See, e.g., the papers collected in Mansbridge (1990) and most of those in Monroe (1991).

REFERENCES

Alchian, Armen A. 1950. "Uncertainty, Evolution, and Economic Theory." *Journal of Political Economy* 58: 211–21.

Alchian, Armen A., and Harold Demsetz. 1972. "Production, Information Costs, and Economic Organization." *American Economic Review* 62: 777–95.

Axelrod, Robert. 1984. *The Evolution of Cooperation*. New York: Basic Books.

Banfield, Edward C. 1962. *The Moral Basis of a Backward Society*. New York: Macmillan.

Banks, Jeffrey S., and Randall L. Calvert. 1990. "Communication and Efficiency in Coordination Games with Incomplete Information." Photocopy, University of Rochester.

Banks, Jeffrey S., and Randall L. Calvert. 1992. "A Battle-of-the-Sexes Game with Incomplete Information." *Games and Economic Behavior* 4: 347–72.

Baron, David P., and John A. Ferejohn. 1989. "Bargaining in Legislatures." *American Political Science Review* 83: 1181–1206.

Boyd, Robert, and Peter J. Richerson. 1985. *Culture and the Evolutionary Process*. Chicago: University of Chicago Press.

Buchanan, James M., and Gordon Tullock. 1962. *The Calculus of Consent: Logical Foundations of Constitutional Democracy*. Ann Arbor: University of Michigan Press.

Calvert, Randall L. 1991. "Elements of a Theory of Society among Rational Actors." Photocopy, University of Rochester.

Calvert, Randall L. 1993. "Communication in Institutions: Efficiency in a Repeated Prisoner's Dilemma with Hidden Information." In W. Barnett and N. Schofield, eds., *Political Economy*. Cambridge University Press, pp. 197–222.

Calvert, Randall L. Forthcoming. "Rational Actors, Equilibrium, and Social Institutions." In J. Knight and I. Sened, eds., *Explaining Social Institutions*. Ann Arbor: University of Michigan Press.

Calvert, Randall L., Mathew D. McCubbins, and Barry R. Weingast. 1989. "A Theory of Political Control and Agency Discretion." *American Journal of Political Science* 33: 588–611.

Coase, Ronald H. 1937. "The Nature of the Firm." *Economica* 4: 386–405.

Coase, Ronald H. 1960. "The Problem of Social Cost." *Journal of Law and Economics* 3: 1–44.

Crawford, Vincent P., and Hans Haller. 1990. "Learning How to Cooperate: Optimal Play in Repeated Coordination Games." *Econometrica* 58: 571–95.

David, Paul. 1985. "Clio and the Econometrics of QWERTY." *American Economic Review* 75: 332–7.

The rational choice theory of social institutions

Demsetz, Harold. 1972. "When Does the Rule of Liability Matter?" *Journal of Legal Studies* 1: 13–28.

Downs, Anthony. 1957. *An Economic Theory of Democracy.* New York: Harper and Row.

Durkheim, Emile. 1938 (1895). *The Rules of the Sociological Method,* 8th ed. Edited by George E. G. Catlin. Translated by Sarah A. Solovay and John H. Mueller. Chicago: University of Chicago Press.

Eggertsson, Thráinn. 1990. *Economic Behavior and Institutions.* Cambridge University Press.

Elster, Jon. 1989. *The Cement of Society: A Study of Social Order.* Cambridge University Press.

Enelow, James M., and Melvin J. Hinich. 1984. *The Spatial Theory of Voting: An Introduction.* Cambridge University Press.

Eulau, Heinz. 1963. *The Behavioral Persuasion in Politics.* New York: Random House.

Farrell, J. 1987: "Cheap Talk, Coordination, and Entry." *Rand Journal of Economics* 18: 34–9.

Frank, Robert H. 1988. *Passions within Reason: The Strategic Role of the Emotions.* New York: Norton.

Frohlich, Norman, Joe A. Oppenheimer, and Oran R. Young. 1971. *Political Leadership and Collective Goods.* Princeton, NJ: Princeton University Press.

Gibbard, Allan. 1990. "Norms, Discussion, and Ritual: Evolutionary Puzzles." *Ethics* 100: 787–802.

Gilligan, Thomas W., and Keith Krehbiel. 1987. "Collective Decision-Making and Standing Committees: An Informational Rationale for Restrictive Amendment Procedures." *Journal of Law, Economics, and Organization* 3: 287–335.

Gilligan, Thomas W., and Keith Krehbiel. 1990. "Organization of Informative Committees by a Rational Legislature." *American Journal of Political Science* 34: 531–64.

Goldberg, Victor P. 1984. "Production Functions, Transaction Costs, and the New Institutionalism." In George Feiwel, ed., *Issues in Contemporary Microeconomics.* London: Macmillan, pp. 395–402.

Habermas, Jurgen. 1984. *The Theory of Communicative Action. Volume 1: Reason and the Rationalization of Society.* Boston: Beacon.

Hardin, Russell. 1982. *Collective Action.* Baltimore: Johns Hopkins University Press.

Hayek, Friedrich A. 1967. "Notes on the Evolution of Systems of Rules of Conduct." In *Studies in Philosophy: Politics, and Economics.* Chicago: University of Chicago Press, pp. 66–81.

Hayek, Friedrich A. 1973. *Law, Legislation, and Liberty. Volume 1: Rules and Order.* Chicago: University of Chicago Press.

Holmstrom, Bengt, and Roger B. Myerson. 1983. "Efficient and Durable Decision Rules." *Econometrica* 51: 1799–1819.

Johnson, James. 1991a. *Symbol and Strategy.* Ph.D. dissertation, Department of Political Science, University of Chicago.

Johnson, James. 1991b. "Habermas on Strategic and Communicative Action." *Political Theory* 19: 181–201.

Johnson, James. 1993. "Is Talk Really Cheap? Prompting Conversation Between Critical Theory and Rational Choice." *American Political Science Review* 87: 74–86.

265

Jordan, J. S. 1991. "Bayesian Learning in Normal Form Games." *Games and Economic Behavior* 3: 60–81.

Keohane, Robert. 1986. "Reciprocity in International Relations." *International Organizations* 40: 1–28.

Knight, Jack. 1992. *Institutions and Social Conflict.* Cambridge University Press.

Koford, Kenneth B., and Jeffrey B. Miller, eds. 1991. *Social Norms and Economic Institutions.* Ann Arbor: University of Michigan Press.

Kramer, Gerald H. 1972. "Sophisticated Voting over Multidimensional Choice Spaces." *Journal of Mathematical Sociology* 2: 165–80.

Krehbiel, Keith, Kenneth A. Shepsle, and Barry R. Weingast. 1987. "Controversy: Why are Congressional Committees Powerful?" *American Political Science Review* 81: 929–45.

Kreps, David M., and Robert Wilson. 1982. "Reputation and Imperfect Information." *Journal of Economic Theory* 27: 253–79.

Laver, Michael E. 1983. *Invitation to Politics.* Oxford: M. Robertson.

Levi, Margaret. 1988. *Of Rule and Revenue.* Berkeley: University of California Press.

Levine, Michael E. 1981. "Revisionism Revisited? Airline Deregulation and the Public Interest." *Law and Contemporary Problems* 44: 179–95.

Lewis, David. 1969. *Convention: A Philosophical Study.* Cambridge, MA: Harvard University Press.

Luce, R. Duncan, and Howard Raiffa. 1957. *Games and Decisions: Introduction and Critical Survey.* New York: Wiley.

Maass, Arthur. 1983. *Congress and the Common Good.* New York: Basic Books.

Mansbridge, Jane J., ed. 1990. *Beyond Self-Interest.* Chicago: University of Chicago Press.

March, James G., and Johan P. Olsen. 1989. *Rediscovering Institutions: The Organizational Basis of Politics.* New York: Free Press.

Margolis, Howard. 1982. *Selfishness, Altruism, and Rationality: A Theory of Social Choice.* Chicago: University of Chicago Press.

Maynard Smith, John. 1982. *Evolution and the Theory of Games.* Cambridge University Press.

Milgrom, Paul, and John Roberts. 1991. "Adaptive and Sophisticated Learning in Normal Form Games." *Games and Economic Behavior* 3: 82–100.

Milgrom, Paul, and John Roberts. 1992. *Economics, Organization, and Management.* Englewood Cliffs, NJ: Prentice-Hall.

Miller, Gary J. 1992. *The Political Economy of Hierarchy.* Cambridge University Press.

Moe, Terry M. 1987. An Assessment of the Positive Theory of 'Congressional Dominance.'" *Legislative Studies Quarterly* 12: 475–520.

Monroe, Kristen Renwick, ed. 1991. *The Economic Approach to Politics: A Critical Reassessment of the Theory of Rational Action.* New York: Harper/Collins.

Myerson, R. 1985. "Bayesian Equilibrium and Incentive Compatibility: An Introduction. In L. Hurwicz et al., eds., *Social Goals and Social Organization: Essays in Memory of Elisha Pazner.* Cambridge University Press, pp. 229–59.

Nelson, Richard, and Sidney G. Winter. 1982. *An Evolutionary Theory of Economic Change.* Cambridge, MA: Harvard University Press.

North, Douglass C. 1981. *Structure and Change in Economic History.* New York: Norton.

North, Douglass C. 1990. *Institutions, Institutional Change, and Economic Performance*. Cambridge University Press.

Olson, Mancur S. 1965. *The Logic of Collective Action*. Cambridge, MA: Harvard University Press.

Ostrom, Elinor. 1990. *Governing the Commons*. Cambridge University Press.

Palfrey, Thomas R., and Howard Rosenthal. 1984. "Participation and the Provision of Discrete Public Goods: A Strategic Analysis." *Journal of Public Economics* 24: 171–93.

Polsby, Nelson W. 1968. "The Institutionalization of the U.S. House of Representatives." *American Political Science Review* 62: 148–68.

Posner, Richard A. 1977. *The Economics of Law*, 2nd edition. Boston: Little, Brown.

Quirk, Paul J. 1990. "Deregulation and the Politics of Ideas in Congress." In J. J. Mansbridge, ed., *Beyond Self-Interest*. Chicago: University of Chicago Press, pp. 183–99.

Radner, Roy. 1986. "Repeated Partnership Games with Imperfect Monitoring and No Discounting." *Review of Economic Studies* 53: 43–57.

Riker, William H. 1980. "Implications from the Disequilibrium of Majority Rule for the Study of Institutions." *American Political Science Review* 74: 432–58.

Rubin, Paul H. 1977. "Why Is the Common Law Efficient?" *Journal of Legal Studies* 6: 51–63.

Rubinstein, Ariel. 1982. "Perfect Equilibrium in a Bargaining Model." *Econometrica* 50: 97–109.

Rubinstein, Ariel. 1985. "A Bargaining Model with Incomplete Information about Time Preferences." *Econometrica* 53: 1151–72.

Samuelson, Larry. 1991. "Limit Evolutionarily Stable Strategies in Two-Player, Normal Form Games." *Games and Economic Behavior* 3: 110–28.

Schelling, Thomas C. 1960. *The Strategy of Conflict*. Cambridge, MA: Harvard University Press.

Schotter, Andrew. 1981. *The Economic Theory of Social Institutions*. Cambridge University Press.

Shepsle, Kenneth A. 1979. "Institutional Arrangements and Equilibrium in Multidimensional Voting Models." *American Journal of Political Science* 23: 27–59.

Shepsle, Kenneth A., and Barry R. Weingast. 1984. "When Do Rules of Procedure Matter?" *Journal of Politics* 46: 206–21.

Shepsle, Kenneth A., and Barry R. Weingast. 1987. "The Institutional Foundations of Committee Power." *American Political Science Review* 81: 85–104.

Somit, Albert, and Joseph Tannenhaus. 1967. *The Development of American Political Science*. Boston: Allyn and Bacon.

Taylor, Michael. 1976. *Anarchy and Cooperation*. New York: Wiley.

Truman, David B. 1951. *The Governmental Process*. New York: Knopf.

Turnbull, Colin M. 1972. *The Mountain People*. New York: Simon and Schuster.

Wallis, John J., and Douglass C. North. 1986. "Measuring the Transaction Sector in the American Economy, 1870–1970." In S. L. Engerman and R. E. Gallman, eds., *Long-Term Factors in American Economic Growth*. Chicago: University of Chicago Press, pp. 95–161.

Weingast, Barry R., and Mark J. Moran. 1984. "Bureaucratic Discretion or Congressional Control: Regulatory Policymaking by the FTC." *Journal of Political Economy* 91: 765–800.

Index